THE CHRISTIAN BOOK FOR MEN

BIBLICAL SOLUTIONS TO THE BATTLES FACING MEN

CHRIS NEAL

VOLUMES ONE AND TWO

The Christian Book for Men – Biblical Solutions to the Battles Facing Men

Copyright © 2019 by Chris Neal.

Graphic design and typesetting by JWC Creative. www.jwccreative.com

For more copies of this book visit www.thechristianbookformen.com

ISBN: 9781794347212

WHAT OTHERS SAY ABOUT THE BOOK AND THE AUTHOR

'The Christian Book for Men' is a plain talking resource for men navigating the Christian journey. With a solid emphasis on Scripture, Neal's openness and own vulnerabilities come through in every chapter, assuring we get a heartfelt and honest appraisal of the issues. Crucially the author doesn't shy away from the difficult subjects, so be prepared to feel a little uncomfortable as you read. All in all, a great new tool for the kitbag.

Michael Cooper – *National Director, England & Scotland, CVM (Christian Vision for Men). www.cvm.org.uk*

Chris has written an honest and transparent view of all the ills that men are facing in today's challenging world. In it, he shares not only from his own experiences but from the Word of God about how men can tackle daunting issues of everyday life and the temptations that are causing so many men to give up and walk away from their faith. This book is one that will encourage Christian men everywhere to open up about what has them bound, and jump into God's Word with renewed vigour and a great expectation that 'with God all things are possible'!

Charlynne Boddie – *Minister/Author/TV and Radio Host/ Charlynne Boddie Ministries. www.charlynne.com*

Chris Neal's book is totally amazing, timely, anointed, blessed and an absolute must for this time we're in…. really, really! I have known Chris and Michele Neal for many years and have seen their passion for God, people and the Bride of Christ. Chris carries the unique ability to see the current issues that are attacking men of our generation, and yet minister the heart and passion of God through this book. One totally hears God's voice through the chapters as these issues are addressed, solutions are offered, and God is revealed as a loving Father.

The love of God is not only evident in this book, but shines out of Chris' life, like a ray of hope to the brokenness in the Nations. This work will set men free to be all they were meant to be.

Francois Botes – *Francois Botes Prophetic and Music Ministry. www.francoisbotes.org*

The days we live in are clouded with darkness. Chris does more than talk about that darkness in his new book; he shines light on it. The illumination in this book will drive out the darkness in your life, as well as those around you. It's time for God's men to be filled with light!

Darren Hibbs – *Christian Author www.darrenhibbs.com*

Chris is honest about his journey in life. To gain understanding about what it means to be a man, he feels the pains and emotions of his human-ness through the mistakes he has already made, yet he strives to get deeper into a real relationship with God, with tears, emotion and passion for wholeness with God. He longs to pass on to other men the things that the Lord has taught him.

Heath Monaghan – *CEO, Aspire Ryde www.aspireryde.org.uk*

Dietrich Bonhoeffer wrote that the call to discipleship is the call to change. Chris has a passion to help disciple Christian men that they may change and better re-present Christ.

Chris writes in his own particular personal style and clearly presents his understanding of the issues he discusses. It is challenging and you may disagree with some points he makes, but his style encourages you not only to think deeper to clarify your own understanding, but to put into practice what you learn. This book is encouraging and a help to Christian men to live out what they learn about their faith.

Revd. Dr. D J Lloyd

I have known Chris since he moved to the Isle of Wight, when he joined the congregation of the Church I pastor; it was a pleasure to get to know him, his wife Michele, and her family.

Chris is a man of passion, drive and energy, who loves the Lord and will do what he can to share the Good News that the Kingdom of God is near.

I always marvel how God brings people together. In our case, there are many things Chris and I agree on and some things we disagree on, especially the football teams we support – the fans are deadly rivals! Through the banter and fun, we have grown to care for one another as Christian brothers, Pastor and church member.

Chris has a real 'father's heart' and a deep desire to support men in their daily battle against the pressures of the world.

One of my greatest pleasures as a Pastor is supporting families at difficult times, especially funerals. I have served Chris and his family, for his father-in law and his own father's funeral. During this time I saw Chris' sensitivity, as a husband, brother and a son. Chris is a very energetic and 'on-the-go' person, and for him to slow down and mourn was important, but through all this, he wanted God to be glorified, through the love of Jesus Christ in the power of the Holy Spirit.

Chris can be a sensitive soul, but there is a steeliness about him also. Whereas men of faith we would pray, worship and reflect on God's love, we could see differences in how we understand the Word of God. These differences would never create a divide among us as men of faith. I sense there may be some things in Chris' writings I may not be comfortable with, but what I love about Chris, is his commitment to seeing God's Kingdom come, be it in his generosity, his passion for worship, his drive to see the Gospel shared, or to see people baptised within the power of the Holy Spirit. For these reasons I encourage you to read his book, let the Spirit of God speak to you and challenge you as it highlights Gospel truths. Act and be changed in the love of Jesus Christ, to show His love in all you do, as Chris tries to do. God Bless you.

Rev Mark Evans - *Minister of Newport Congregational Church (Isle of Wight).*

'How beautiful and delightful on the mountains are the feet of
him who brings good news, Who announces peace, Who brings
good news of good [things], Who announces salvation,
Who says to Zion, "Your God reigns!" '

Isaiah chapter 52:7

DEDICATION

In loving memory....

Dear Dad, you had no idea I would write this book, and sadly, you never lived to see its publication. Thank you, Father God, for my dad, and thank you from the bottom of my heart that he and mum – both of whom came to love and follow you – are now experiencing life face-to-face with You in Your eternal kingdom, along with all others who believe and trust in Jesus Christ for their salvation.

ACKNOWLEDGEMENTS

Firstly, I wish to thank God for taking a risk in believing that He could use me to write a series of 'Men's Ministry Training Modules' which I believe, with all my heart, He wants to use to disciple ordinary men like you and me into a much deeper relationship with Him. I also believe that as a result of this teaching, He wants each of us to enjoy a deeper relationship with one another as brothers in Christ, and with our sisters in Christ too, *"that they may be one just as We are one."* (John chapter 17 verse 22).

The completed training modules will be used specifically in Christian Men's Ministry settings.

Whilst I was writing the modules, I felt God impress upon me that the content of the modules needed to be presented first as a book. That was a scary thought, having never before written a book! But I didn't need to worry because God is good – if He asks you to do something He promises to help you fulfil it!

And so I thank God that each day I sat down to type, not knowing what God wanted me to type, He was faithful and He made the words flow, just as He did for my wife Michele, when she obediently wrote her three books for His glory.

Secondly, I want to thank those many church leaders who have encouraged me over the last twelve years or so to get involved with men's ministry; firstly with the organising of men's social events, then with presenting some teaching, and latterly with the writing of the training modules and subsequently this book. I want to single out the Reverend Mark Evans for not only the encouragement he has given me in the area of men's ministry, but also going the extra mile to support my family and I during some painful times of bereavement which we have gone through in the last three years.

Thirdly, I want to especially thank the Reverend Dennis Lloyd (retired) who kindly read through every chapter of Volume One and offered advice on how to improve the content.

Fourthly, I want to record my genuine thanks and heartfelt gratitude to Michael Cooper for taking time out to write the Foreword of this book and I also want to thank all those others (including Michael) who felt the book worthy of writing some kind words, by way of an endorsement. I say to each of you… "I know you are incredibly busy people and I know it takes commitment to make time to read somebody else's manuscript. Thank you **so** much for your encouragement and support in this work that God has called me to do."

Finally, I want to thank Michele - my amazing wife - for tirelessly editing every chapter (and making many paragraphs make better sense!) as well as assisting me with the onerous task of proof-reading. She is a rock, and without her loyalty, love and commitment to seeing God's will done in our life, this book would have never been published.

FOREWORD

At CVM we are in the business of telling blokes about Jesus. By every means possible, the emphasis is on supporting, encouraging, resourcing and equipping men's groups and local churches in their evangelism to men. For thirty years, God has used CVM to win thousands of men into the Kingdom, but for each this is just the start of a journey. A journey littered with highs and lows, laughter and tears, celebration and pain.

The fact is, becoming a Christian is not the easy option; when we make that decision to follow Jesus we're not given some sort of "Get Out of Jail Free" card or special immunity from the dark and dangerous stuff of life. Instead, at the risk of mixing metaphors, we stand high above the parapet wearing a huge target on our back. In Volume One Chapter Three Chris Neal puts it like this: *"You have - without necessarily realising it - walked onto a spiritual battlefield, where the forces of good are at war with the forces of evil."* Acknowledgement of what it is we step into as new Christians is perhaps underplayed. Add to that the tendency men can have of walking a path of denial or setting about to 'fix the problem' (without the aid of the instructions of course), and you have a journey heading in the wrong direction.

Where are you on your journey? How prepared for the stuff of life are you? Who is alongside you in the battle? What weapons should you carry and are you properly trained in their use? I believe that **The Christian Book for Men** will help you to answer these and, I pray, many other questions about what it means to live as a man of God. The truth and wisdom of God's word, the Bible, underpins everything that you'll read in the pages ahead and all of it is helpfully woven together with stories from Chris' own journey.

As an evangelist, I also share the author's great passion to see men discipled, trained, and transformed by obedience to the Word of God. I pray that this book will help to keep your journey heading in the right direction and thereby that you will discover everything God has planned for you. Evangelism is most effective when we are good and authentic witnesses to what God has done in our lives through the Lord Jesus. By placing Jesus at the centre, we live as God created us to be and, by His grace, are able to inspire others to embark on their own life changing journey.

Every blessing,

Michael Cooper, National Director, England & Scotland, CVM (Christian Vision for Men). www.cvm.org.uk

CLAY IN THE POTTER'S HANDS

As Chris' wife, I felt it might be helpful if I wrote something to give you a glimpse of the person he used to be, the man he now is by the grace of God, and how this book came to be written.

In 2006 I married Chris. At that time, he was a self-made businessman, with the flashy car and expensive clothes! He was a man driven by success and a need to impress others. In his own mind he 'knew it all' and had a tendency to make insensitive jokes at others to bolster up his own ego.

His ability to listen to other people and validate their views and feelings was almost non-existent. He was 'right' and everyone else was 'wrong'! This is how our marriage started, and most people openly told us that we had no chance of getting past the first two years.

Twelve years later, we are still married, and Chris is a very different man. He is thoughtful, sensitive, and willing to listen, empathise and understand; he confesses his faults, apologises for his failings, asks for forgiveness and offers to put right the things he has done wrong and the hurts he has caused to others. Gone are the flashy cars and the expensive clothes. Gone is his need to impress others – now, whatever he does is done with one sole motive… to do God's will and to bring glory to Him.

So, how did Chris change from a man full of his own self-importance to 'a man after God's own heart'; a man who truly wants to demonstrate to others what God can do to us when we have spent our life making idols of ourselves? The answer to that question is through God's determined pursuit of him since 2008, relentlessly revealing to him the true state of the condition of his soul before a Holy God; exposing the sins and hypocrisy that lay hidden in the deepest recesses of his heart, and bringing upon him great conviction and godly sorrow, leading him into a place of genuine repentance with a holy desire to change from a follower of Christ who is living his life in 'the flesh', to a follower of Christ whose whole desire is to now live his life 'in Christ' and for Christ.

Over these past ten years God has spoken deep into his soul and revealed to him from His Word what it means to be a man of God, in every aspect of a man's life; as husband, father, son, brother, businessman and colleague, friend and neighbour.

God has had to spiritually batter Chris into the shape of the vision that He has been revealing to him, throwing him onto The Potter's Wheel and spinning him round and round, reshaping him time and time again into a vessel that He could use. Chris has not found this process easy and has often rebelled against the methods that God has used to instruct, discipline and correct him.

Many times Chris has closed off his ears and retreated into his 'cave' of self-pity, arguing against God and wishing that God had never given him a vision concerning the hearts and the lives of men who profess to be followers of Christ. But by God's grace, even whilst carrying on with his day to day paid employment, Chris has risen to the challenge of completing this book for God's glory.

For ten years, I have watched Chris fight the battle to put into practice the things God has revealed to him. I have witnessed the blood, the sweat and the tears that have accompanied his lonely, heart-breaking, soul searching journey of deliverance from a man of the flesh to a man after God's own heart. I have joined him in shedding many tears as he struggled against the world, the flesh and the devil in order to complete this book.

What you are now holding in your hands is a work that has been forged in the fiery-furnace of an immense burden to raise up men of God from the world's dust-heap of insignificance and irrelevance; to raise men up from the tsunami of worldly opinion that has sucked the very life and soul out of them.

God has a holy purpose for His men in every aspect of their lives, and this book, which Chris has written out of painful experience and obedience to God, is his gift, given in brotherly love, to every man who yearns to be raised from a life that seems meaningless, to a life that shines with the glory of God, in their every thought, word and deed.

This book is not a work of 'self-righteousness'. It has been born in the crucible of much suffering – emotionally, physically and spiritually. I pray that every man who lays hold of this book will be challenged, convicted and changed by what is written within these pages, so that God receives all the glory for the transformation of their lives.

I would like to encourage every woman to read this book too, so that you may learn how to help your man become all that God wants him to be, and all that God expects of those He has called His sons.

"My son, do not reject or take lightly the discipline of the LORD [learn from your mistakes and the testing that comes from His correction through discipline]; Nor despise His rebuke, for those whom the LORD loves He corrects, even as a father corrects the son in whom he delights." – Proverbs 3:11-12.

"… you have forgotten the divine word of encouragement which is addressed to you as sons, "My son, do not make light of the discipline of the Lord, and do not lose heart and give up when you are corrected by Him." - Hebrews 12:5.

"You must submit to [correction for the purpose of] discipline; God is dealing with you as with sons; for what son is there whom his father does not discipline?" - Hebrews 12:7.

"For our earthly fathers disciplined us for only a short time as seemed best to them; but He disciplines us for our good, so that we may share His holiness. For the time being no discipline brings

joy, but seems sad and painful; yet to those who have been trained by it, afterwards it yields the peaceful fruit of righteousness [right standing with God and a lifestyle and attitude that seeks conformity to God's will and purpose]." – Hebrews 12:10-11.

"Those whom I [dearly and tenderly] love, I rebuke and discipline [showing them their faults and instructing them]; so be enthusiastic and repent [change your inner self—your old way of thinking, your sinful behavior—seek God's will]." – Revelation 3:19.

Michele Neal

CONTENTS

Volume One – Overcoming Soul Battles

Volume Two – Overcoming Behaviour Battles

VOLUME ONE

OVERCOMING
SOUL BATTLES

INTRODUCTION

If you aren't a Christian man, but picked up this book to see what it's all about, that's brilliant. This book contains vital information which I believe can help you become - for want of a better term - a *'better man'* – specifically a better husband, a better father, a better son, a better work colleague. That's because the information in this book comes from the mouth of the Creator of the Universe. By that, I mean it is almost entirely based on the words of Holy Scripture; the words of Life and Truth. Each one of the chapters in each of the two volumes making up this book is complete in itself. So if, for example, you are particularly interested in *conflict resolution* and the amazing improvements that this can bring to your everyday life, then begin reading at the end! – Volume Two - Chapter 5.

If you <u>are</u> a Christian man, then like it or not, you are in a spiritual battle!

This biblically inspired book has been written to give you the tools that will help you be victorious against everything the enemy will hurl at you! If you are like me, you may have noticed that some of the 'stuff' going on in the world around you makes even less sense than it did just ten years ago. That's because the enemy knows his time is running out and he is ramping up the levels of evil upon the earth, causing extreme levels of pain and hardship among much of humankind.

Why is Satan doing this?

Because Jesus Christ – the King of kings and Lord of lords – promised that He is returning and Satan isn't happy about that. But in the meantime Jesus is relying on men of God like you and me to put our heads above the parapet and, in Jesus' Name and in His power and authority, demolish the strongholds of Satan and his minions. The question is, can God count on you and me to stand up to the fiery darts of the enemy, and overcome the onslaught, for the sake of the advancement of God's Kingdom?

My prayer is that the God-inspired words of this book will provide you with the encouragement and inspiration you need to undertake God's will, always for His glory.

Richest blessings….

Chris J Neal

Chapter 1

YOU HAVE GOD-GIVEN TALENT – USE IT FOR HIS GLORY!

'Just as each one of you has received a special gift [a spiritual talent, an ability graciously given by God], employ it in serving one another as [is appropriate for] good stewards of God's multi-faceted grace [faithfully using the diverse, varied gifts and abilities granted to Christians by God's unmerited favour]. Whoever speaks [to the congregation], is to do so as one who speaks the oracles (utterances, the very words) of God. Whoever serves [the congregation] is to do so as one who serves by the strength which God [abundantly] supplies, so that in all things God may be glorified [honoured and magnified] through Jesus Christ, to whom belongs the glory and dominion forever and ever. Amen.' (1 Peter chapter 4 verses 10 and 11).

I'd like to begin by telling you a little about myself, by way of sharing part of my testimony, but also to combine it with some words intended to encourage you.

But before I do, I feel the need to inform you that throughout this book, I will mention several words and highlight some sinful practices that would likely cause some members of a congregation to walk out if I mentioned them when preaching in church. I've certainly never heard them mentioned in church publicly. Let me reassure you that they are not 'rude' words, they are just frank words describing things as they are, and which are things that we men need to 'man-up' about and learn to deal with head-on if we are going to be set free from sin and *'enjoy life, and have it in abundance [to the full, till it overflows].'* (John chapter 10 verse 10).

In 2008, my wife and I were present at the ordination of the curate of the church we attended in Melton Mowbray, Leicestershire, UK. He was a wonderful, caring man of God, and his calling into the priesthood of the Church of England was an event that the whole congregation looked forward to attending.

Michele and I took our places in the pews and watched eagerly as the ordinands filed their way in and sat in the front rows of the Cathedral. It was difficult to see them from where we were sitting but as they went up to be ordained by the bishop, Michele and I noticed something simultaneously, although neither of us communicated to each other what we were thinking until after the event.

As I looked, I was struck by the fact that our curate was the only man present who was being ordained. Every other ordinand was a woman. At the very moment that I saw this, I whispered a question to the Lord, "Where are all the men?" All of a sudden I heard some very powerful words spoken deeply into my spirit. Those words were from God, and those words were, **"If My men will not rise up, I will use My women."** To clarify, God spoke those words to me in such a way as to mean, "If men will not respond to the call I have put upon them to become ordained, then I will not hesitate in using My women instead." I did not feel that God was changing His mind from what is written in His Word concerning His decree that __men__ are to be the overseers of the Church, but rather that in circumstances where men disobey or forsake His call on their lives, He will use women to undertake the work that He originally intended for men to fulfil.

After the ceremony, as I told my wife what God had revealed to me during the service, she said that shivers went down her spine, because at the very moment that she had looked at all the ordinands, she also noticed that our curate was the only man being ordained, and she also asked the Lord the very same question, **"Where are all the men?"**

Looking back, I am now able to see that that unforgettable moment was the beginning of the birth of this book.

Nothing happened for a year, and then in 2009, I felt God calling me to some kind of ministry to disciple Christian men.

Many folk are involved in evangelising men but God was making me very aware that His men need discipling. After all, in the Great Commission given to us by Jesus Christ in Matthew chapter 28, He tells us we are to **MAKE** disciples, not *'become'* disciples!

I've been a church-goer since I was a young boy, but I have only been born again and Spirit-filled since 1991. By the way, just because I am Spirit-filled doesn't mean I'm <u>always</u> full of the Spirit, because, regrettably, I leak - and to be honest, sometimes I find myself running on empty. That's when sin can more easily enter the camp. The Holy Spirit and sin cannot dwell in the temple (our body) together, so if you or I choose to sin, the Holy Spirit has to withdraw from us.

We will see, as we discuss the Word of God, that if and when our flesh sins, we have to confess it and repent of it; then we can ask God to fill us with His Holy Spirit again!

Since January 2010, God has been challenging me to get up off my backside and spend some time encouraging and exhorting any man who might be interested, that despite the fact that we live under the new covenant of God's amazing grace, nevertheless God wants and expects us, His men, to live godly, righteous, blameless, pure and holy lives. Moreover, we can only find out how to live like this, by checking out our instruction manual – **the Bible,** the Word of God.

The enemy of God (the devil) does his best to blind us to the truth God has written for all time in His Holy Scriptures, and in my experience, we constantly need the Holy Spirit to bring it back to our attention. I'll come on to tell you why I have a real heart for this subject shortly.

I'M TEACHING MYSELF TOO!

By writing this book for men, it does not mean in any way that I have personally 'got it altogether' - practically or spiritually. I struggle with one sin or another probably every day of my life. When we look at our church-leaders, the enemy tries hard to persuade those of us in the congregation, us 'ordinary folk' that those in spiritual authority have 'made it' – that they don't struggle with sin like us ordinary men do, but that is a lie.

The Bible says *'All have sinned and continually fall short of the glory of God.'* (Romans chapter 3 verse 23).

By the way, it wasn't Hitler who said he was the greatest sinner, it was St Paul, God's chosen evangelist to the gentiles. Imagine that, the man who wrote around two thirds of the New Testament said in all seriousness and humility that **he** was the greatest sinner. Clearly, he knew the only standard against which we can compare ourselves, and know whether or not we are sinners, is our Lord and Saviour Jesus Christ.

Where sin is concerned, it is no good comparing ourselves against what other people do or don't do. Our only benchmark is Jesus Christ - the pure, sinless, Lamb of God and what He has to say about it.

Later in this book, there is a chapter dedicated to the subject of sin and so we will revisit this subject later.

For now, I want to get back to talking to you about the heart God has given me for discipling men, and I want to keep reminding you that He wants to **encourage you** to develop whatever gift and deep desire He has given you, rather than you listening to the lies of Satan constantly telling you that you are not up to the job!

<u>GOD WANTS TO SEE ALL MEN DISCIPLED</u>

Whenever we take a stand for God or 'put our head over the parapet' and begin to do His work, many readers will know that immediately we do that, the devil ramps up his onslaught.

Sure enough, I have found myself coming under attack many times during the writing of this book! The enemy told me, right at the beginning, that I simply wasn't qualified to do this work.

You may know his tactics; he brings some facts to mind and causes us to dwell on them. Facts like 'I am a nobody. I've no theological qualifications, never been a church leader, and most days I fail to reach God's perfect but achievable standards for my life'. But as somebody said to me recently, "God does not call the qualified; He qualifies the called!" If God has called you, He **will** qualify you. He will give you the words to speak or open the doors that you are unable to budge.

Also it is important to listen out carefully for the still small voice of God.

When I felt inadequate, I listened and began to hear **Him** giving me some facts.

He reminded me what it says in His Word, that the devil (Satan) is the accuser of the brethren. In Revelation chapter 12 verse 10, looking to a future time when Satan will receive what is due to him, it says this:

'Then I heard a loud voice in heaven, saying, "Now the salvation, and the power, and the kingdom (dominion, reign) of our God, and the authority of His Christ have come; for the accuser of our [believing] brothers and sisters has been thrown down [at last], he who accuses them and keeps bringing charges [of sinful behaviour] against them before our God day and night'.

But when Satan accuses us before almighty God, just remember, Romans chapter 8 verse 34 tells us that Jesus intercedes for us.

Praise His Holy Name!

I want to encourage all men of God who have visions and dreams of being used by Him, but tend like me, to focus on our weaknesses rather than our God-given strengths. The truth about you is very different to what you might think, or the lies you might have listened to!

In John chapter 15 verse 16 (NKJV), Jesus, talking to His disciples (that is His followers) said this, and He is saying it to every follower of His today: ***"You did not choose Me, but I <u>chose you and appointed you</u> that you should go and bear fruit, and that your fruit should remain."*** (Author's emphasis).

Be encouraged – Jesus has chosen **<u>you</u>** and appointed **<u>you</u>** to achieve for Him whatever calling or ministry He has placed on your heart.

Let me tell you what I believe God told me about myself, on one of the many occasions that I thought "I am not up to this". Bear with me as I share these words and explain them because I don't want this to sound 'self-righteous.' It may sound so, but it is not intended to be!

This is what I felt the Lord say to me. *"Chris you are my chosen instrument. You are indeed well qualified to do this work for Me. You have something in common with Paul the apostle".*

Believe me, I was stunned at those words and wondered what God meant. If my sharing those words with you sounds like I am boasting, then please stay with me and believe that if I am boasting, it is in Christ Jesus my Lord. You see, in 2 Corinthians chapter 11 verse 6 (NIV), Paul said: ***"I may indeed be untrained as a speaker, but I do have knowledge."***

And God has given me knowledge, and He has given **<u>you</u>** knowledge too!

Firstly I am a man – so I feel qualified to write to men <u>about men.</u>

Secondly, throughout my life, I have made most of the mistakes I now seek to help others address or avoid altogether, and sometimes I still fall back to my ungodly flesh, or the pleasures of this world, or Satan's deception; all of these things can cause me to sin.

Thirdly, I've gained knowledge by reading some godly books written by Christian men in a way that I could relate to.

Fourthly, I am married to the most amazing wife who has helped me in so many ways by sharing a godly woman's perspective on the subject of sin. You may have read one of her books, *Come on Church! Wake Up! – Sin Within the Church and What Jesus Has to Say About it.*[1]

On another occasion, God told me He has given me a new name. **"Your name is VALIANT WARRIOR";** He told Gideon something similar in Judges chapter 6. I found that very humbling!

To encourage me further to undertake this work, God has given me much revelation about what some godly men get up to when they are stressed, feeling guilty, alone or weary. This has come not only from studying the subject but also from personal experience and that of trusted brothers in Christ.

So I have reason to believe God has given me knowledge, just as He did Paul **and** just as He will give or has already given to you concerning His plan for your life. But furthermore I have no less than three things in common with the disciples Peter and John! Now, before you pre-judge me on this and think I'm 'off my trolley' just take a look at what I mean by this in the following Scripture…

In Acts chapter 4 verse 13 (NIV) we read:

'When they saw the <u>courage</u> of Peter and John and realized that they were <u>unschooled, ordinary men</u>, they were astonished and they took note that <u>these men had been with Jesus.</u>' (Author's emphasis).

So, the Bible says that Peter and John were unschooled, ordinary men, but they had the courage to speak God's Word, and they had spent time with Jesus.

So what do I have in common with those two mighty men of God? What do you have in common with them?

Well, I am an ordinary bloke, and although I went to school, and college, I have no *theological* training or qualifications.

For sure, God has given me courage, because in early 2017 I seriously began to obey Him and do what, in the natural, I simply could not have done. As a direct response to my - albeit delayed - act of obedience, He enabled and equipped me to put together this book and a series of teaching modules. Trust me, in my own strength this would have been impossible *and* unthinkable.

GOD IS PATIENT

I put it off for years, but God is patient with me, and He will be patient with <u>you too</u> if you have put off doing something you know He has called you to do!

On many occasions the enemy told me I was wasting my time, and so for years I was disobedient to God's call on my life.

God began to show me, as I hungered for His Word, and read the Bible daily, that every man in history who achieved anything for God had to **use** the gift He gives all of us men – that is, the gift of **courage**.

Throughout my life I have worked in the field of industrial sales and marketing. To talk to an audience about a subject I know and understand well, became like 'falling out of bed' for me. It was 'water off a duck's back.' But to talk and write about God and discipling men – in the natural? NO WAY! Not a chance.

The initial thought of doing this, years ago, struck me with fear. I am telling you this to encourage you to walk into God's plan for your life, even if it feels frightening.

A dear friend of mine, Reverend Mark Evans who is the Minister of the Congregational Church in Newport, Isle of Wight, England, used to sign off his emails with the phrase **'Take RISKS for the glory of God.'** He did this because, like me, Mark has a desire to step out in faith to do things for the Lord, to be on the edge, and not to always play it safe! Mark would say that, as Christians we need to remember our Christian heritage, consider those who gave it all, those martyred for their faith in Christ and also (in more recent times) those who have spoken out when they have seen injustice in religion or within their nation. Mark and I like to think that in today's health and safety conscious world, we need to encourage others to step out in faith a little more, whether that be in word or deed. The time has come to 'rock the boat a little', for the Glory of God.

In Zechariah chapter 4 verse 6 (NIV) the Lord Almighty says to you and to me:

"Not by might nor by power, but by my Spirit."

Once we realise that God will do the work by His Spirit, once we take a step of faith in obedience to Him, then we will be more likely to take the risks that come with the calling. Taking a risk requires us to be men of courage!

WE NEED COURAGE!

In the amazing book of Joshua, chapter 1 verses 1 to 9, God felt it necessary to repeat to His chosen warrior *three times* the same command *"Be strong and (very) courageous"*.

In case he forgot, God reminded him again in verse 18. Maybe it's time for you to be 'strong and courageous!'

Joshua was about to take ground away from the enemy for the purposes of God, and I am convinced every time you or I obey God, we are advancing the Kingdom and taking something back from the enemy.

Satan doesn't sit back when God calls us to gain ground for God's Kingdom and take back what belongs to Him. No, Satan hates every God-fearing man and woman, and wants to bind every one of us up and make us ineffective for God.

God, on the other hand, wants to set men free from the slavery of sin. We, as men, are called to take back what the enemy has stolen, whether that's our peace of mind, our purity, our holiness, our loved ones, the lost, a village, or a nation.

I said earlier that I discovered I have three things in common with Peter and John, who were unschooled, ordinary men, who hung around with Jesus...

I have also hung around with Jesus. Quite closely for the past twenty five years, but off-and-on in total for nearly fifty years.

Well OK, if we are going to be factually correct I haven't hung around with *Jesus Himself,* but with His Holy Spirit, who as you know, takes up residence inside every follower of Jesus Christ.

But, enough about my qualifications, or lack of. Why do I believe God wants to speak through me to disciple men in the ways that He wants us to behave in our daily lives?

Well, many years ago, I asked God to give me His heart for His people.

You can't mess with God you know. When you ask Him for something, you have got to be prepared that He will give you what you ask for, provided you mean what you say!

Jesus says in Matthew chapter 7 verse 7 (NLT), ***"Keep on asking, and you will receive what you ask for. Keep on seeking, and you will find. Keep on knocking, and the door will be opened to you."***

So, if God hasn't answered you yet, KEEP ON! Keep on keeping on; keep asking and expecting.

One of the ways He started to show me something of His heart, was to make me get righteously angry every time I read about or heard about a woman being abused by a man. He made me angry with Satan, who does his evil works through a man, rather than me having anger towards the man who committed the abuse. Remember, Jesus said we are <u>to love</u>, even our enemies.

I started feeling a godly anger too when I heard about the acts perpetrated by men against women in wars; and likewise when I discovered that men in some third world countries sell their daughters into the sex trade in order that the rest of their family might simply buy some food to enable them to survive a little longer. I got angry! My ability to weep, improved with every act of evil I heard about.

I had the same problem when I read that lorry drivers in some parts of India expect to park up their lorries overnight and have young women made available for sex favours. I gather this is simply the culture of certain groups of people in that country.

I read in a Tearfund Prayer Diary in 2018 that *'gender based violence causes more deaths and disability among women aged 15 to 44 than cancer, malaria, traffic accidents and war.'* [2]

That is a shocking statistic; can you believe it?

I repeat, my godly anger was not directed at the men who perpetrated such evil acts because, as Scripture tells us (Ephesians chapter 6 verse 12, NIV) *"Our struggle is not against flesh and blood, but against the rulers, against the authorities, against the powers of this dark world and against the spiritual forces of evil in the heavenly realms."*

WAKE UP MEN, THE DEVIL IS REAL!

If you do not believe in the devil or demons, it's time to wake up, men! WAKE UP!

My anger was directed at Satan and his minions, and recently I have found myself getting increasingly angry at the way Satan is causing men and women pain - in the area of relationships. My own first marriage was destroyed by my sin and my wife's sin - and looking back I can see Satan's hand it that too.

Thankfully, God had mercy on me and forgave me and blessed me with my second wife Michele. Sure, we all have choices to make and have to accept responsibility for our actions, but Satan is usually always working away behind the scenes to bring the people of God down.

Satan doesn't focus on those who are already his (unbelievers), but on followers of Christ who can damage his kingdom, his domain, his territories and principalities.

The enemy is primarily interested in those of us who know the power we have in Christ, and who are willing to put our heads above the parapet, use God's power, and forcibly take back our relationships, our children, our neighbourhood, and all the things, and the people, the devil has stolen from us.

In the Bible, we see examples of the arrogance and the evil, selfish, attitudes men have towards women. You may recall that in John's Gospel chapter 8, a woman caught in adultery was brought to Jesus - and to test Him the local men asked Jesus what should be done *to her*. They wanted *her* killed.

Did it ever occur to you that there was actually **a man** involved in that act of adultery? Yet the men picked solely on the woman.

Interestingly, the Mosaic Law stated that both <u>the man and the woman</u> must be stoned to death. Leviticus chapter 20 verse 10 (NIV) states clearly *"If a man commits adultery with another man's wife - with the wife of his neighbour--both the adulterer and the adulteress must be put to death"*.

So where was the man with whom this woman committed adultery, and why weren't the men in the crowd accusing him, too? Personally I reckon he was there in the crowd well known to the other men, jeering at the woman, along with all the others. No wonder Jesus hated hypocrisy.

WOMEN ARE OUR EQUAL

We are called to love our wives and to acknowledge we as our equal in Christ. In Ephesians chapter 5 (NLT) it says *'For husbands, this means love your wives, just as Christ loved the church. He gave up his life for her to make her holy and clean, washed by the cleansing of God's word.'*

The Bible states that the man is the spiritual head – and, based on what we read in 1 Timothy chapter 3 and Titus chapter 1 it is God's will that only a man can be the overseer of a church, but New Testament teaching is clear that women and men are equal before God. *'There is [now no distinction in regard to salvation] neither Jew nor Greek, there is neither slave nor free, there is neither male nor female; for you [who believe] are all one in Christ Jesus [no one can claim a spiritual superiority]'*. (Galatians chapter 3 verse 28).

God has shown me that prejudice towards women still exists today. I have noticed it in many of the churches I have attended over the last 25 years, as well as throughout the secular world.

Talking of this, we will look at the subject of husbands and wives in Volume Two chapter One.

God has also made me aware of all sorts of other things going on in the world that He's not happy with – and how so much of it happens behind closed doors.

For example, elderly people being abandoned by their children and grand-children; single mum's being ignored by the state and abused by society; Third-World presidents siphoning off millions or even billions of dollars from their poverty-ridden citizens so *they* can live in palaces (etc, etc).

Please don't get me wrong, I am not suggesting that all of us men are caught up in some conspiracy against women, or are caught up in wickedness.

But God, by showing me His deep grief about the pain and

hardship suffered by so much of His beloved human race, has challenged me to bring to the notice of God-fearing men how He wants us to take up the challenge and make a difference. The starting point is with ourselves, our families and our community. Someone once said "God bring revival, start with **me.**"

Jesus says in Matthew chapter 5 that we are *'the salt of the earth'* and also *'the light of [Christ to] the world.'* We are not to hide away, keeping ourselves to ourselves. And when people meet with us and see how we talk and behave, God wants them to look at us (God's men) but see God!

In order for that to happen, I believe we need to admit that we are not the 'finished article'; we need to humble ourselves and ask God to enable us to renew our minds by believing and obeying His Word, and for God Himself to 'fix' the bits in us that are beyond our own ability to redeem and repair.

NONE OF US ARE YET THE FINISHED ARTICLE.

You may feel that in your case, there is nothing for Him to fix, that you've got it all together. If that's what you think, my prayer is that when you have finished reading this part of the book, God will have spoken to you and shown you there is indeed something that needs fixing in you; there is certainly still much for God to fix in me!

What I am about to say may appear like a total digression onto another subject but it isn't, so please bear with me.

When we look at what is happening in the world today, many are wondering what is going on. Jesus warns believers that these things will escalate in the End Times. Things are really hotting up and the internet is awash with the fulfilling of End Times prophecy, which will culminate in the Rapture of the Church and the millennial reign of Christ upon the Earth.

From the way things appear, it would seem that time is running out. I am not prophesying when the end will be – that would be utter folly, as the Bible is clear – no one except God knows when His Son will return. If you are not familiar with this, take a read of Mark chapter 13 and Matthew chapter 24.

But, Jesus *did* tell us to keep watch and look for signs in the heavens and on the earth. And He told us what to look out for. Referring to the End Times, He said (Matthew chapter 24 verse 6 to 8, NIV) *'You will hear of wars and rumours of wars, but see to it that you are not alarmed. Such things must happen, but the end is still to come. Nation will rise against nation, and kingdom against kingdom. There will be famines and earthquakes in various places. All these are the beginning of birth pains.'*

And Paul was clearly given a revelation by God about the events leading up to the End Times. This is what he said in 2 Timothy chapter 3 (NIV):

"But mark this: there will be terrible times in the last days. People will be lovers of themselves, lovers of money, boastful, proud, abusive, disobedient to their parents, ungrateful, unholy, without love, unforgiving, slanderous, without self-control, brutal, not lovers of the good, treacherous, rash, conceited, lovers of pleasure rather than lovers of God-- having a form of godliness but denying its power. Have nothing to do with them. They are the kind who worm their way into homes and gain control over weak-willed women, who are loaded down with sins and are swayed by all kinds of evil desires, always learning but never able to acknowledge the truth."

To my mind, what Jesus prophesied nearly 2,000 years ago is what we now hear about regularly broadcast as 'Breaking News' in the media. And what Paul warned us of, is behaviour that is becoming not only common, but even condoned by some in society. In January 2017, the UK news media had just reported of the horrific killing in cold blood in this country of a beautiful seven year old girl by an obviously disturbed fifteen year old girl.

<u>THE TIMES ARE CHANGING!</u>

When I was a child (in the 1950's and 1960's), all my friends lived with their mum and dad in a relatively loving family relationship. Home was essentially pleasant and safe. All my relatives got married (or remained single) and most went on to celebrate their silver, ruby and golden wedding anniversaries. Dads (and mums) brought up their children to behave themselves, especially in public, to respect their elders and those in authority.

Today, fifty to sixty years later, the picture is very different. Things unheard of then, are commonplace today: men 'married' to men, women 'married' to women, divorce rates at over 50%, 'partners' living together in sin, homosexuality practiced overtly, paedophilia, pornography, terrorism, even children murdering children.

When I see - both in the Church and in the world – the breakdown of marriage relationships, parent/child relationships and other family relationships, at ever-increasing and alarming rates, I believe it is time we had church programmes in place aimed at helping us **men** understand how to ensure we prevent these issues from happening - not just within the Church or within our communities - but most importantly within our own immediate family.

Like it or not, if you are a Bible-believing Christian, you and I are the spiritual head of our households, and God will hold us men accountable for a number of things.

I say 'like it or not', because for years I didn't like it or even know what it meant to be the 'spiritual head', and due to what I can only call spiritual apathy, I certainly didn't want to rise to that God-given challenge.

The pride in some of us men may cause us to like the title 'spiritual head' but we don't want to wear the mantle of all that God requires of that responsibility. One of our main tasks as the spiritual head of the home is to ensure we keep the enemy away from our family, so is it any wonder that many men feel so overwhelmed at the thought of their God-ordained role as the spiritual head of the home?

YOU AND I ARE THE SPIRITUAL HEAD OF OUR FAMILY.

The very first man that God created, completely abrogated his primary responsibility; which was to keep the enemy out of the Garden of Eden, or 'the home' if you prefer. When the enemy, in the form of a snake, came in and tempted Adam's wife to sin by disobeying God's Word, Adam was not away on a sabbatical somewhere, blissfully ignorant of his wife's sin. No, the Bible says Adam was right there with her! But Adam as the spiritual head, did *nothing* to stop something that was about to turn his and his wife's relationship with God upside down; and as a direct result, cause pain and suffering to all humanity from that moment on. If you are a believer, and read your Bible, you will know the whole history of the plight of the human race was changed for eternity that day. We refer to the event on that day as 'The Fall' - it was the day that sin entered the human race.

It was the day the first created man chose not to perform his God-given responsibility; to his wife, to his home (the garden of paradise), and actually to God as well.

The Bible says in Genesis chapter 3 verse 6 (NIV), that when Eve took of the forbidden fruit, she also gave some to her husband, ***'who was with her, and he ate it'.*** Until that moment Adam and Eve enjoyed perfect communion with almighty God. The three of them walked the garden together. Paradise!

So, beware; one moment of lust or carelessness on your part and, just as it was for Adam, the most important relationship in your earthly life could be ruined – possibly forever. I know - it happened to me – in my case, divorce was the result.

I believe we need a form of teaching that will help us men learn, like never before, how to go back to Scripture and recall how God intended us to live godly lives, and handle relationships <u>in biblical ways</u> because God's ways are best, and everybody benefits when we are obedient to Him.

The problem is, mankind does not like the word 'obedient.' We prefer words like 'freedom, grace, choice, pleasure' and the original lie of pride that says: 'I know best.'

<u>YOU AND I ARE IN A BATTLE!</u>

I, like many others, believe God's men are in a spiritual battle. And the battle is for your soul; and it starts in your mind. If Satan can get us to believe a lie – however subtle – and act upon it, we and others will suffer the consequences of our actions. The Bible warns us in Proverbs chapter 23 verse 7, *'As [a man] thinks in his heart, so he is'*.

So, here now is the warning of some frank words that I mentioned at the start of this chapter…

If I think it doesn't harm anybody if I look at sexually explicit images on the internet then I will have no problem doing it. If I think it's OK to masturbate because my wife is not meeting my sexual needs often enough, I will have no qualms about gratifying myself.

I am sorry if my choice of explicit words has shocked you, but God has told me it is time for men to be raised up in the Church who will have the courage to <u>get real</u> with brothers in Christ, by bringing things that are hidden in darkness out into the light.

The fact is pornography, masturbation, homosexual sex, same-sex marriage, fornication, paedophilia, drugs abuse, alcohol abuse, gambling – these things are wrong. God's Word says so! In this book I will show you Scriptures to support what I have just said, but in any case in 1 Corinthians chapter 6 verse 20 it says *'Honour and Glorify God with your body'*. I put it to you that these things do not honour and glorify God in any way whatsoever.

You may not struggle with any of the sins I have listed above, but in God's eyes they are no different from other more commonplace sins such as swearing, gossiping, cheating, lying, cursing, rage, being economical with the truth; the list goes on and on.

In God's eyes, sin is sin!

And if you think you are not caught up in any sin, please can I recommend you keep in mind Paul's warning about such thoughts:

'Therefore let the one who thinks he stands firm [immune to temptation, being overconfident and self-righteous], take care that he does not fall [into sin and condemnation]'. (1 Corinthians chapter 10 verse 12).

Secondly may I suggest you buy yourself a copy of a great piece of work – a 'classic book' by Jerry Bridges called 'Respectable Sins' [3]. He believes that many Christians have become preoccupied with so-called 'major sins' – so much so that we have lost sight of our need to deal with the more subtle ones.

He addresses these 'respectable sins' and opens up a new door to God's forgiveness and grace. This book helped me personally accept God's verdict on things I never thought twice about doing earlier in my walk of faith. I will look closer at this in Chapter Three of this first Volume, and you will find Bridges' complete list of 'respectable sins' listed there.

Whether you consider your sins are major or minor, sin is sin before God, and sin has consequences because it is wrong. And it is only a matter of time before we will suffer - in some minor or even catastrophic way - from our sins. Sin is a slippery slope and many are the Christian men who have engaged in acts of sin, often in secret, only for it to become exposed, and in some cases the consequence was not only a falling from grace but imprisonment. I know of such men personally and my heart goes out to them, their families, and those who have been affected by their actions.

'As [a man] thinks in his heart, so is he'. We must protect our minds from the supposedly 'nice' appealing, subtle lies of Satan and his demons.

Somebody once said *'Too many Christians treat sin like a strawberry milkshake, instead of like a deadly rattlesnake'.*

It's because I believe, in these last days, that Satan is working hard to 'take men out' of the Church and also cause those men who <u>do</u> practice their faith to listen to and accept Satan's subtle lies concerning our God-given calling and God's verdict concerning unrepentant sin in our life, that I want to look in Volume Two of this book at how we can be better witnesses to our children, our wives, and other family members and also to those we meet in the workplace.

This book is based not on tried and tested secular techniques, but primarily on the power and absolute timeless truth of Scripture alone!

I now want to encourage you further by showing you that in order for God to use you, you do not need to be perfect. I want to look, in the next chapter at a man God was able to use mightily for His purposes even though he, like all of us, was human and made mistakes.

Chapter 2

BECOMING A MAN AFTER GOD'S OWN HEART

'...He looked at Eliab [the eldest son] and thought, "Surely the LORD'S anointed is before Him." But the LORD said to Samuel, "Do not look at his appearance or at the height of his stature, because I have rejected him. For the LORD sees not as man sees; for man looks at the outward appearance, but the LORD looks at the heart." ' (1 Samuel chapter 16 verses 6b and 7).

In this chapter, I want to reassure you from God's Word – the Holy Scriptures - that God loves you **and** if you will open your ears and your mind to hear, there are things He wants you to know that will help you become a better man; a transformed man – <u>a man after God's own heart.</u>

And why should you want that? Because not only will you have a healthier, more peaceful, more joyful life, if you can put into practice God's plan for your life, but also everyone you relate to – those at home, at work, at church, those you meet each and every day of your life – will also benefit from your changed heart and your transformed life. They will see more of God's heart in you and hopefully less of your human-ness – your fallen, sinful, human-ness.

How then can we best learn to become '**A Man after God's Own heart**'?

Who can be our best role model? The answer to that question is of course Jesus.

We should only compare ourselves with Jesus Christ and not with other men, no matter how godly and righteous other men may appear to us. After all, only God can see the hearts of men, and no matter how well you think you know a righteous God-fearing man, he may not be walking in the light all of the time. Few of us are.

Although Jesus is our *perfect* role model, there is a 'fallen' human being in the Bible whose life is able to teach us how to be a man after God's own heart. Unlike Jesus, no man or woman is perfect. In fact, human beings are incapable of living perfect lives this side of the grave. However, **despite** our weaknesses and failings, God *can* and *will* use us in mighty ways if we will yield to Him and obey His Word. That truth is established throughout the Bible and is echoed in the life of the man I want to talk about here.

This man is the only man referred to in the Bible as 'A man after God's own heart'. And that man is **King David**, the second king of Israel.

Before we begin, I want to establish **three foundational factors** or pre-requisites that will enable us to be discipled by God. Without coming to terms with these factors, discipleship for any man is going to be difficult.

The first important factor I want to highlight is this…

The Bible is The truth.

How can we make such a declaration? Well, in John chapter 14 (NKJV), Jesus said *'I am the way, the Truth and the Life'.* So Jesus is the truth. What about the Bible?

In John chapter 1 we learn that Jesus is the Word made flesh (verse 14 says *'the Word (Christ) became flesh, and lived among us'*).

Here *'the Word'* is referring to the 'Word of God' which in its written form is the Bible. What I am about to say is a concept some may struggle with, but if the Bible says Jesus is *'the Word made flesh'* then the Bible is declaring that **Jesus Christ is <u>the Bible</u> in fleshly form.**

If Jesus Christ says He is *'The Truth',* and the Bible says *'Jesus is the Word (of God) and He became flesh',* then to me it's clear that the Holy Bible <u>is real truth and absolute truth.</u>

I concede that for many, this concept is very difficult to understand. It is for me too! What is required is not that we understand it but that we *believe* it, with simple child-like faith.

In 2 Timothy chapter 3 and verses 14 to 17 (NLT), Paul who is instructing Timothy, the leader of a church in Colossae, says this:

'You must remain faithful to the things you have been taught. You know they are true, for you know you can trust those who taught you. You have been taught the Holy Scriptures from childhood, and they have given you the wisdom to receive the salvation that comes by trusting in Christ Jesus. <u>All Scripture is inspired by God and is useful to teach us what is true and to make us realize what is wrong in our lives.</u> It corrects us when we are wrong and teaches us to do what is right. God uses it to prepare and equip his people to do every good work.' (Author's emphasis).

If you are a Christian but you do not believe the Bible is truth then you must examine your beliefs, line them up with God's Word and get back in your 'closet' with God. Because in these End Times the devil is using *whoever* he can and *whatever technique* he can to convince you that the Bible is not truth.

So *all* Scripture (that includes the Old Testament and the New Testament) is used by God to equip you and me to do every good work He calls us to do. Some of us may need to get back to basics and get our dusty Bibles out again, read them, and put its truth into practice.

Furthermore, we need to know how to understand and interpret Scripture. American Christian author Tim LaHaye says this, and I and many others agree with him:

"The Bible was written to ordinary people like you and me, and most passages are easy to understand and believe if we apply the golden rule of interpretation to the passage:

'When the plain sense of Scripture makes common sense, seek no other sense, but take every word at its primary, literal meaning, unless the facts of the immediate context clearly indicate otherwise.'" [1]

Therefore, for example, when it says in the Old Testament book of Leviticus chapter 20 verse 13 (NIV): **'If a man has sexual relations with a man as one does with a woman, both of them have done what is detestable',** we are to accept that these words are as plain as the light of day – they require no other interpretation. And since **'Jesus Christ is [eternally changeless, always] the same yesterday and today and forever'** (Hebrews chapter 13 verse 8), He has not changed His mind. Do not allow yourself to be fooled by liberal theologians; it is clear that God is telling us that homosexual sex is detestable, and in fact, that verse in Leviticus goes on to tell us that in those days such people were to be put to death. The Good News is that today we live under the New Testament of God's grace, and whilst the Bible makes it clear that **all** who sin in <u>any way</u> are deserving of death, God offers those of us who believe and trust in the Lord Jesus as our Saviour the prospect of forgiveness provided we confess and turn from our sin (repent) as I will discuss later.

On the other hand, where it says twice in John chapter 1 that Jesus is *'The Lamb of God',* it is obvious that the literal meaning of the word 'lamb' cannot be truth. Jesus was God incarnate – almighty God in the human form. He was not an animal. He was not a 'baby sheep'. So we need to interpret that specific Scripture. What does it mean - 'The Lamb of God'? The answer is that Jesus is our Saviour and that He was the only pure and spotless one who could die in our place in order that those of us who believe and trust in Him and confess and repent of our sins, could have our sins forgiven, and thereby spend eternity in Heaven with God, with the angels and with other believers, after our physical death. After the death and resurrection of Jesus Christ (the 'Lamb' of God), the Old Testament sacrifice of a Passover Lamb was no longer necessary for our forgiveness. Jesus died once, and for all humanity, so that our sins could be forgiven. The condition required for us to be saved is that we believe in Jesus as our Lord and Saviour, turn from our sins and obey His Word.

The Second important factor I want to share with you is something the Bible tells us we need to do, and this, by the way, in my experience, is the most painful thing we will probably ever need to do in our lives. What is it? It is to…

'Crucify the Flesh.'

Jesus used several phrases to illustrate what this meant, as well as actually fulfilling it literally on the Cross, in order that you and I might have the door to salvation opened to us.

He said in Matthew chapter 16, verse 24, *"Whoever wants to be my disciple must deny themselves and take up their cross and follow me."* (NIV).

He also said unless you leave your parents, children, etc., and follow Him you cannot be His disciple. What He meant by this is everything that is more important to you in your life than following Jesus, must become secondary to you. Jesus is saying that becoming a disciple of His must become the number one priority in your life. It doesn't mean you can't have a social drink from time to time in moderation, or that you must give up your favourite pastime, but following Jesus and behaving in a Christ-like way is to become your 'default position'. When we are obedient like this, God will bless us abundantly in new ways.

In the context of worrying about material things, Jesus said in Matthew chapter 6 verse 33, *"But seek first the kingdom of God and His righteousness, and all these things shall be added to you.*" (NKJV). The riches you will receive by following Jesus (the consequence of which may mean becoming ridiculed or despised by some of those old friends of yours), are infinitely better for you.

It was the apostle Paul who, inspired by the Holy Spirit, used the phrase 'Crucify the flesh' (See Galatians chapter 2 verse 20). I believe what Jesus and Paul meant was this....

You and I are a spirit, we have a soul, (our mind and emotions), and we live in a body (i.e., our flesh) which, because of 'The Fall', is predisposed to sin. Our natural (fleshy) desires want what is wrong in God's eyes. Our flesh (that is our body) lives in rebellion to God, and lusts after things that the devil entices us to believe are good, or enjoyable, or will satisfy that desire inside us that says "I must have it now". When Adam and Eve fell for this lie, in the Garden of Eden, sin entered the camp. Our job as men, is to remove sin first from ourselves, then from our family and - insofar as we can - from our church and our community.

I believe with every fibre of my being that this is possible only if we learn how to become a man after God's own heart, and the starting point to being able to crucify the flesh is to be filled with the Holy Spirit (in other words to be born again).

The third important thing is…

Being 'born again.'

It is the act of being 'born again' that makes a man hungry to be discipled. But what does it really mean to be 'born again'?

John chapter 3 verses 1 to 8 is the key passage of Scripture concerning being 'born again':

'There was a man named Nicodemus, a Jewish religious leader who was a Pharisee. After dark one evening, he came to speak with Jesus. "Rabbi," he said, "we all know that God has sent you to teach us. Your miraculous signs are evidence that God is with you."

Jesus replied, "I tell you the truth, unless you are born again, you cannot see the Kingdom of God."

"What do you mean?" exclaimed Nicodemus. "How can an old man go back into his mother's womb and be born again?"

Jesus replied, "I assure you, no one can enter the Kingdom of God without being born of water and the Spirit. Humans can reproduce only human life, but the Holy Spirit gives birth to spiritual life. So don't be surprised when I say, 'You must be born again.' The wind blows wherever it wants. Just as you can hear the wind but can't tell where it comes from or where it is going, so you can't explain how people are born of the Spirit." (NLT)

Now this is a deep spiritual truth and a very profound paragraph of Holy Scripture. It is vital that you understand that, in order to understand His Holy Word, and in order to be a man after God's own heart, you must first of all be 'born again'. So what does this Scripture mean? In a few words, what Jesus is talking about here (to Nicodemus) is that we must, in effect, be 'filled with the Holy Spirit', just as the disciples were on the day of Pentecost (see Acts chapter 2). It was when the Holy Spirit fell upon them on that historic day, that the scales fell off their eyes and they could see what they couldn't see or understand before. It means that once we are filled with the Holy Spirit, He can then do in us what we cannot do in our flesh. He transforms us into the likeness of Christ. Transformation is a process, and for some of us the process is very rapid and for others much slower, depending on our willingness to yield to the Lord's Will through obedience to His Word.

Many times in the Gospels, we hear Jesus say that His followers didn't understand what He was talking about and, for sure, the religious leaders didn't understand either. But when we are filled with the Holy Spirit and when we crucify the flesh – our own selfish desires – and let the Holy Spirit lead us, then we can be transformed into the likeness of Christ.

I have now established the three prerequisites, for being open to God's desire and His hunger <u>to teach you more deeply</u> about His ways, and for you to learn how He longs for you to live and act. To reiterate, these are:

There is no such thing as 'relative truth', the Bible is _The Truth_.

We must be willing to <u>crucify our flesh</u>.

We need to be <u>born again</u>.

I said right at the beginning of this chapter that God loves everyone unconditionally. Let me ask you a question. How much do you love God?

How much do you want to be like Him? Are you willing to behave towards others as He does? Are you prepared to love your enemies, and do good to those who hate you (by the way, those are Jesus' commands to us, they're not my words!).

How much do you want to be a man after God's own heart?

Well, hopefully you are reading this book because that's exactly what you want. But it's hard. I've been trying for decades and it's tough, very tough… It is usually the sins of stubbornness, pride and rebellious independence that make it so difficult to obey God.

Having established some important foundational truths, I am now at the place where I am ready to share with you about the man whom the Bible tells us was a man after God's own heart. There is much we can learn from that great man of God. He was a true warrior-man who fought bravely with his loyal men to take so much ground back from the devil for God.

I want to begin by looking at 1 Samuel chapter 16 verses 1 to 13 (NLT)…

'Now the LORD said to Samuel, "You have mourned long enough for Saul. I have rejected him as king of Israel, so fill your flask with olive oil and go to Bethlehem. Find a man named Jesse who lives there, for I have selected one of his sons to be my king."

But Samuel asked, "How can I do that? If Saul hears about it, he will kill me."

"Take a heifer with you," the LORD replied, "and say that you have come to make a sacrifice to the LORD. Invite Jesse to the sacrifice, and I will show you which of his sons to anoint for me."

So Samuel did as the LORD instructed. When he arrived at Bethlehem, the elders of the town came trembling to meet him. "What's wrong?" they asked. "Do you come in peace?"

"Yes," Samuel replied. "I have come to sacrifice to the LORD. Purify yourselves and come with me to the sacrifice." Then Samuel performed the purification rite for Jesse and his sons and invited them to the sacrifice, too.

When they arrived, Samuel took one look at Eliab and thought, "Surely this is the LORD's anointed!"

But the LORD said to Samuel, "Don't judge by his appearance or height, for I have rejected him. The LORD doesn't see things the way you see them. People judge by outward appearance, but the LORD looks at the heart."

Then Jesse told his son Abinadab to step forward and walk in front of Samuel. But Samuel said, "This is not the one the LORD has chosen." Next Jesse summoned Shimea, but Samuel said, "Neither is this the one the LORD has chosen." In the same way all seven of Jesse's sons were presented to Samuel. But Samuel said to Jesse, "The LORD has not chosen any of these." Then Samuel asked, "Are these all the sons you have?"

"There is still the youngest," Jesse replied. "But he's out in the fields watching the sheep and goats."

"Send for him at once," Samuel said. "We will not sit down to eat until he arrives."

So Jesse sent for him. He was dark and handsome, with beautiful eyes.

And the LORD said, "This is the one; anoint him."

So as David stood there among his brothers, Samuel took the flask of olive oil he had brought and anointed David with the oil. And the Spirit of the LORD came powerfully upon David from that day on.' Then Samuel returned to Ramah.'

David, the youngest son of Jesse, who was not considered of any importance by his father, and who was hidden away in the fields tending sheep – he, it was, who was God's chosen man.

I now have six new points to make, my first new point is this…

Somebody that others have discounted, can be used by God.

If you are somebody that has been overlooked, either by your father or anyone else in 'authority'; if you think you are too young or too old; if you are perhaps physically weaker than the older more mature men in your church, God can and will use you! The proviso is just this – Is your heart right with God?

If you doubt this truth, remember what God said to Samuel:

"For the LORD sees not as man sees; for man looks at the outward appearance, but the LORD looks at the heart."

Why does God look at our hearts when judging us? Jesus gives us the answer:

"For out of the heart come evil thoughts and plans, murders, adulteries, sexual immoralities, thefts, false testimonies, slanders (verbal abuse, irreverent speech, blaspheming)". (Matthew chapter 15 verse 19).

How is your heart today? Is it right with God?

Your flesh may be weak, like mine, but so long as **your spirit is willing**, God **can** use you.

If you know your heart isn't right with Him, but you want it to be, don't write yourself off; confess, repent, ask God to forgive you, seek prayer from a trusted man of God, find a mentor to stand with you and encourage you.

The Bible says that David was a man after God's own heart, and that is why I want to study aspects of his life, to see what we can learn from him. Samuel anointed David to become the next King of God's people, and it was to David's predecessor - King Saul - that God said through the prophet Samuel in 1 Samuel chapter 13 verse 14:

"But now your kingdom (Saul) *shall not endure. The LORD has sought out for Himself a man (David) <u>after His own heart</u>, and the LORD has appointed him as leader and ruler over His people, because you have <u>not kept (obeyed) what the LORD commanded you.</u>"* (Author's emphasis and inserted word).

<u>**My second point is this…**</u>

<u>**God is looking for men with a right heart.**</u>

If your heart is right with God, it means you will want to keep God's commands. God is looking for men who will obey Him.

Obedience is not a popular word today is it? We prefer other words from the Bible like….. Grace, love, blessings, forgiveness.

God wants men who will be obedient to His Holy Word **and** to His call on their life.

Will you obey the Lord your God? Will you get up off your backside, stick your head over the parapet and fight for the things of God in this ever-increasingly lawless world; or for lost souls, or for whatever God has laid on your heart?

It will probably be costly; you will almost certainly need to make a sacrifice.

Are you up for it? If so, God will use you. If not, you can repent of your fear and He will still use you!

Let's take a look at David's life, firstly while King Saul was still reigning as King. Let's look at David's attitude to <u>obedience</u>. In addition to his undaunted willingness to obey God, many examples of David's character and obedience are demonstrated in how he showed respect for his elders and those in authority – especially King Saul, who was appointed by God.

David, too young to be a member of the army, was sent by his father, Jesse, at the age of just fifteen, to see how David's three elder brothers were doing on the front line.

There, he learns that Goliath, the finest, strongest, undefeated Philistine fighter, is taunting the Israelites to come and fight him, hand to hand. Saul's army are terrified! But David wants to stand up to him. However, his eldest brother was angry with him. This is what we read in Samuel chapter 17 verses 28 to 30 (NLT):

'But when David's oldest brother, Eliab, heard David talking to the men, he was angry. "What are you doing around here anyway?" he demanded. "What about those few sheep you're supposed to be taking care of? I know about your pride and deceit. You just want to see the battle!"

"What have I done now?" David replied. "I was only asking a question!" He walked over to some others and asked them the same thing and received the same answer.'

In the face of taunting and ridicule, David did not slander his elders but simply and politely stated facts. "What have I done? I was only asking a question."

He then managed to get an audience with King Saul on the battleground, and here we learn something of David's walk with the Lord whilst still a simple shepherd boy. We learn in 1 Samuel chapter 17 verses 34 to 37 that, as a shepherd, God had given David so much courage and fearlessness that he was able to kill lions and bears with his bare hands. Clearly, he was no ordinary teenager. He had supernatural power – the power of God's mighty

Spirit rested upon him from an early age.

After persuading King Saul to allow him to take on Goliath personally, he is taunted again. This time by his enemy - Goliath himself. But David is not afraid. His language changes totally.

In the face of being taunted by Goliath - the most experienced giant of a Philistine warrior, - fifteen year old shepherd-boy David responds with this awesome statement of faith, courage and righteous indignation, written in verses 45 onwards. I love it!

'Then David said to the Philistine, "You come to me with a sword, with a spear, and with a javelin. But I come to you in the name of the LORD of hosts, the God of the armies of Israel, whom you have defied. This day the LORD will deliver you into my hand, and I will strike you and take your head from you. And this day I will give the carcasses of the camp of the Philistines to the birds of the air and the wild beasts of the earth, that all the earth may know that there is a God in Israel. Then all this assembly shall know that the LORD does not save with sword and spear; for the battle is the LORD's, and He will give you into our hands."'

What a wonderful declaration of faith!

Every word David spoke was fulfilled by God Almighty, that very day!

So what else can we learn from David?

My Third Point is this…

Fear can be conquered by *courage* and *faith* in the Lord.

How strong is your faith? Are you a man of courage, or 'do you get going when the going gets tough?'

Are you aware that the battle is not yours but the Lord's? That should be a great relief to us all!

Man of faith, God will give your enemy into your hands if you will be a man after God's own heart. That is, if you are Spirit-filled and if you obey God's commands and stand before the enemy with the confidence that God will remove or destroy him.

We all have enemies – and most of them are in the spirit realm.

We will study spiritual warfare in the next chapter, but know for now that the battle is the Lord's. Your boss is not the enemy, neither is your wife, nor a problem son or daughter, nor anybody else. The enemy is Satan, or one of his demons. It is they who tempt people to sin and cause ungodly behaviour. Check out Ephesians chapter 6; the battle is in the spirit realm, and, as I said, we will look at that in chapter Three.

Sometimes, it appears that God seems to sit on His hands and doesn't defeat our enemy for some years. And in our flesh that can be very frustrating. But, we are in good company because the next thing I want to highlight from David's life is that God had to teach him patience. David had to wait upon the Lord, and many is the time that we will have to do so too.

As I said, Samuel was told by God to anoint David as the next King of Judah when he was just fifteen years old, but it turns out that he had to wait something like fifteen further years before he replaced Saul as King. He then waited a further seven years (over twenty in total) before also being made King of Israel. During that time God taught him character and patience.

<u>My Fourth Point is this…</u>

<u>We must learn to wait upon the Lord</u>

Do not run ahead of Him. Learn to be patient. Remember, Peter reminds us what the Psalmist wrote (2 Peter chapter 3 verse 8, NIV) ***'With the Lord, a day is like a thousand years, and a thousand years are like a day.'***

There is also something important we need to learn from King Saul. The reason that God told Samuel to anoint David, was because Saul started to disobey God. Disobedience can result in the removal of our anointing. It was God's will for Saul to continue for many years as King even after God decided he was to be removed; it is important that we learn that disobedience can result in the beginning of the end of our ministry.

In 1 Samuel chapter 15 and verses 22 and 23 (NLT), Samuel, addressing King Saul says:

"What is more pleasing to the LORD: your burnt offerings and sacrifices or your obedience to his voice? Listen! Obedience is better than sacrifice, and submission is better than offering the fat of rams. Rebellion is as sinful as witchcraft, and stubbornness as bad as worshiping idols. So because you have rejected the command of the LORD, he has rejected you as king."

So our obedience to God is more important than making sacrifices in our life for God. Sacrifices, fasting, tithing; these things are good and they are right. But God says <u>obedience is better.</u>

As a short digression, as I proof-read the draft of this book, I noticed my reference to tithing above and God reminded me that tithing is the only area in the entire Bible where God challenges us to actually test Him. In Malachi chapter 3 verses 8b to 10 (NLT) we read this:

"You have cheated me of the tithes and offerings due to me. You are under a curse, for your whole nation has been cheating me. Bring all the tithes into the storehouse so there will be enough food in my Temple. If you do," says the LORD of Heaven's Armies, "I will open the windows of heaven for you. I will pour out a blessing so great you won't have enough room to take it in! Try it! Put me to the test!"

I battled with God for years over the matter of tithing. The day I gave in to God and said *"OK I will obey"*, I will never forget that in the post the very next morning arrived, what in those days (the early 1990's), was a very significant cheque for over £2,000; a tax refund from the Inland Revenue that was a total surprise to me. God loves to bless us as we walk in obedience to His Word!

Right back in the Old Testament book of Leviticus, chapter 26, we see that God gives blessings in return for obedience. The blessings are listed there for you to read if you wish to do so.

<u>My fifth point is this…</u>

<u>**To be a man after God's own heart,**</u>
<u>**we must learn to obey God, at every opportunity.**</u>

Returning now to King David, he was blessed abundantly by God for his obedience. And the level of his obedience was quite astonishing. I'm linking obedience with character because, to my way of thinking, the two are closely intertwined.

Let's look at examples in the Scriptures of David's God-like character.

King Saul became so jealous of David that many times he wanted to kill him. David knew this, and David himself had a number of opportunities to kill Saul, **but** David consistently resisted the taking of those opportunities!

Saul's jealousy of David began soon after he appointed him in charge of his fighting men. After a major coup with David 'at the helm', the army returned home from battle, and as they did so the women sang a song praising David more than Saul. 1 Samuel chapter 18 verses 6 to 9 (NLT) says:

'When the victorious Israelite army was returning home after David had killed the Philistine, women from all the towns of Israel came out to meet King Saul. They sang and danced for joy with tambourines and cymbals. This was their song:

"Saul has killed his thousands, and David his ten thousands!"

This made Saul very angry. "What's this?" he said. "They credit David with ten thousands and me with only thousands.

Next they'll be making him their king!" So from that time on Saul kept a jealous eye on David.'

Then in verses 10 and 11 (NLT) we read:

'The very next day a tormenting spirit from God overwhelmed Saul, and he began to rave in his house like a madman. David was playing the harp, as he did each day. But Saul had a spear in his hand, and he suddenly hurled it at David, intending to pin him to the wall. But David escaped him twice.'

Please heed this warning - jealousy is a terrible thing, and in the case of Saul it resulted in him wanting to commit murder, ironically of the very man that was totally loyal to him and who did everything in his and his army's power to destroy Saul's enemies. However, perhaps what taunted Saul even more was what Samuel had told Saul to his face in 1 Samuel chapter 15 and verse 28, that God had decided to give Saul's kingdom to *'a better man than Saul!'*

Jealousy is a terrible thing.

My first marriage ended in divorce, after 28 years of what I thought was blissful happiness and God's blessing on my life. It would not be right to go into the details here, but what I will say is that jealousy of somebody that Satan used to end my first marriage could easily have created in me, feelings of wanting to commit murder. Even as Christians, I believe we are all still capable of the most horrendous sin and evil, when we allow our flesh to rise up and dominate our minds and hearts in the face of adversity. This is why it is so vital that we crucify our flesh and live our lives being led by the Holy Spirit, and being obedient to God's Word.

Returning to David again, Saul's persistent desire to kill David drove David away from him. God tested David to see if he would obey God and be a worthy King when his time came. Not only was David patient, but the depth of his character and integrity just blows me away. When I read about David's life, I am in awe of him. Could I have been like him? Could you?

Despite David knowing Saul wanted to kill him, let me remind you of some examples of how he behaved towards Saul, who David recognised as God's anointed king, yet who showed himself to be David's enemy.

He allowed himself to be alone in the palace, with Saul, while he played the harp for Saul, to soothe his mind. He did this for some time, but you will find if you read 1 Samuel chapter 19 and verses 9 and 10, that Saul tried to kill him again with his spear while David was playing to him. David finally fled from Saul altogether without trying to take revenge.

Saul tried to find David to kill him, and in chapters 20 to 24 you can read all about Saul's evil exploits, indiscriminately killing priests and others along the way.

Then in chapter 24, Saul goes into a cave to relieve himself and we read this (verses 3b to 19, NLT):

'But as it happened, David and his men were hiding farther back in that very cave!

"Now's your opportunity!" David's men whispered to him. "Today the LORD is telling you, 'I will certainly put your enemy into your power, to do with as you wish.'" So David crept forward and cut off a piece of the hem of Saul's robe.

But then David's conscience began bothering him because he had cut Saul's robe. He said to his men, "The LORD forbid that I should do this to my lord the king. I shouldn't attack the LORD's anointed one, for the LORD himself has chosen him." So David restrained his men and did not let them kill Saul.

After Saul had left the cave and gone on his way, David came out and shouted after him, "My lord the king!" And when Saul looked around, David bowed low before him.

Then he shouted to Saul, "Why do you listen to the people who say I am trying to harm you? This very day you can see with your own eyes it isn't true. For the LORD placed you at my mercy back there in the cave. Some of my men told me to kill you, but I spared you. For I said, 'I will never harm the king—he is the LORD's anointed one.' Look, my father, at what I have in my hand. It is a piece of the hem of your robe! I cut it off, but I didn't kill you. This proves that I am not trying to harm you and that I have not sinned against you, even though you have been hunting for me to kill me.

"May the LORD judge between us. Perhaps the LORD will punish you for what you are trying to do to me, but I will never harm you. As that old proverb says, 'From evil people come evil deeds.' So you can be sure I will never harm you. Who is the king of Israel trying to catch anyway? Should he spend his time chasing one who is as worthless as a dead dog or a single flea? May the LORD therefore judge which of us is right and punish the guilty one. He is my advocate, and he will rescue me from your power!"

When David had finished speaking, Saul called back, "Is that really you, my son David?" Then he began to cry. And he said to David, "You are a better man than I am, for you have repaid me good for evil. Yes, you have been amazingly kind to me today, for when the LORD put me in a place where you could have killed me, you didn't do it. Who else would let his enemy get away when he had him in his power? May the LORD reward you well for the kindness you have shown me today." '

So David had his chance, but decided not to take it, out of loyalty, both to God **and** to His anointed king - Saul.

I wonder if you or I would have shown that degree of restraint and character...

You may know this story well. If not, you may hardly believe it but despite what Saul said to David in the above passage, Saul later takes another opportunity to try to kill David and sets off to do so. But God spares David, God's chosen successor of Saul, once again.

In chapter 26 we learn that Saul discovers that David and his men are hiding on a hill, and Saul and his men set off and camp overnight nearby.

Once again, God tests David. Will he show grace to Saul or will he take his revenge and strike him dead?

This is what verses 7 to 12 tell us:

'David and Abishai went right into Saul's camp and found him asleep, with his spear stuck in the ground beside his head. Abner and the soldiers were lying asleep around him.

"God has surely handed your enemy over to you this time!" Abishai whispered to David. "Let me pin him to the ground with one thrust of the spear; I won't need to strike twice!"

"No!" David said. "Don't kill him. For who can remain innocent after attacking the LORD's anointed one? Surely the LORD will strike Saul down someday, or he will die of old age or in battle. The LORD forbid that I should kill the one he has anointed! But take his spear and that jug of water beside his head, and then let's get out of here!"

So David took the spear and jug of water that were near Saul's head. Then he and Abishai got away without anyone seeing them or even waking up, because the LORD had put Saul's men into a deep sleep.'

We go on to learn that David confronts Saul again, and once more Saul is (or so he says) so sorry for wanting to kill David.

So, my final point is this…

We must allow God to build character and integrity in us, if we want to be a man after God's own heart.

Later Saul dies, along with his son Jonathon, in battle - and how did David respond knowing that his life would, at last be safe, and that he would be anointed as Saul's successor? Did he throw a party as you and I might have done?

No! In 2 Samuel chapter 1 and verses 11 and 12 (NLT), this is how David reacted when he learned first-hand of Saul's death:

'David and his men tore their clothes in sorrow when they heard the news. They mourned and wept and fasted all day for Saul and his son Jonathan, and for the LORD's army and the nation of Israel, because they had died by the sword that day.'

David was described by God, as a man after His own heart. As men, you and I are called to be like this. We also need to be Spirit-filled, because I put it to you that if we operate only in our flesh, none of us could act like David acted. The flesh, if not checked, seeks revenge on others and causes us to follow the ways of the evil one. Saul's kingship came to an end because he disobeyed God and he would not repent; instead he went back to his old fleshly ways.

Only if we are walking in the Spirit with God, like the patriarchs of the Bible did, can we hope to live a godly life.

Even though King David was described by God as 'A man after God's own heart' if you know the story of this godly King, you will know that in a moment of weakness, David in later life gives in to his own flesh and commits the sins of adultery, then cold-blooded murder of the adulteress' husband – who was ironically a man who showed great loyalty to King David himself. Sadly for David his sin came back to haunt him because God, being a just God as well as a merciful one, allowed the consequences of David's sins to affect David and his family forever. His first son, conceived through his adultery with Bathsheba, died and this broke David's heart. Furthermore, because of David's sin, God withdrew His promise to David that he would build God's Temple. God said this would now pass to his second son, Solomon.

Perhaps I will close this chapter by reminding you that the New Covenant of grace, under which we now live, does not exempt us from the consequences of any sin that we may commit. Yes, when we confess and repent of our sins, we receive God's forgiveness, but our lives will still bear the consequences of our sins. This is because God is both merciful <u>and just</u>.

But if you confess, repent and overcome sin, walk in the Spirit, and obey the Lord - obeying His Holy Word and His plan for your life - then you can experience His power, peace and joy in your daily life.

And if you overcome and become a man after God's own heart, He can and will use you in **<u>mighty powerful ways</u>** to work for His Kingdom here on earth for His glory.

Chapter 3

DEALING WITH TEMPTATION – SPIRITUAL WARFARE

*'...having strapped on YOUR FEET THE GOSPEL OF PEACE
IN PREPARATION [to face the enemy with firm-footed stability
and the readiness produced by the good news].'*
(Ephesians chapter 6 verse 15)

*"'Troops, the believer who is fully armed is near impossible
to destroy. To make your armed opponent vulnerable, simply
persuade him to remove a piece of his armour. You'll be
pleasantly surprised to discover just how easy it is to do so."
– SATAN'*

(Taken from 25 *Truths about Demons and Spiritual Warfare* by
David Diga Hernandez). [1]

*"For though we walk in the flesh [as mortal men], we are not
carrying on our [spiritual] warfare according to the flesh and
using the weapons of man. The weapons of our warfare are not
physical [weapons of flesh and blood]. Our weapons are divinely*

powerful for the destruction of fortresses. We are destroying sophisticated arguments and every exalted and proud thing that sets itself up against the [true] knowledge of God, and we are taking every thought and purpose captive to the obedience of Christ, being ready to punish every act of disobedience, when your own obedience [as a church] is complete." (2 Corinthians chapter 10 verse 3 to 6).

If you are a godly man, **you are in a battle!**

To mature Christian readers, that will be a statement of the obvious. However, if you should doubt this biblical truth, and many do, there are some great books out there to help you come to terms with it. I have listed some at the back of this book under the heading 'Recommended Reading'. There is another truth to keep in mind, and that is that God has an enemy, Satan, who wants to keep secret this fact that <u>you are in a battle</u>, the moment you commit your life to Jesus.

If you're sceptical about this statement, then I hope to convince you of its truth from God's Word.

Firstly, the Bible is clear, that God wants all Christians - not just men - to understand that if you have given your life to Christ, then by that very act, you have become an enemy of the devil. Every Christian is a target of Satan, and he will stop at nothing in his attempt to 'take you out' (make you ineffective for God or even destroy you), and prevent you from being used by God on the battlefield of this earthly life! The devil has **no fear of any unbelieving soul** – his only fear regarding unbelievers is that he or she may turn to Christ. At the point of surrendering your life to Christ, the devil musters his troops to try to come against you. If you have recently come to Christ, knowledge of how to overcome the devil and his troops (his demons), is of paramount importance to you, and equipping you to overcome your spiritual enemy is the purpose of this chapter.

So to recap, if you are a believer in Christ Jesus, you have become a target of the devil because he knows that your faith in Jesus Christ will lead you to being saved from spending eternity in Hell. You have also become a danger to the devil, because he knows that *in Christ* you have power to take back from him what he has stolen away from the Kingdom of God. You have - without necessarily realising it - walked onto a spiritual battlefield, where the forces of good are at war with the forces of evil. The purpose of this chapter is to explain this to you clearly.

Secondly, the good news is that God wants to equip and enable **all of us** to win that battle. He wants us to win it, for **Himself**, for **ourselves**, for **those we love,** for those **we work with,** and for **all those with whom we come into contact.**

'The Lord is faithful, and He will strengthen you and protect you from the evil one' (2 Thessalonians chapter 3 verse 3, NIV), BUT we all have an important part to play as we are now about to explore.

One exceptional and compelling book that will help you to understand and believe this reality is called '**25 Truths about Demons and Spiritual Warfare'** by David Diga Hernandez. I can't recommend it strongly enough.[2]

I'd like to begin this chapter taking a look at the key Scripture in the New Testament concerning spiritual warfare.

Ephesians Chapter 6 (verses 10 to 20):

'In conclusion, be strong in the Lord [draw your strength from Him and be empowered through your union with Him] and in the power of His [boundless] might. Put on the full armour of God [for His precepts are like the splendid armour of a heavily-armed soldier], so that you may be able to [successfully] stand up against all the schemes and the strategies and the deceits of the

devil. For our struggle is not against flesh and blood [contending only with physical opponents], but against the rulers, against the powers, against the world forces of this [present] darkness, against the spiritual forces of wickedness in the heavenly (supernatural) places. Therefore, put on the complete armour of God, so that you will be able to [successfully] resist and stand your ground in the evil day [of danger], and having done everything [that the crisis demands], to stand firm [in your place, fully prepared, immovable, victorious]. So stand firm and hold your ground, HAVING TIGHTENED THE WIDE BAND OF TRUTH (personal integrity, moral courage) AROUND YOUR WAIST and HAVING PUT ON THE BREASTPLATE OF RIGHTEOUSNESS (an upright heart), and having strapped on YOUR FEET THE GOSPEL OF PEACE IN PREPARATION [to face the enemy with firm-footed stability and the readiness produced by the good news]. Above all, lift up the [protective] shield of faith with which you can extinguish all the flaming arrows of the evil one. And take THE HELMET OF SALVATION, and the sword of the Spirit, which is the Word of God.

With all prayer and petition pray [with specific requests] at all times [on every occasion and in every season] in the Spirit, and with this in view, stay alert with all perseverance and petition [interceding in prayer] for all God's people. And pray for me, that words may be given to me when I open my mouth, to proclaim boldly the mystery of the good news [of salvation], for which I am an ambassador in chains. And pray that in proclaiming it I may speak boldly and courageously, as I should.'

As I explore this passage, my prayer is that these truths will give you **fearless overcoming power** and **faith in God** who, remember, is fighting the battle for you in the spirit realm. Although He fights the battle *spiritually*, you have to fight it in the *physical* realm. If you are not willing to do so, you could be taken out of the battle with one swift mighty blow of the enemy. But, once you decide to go into battle, the battle is the Lord's and if you are in Christ, God will win the battle for every man who steps out in faith, provided that man is wearing the spiritual armour which is described above in Ephesians chapter 6. You will recall in Chapter Two *'Becoming a man after God's own heart'*, I looked at David and how he did what was impossible in the natural – he killed Goliath. This is actually a great example of spiritual warfare. The enemy of God's chosen people had come to wipe them out. The Israelites and their army were all shaking with fear; all that is, except the young teenager, David.

Let me remind you what David said to Goliath who, in the spirit realm, was the devil's strongest warrior. (1 Samuel chapter 17 verse 45 and 47, NKJV)…

"You come to me with a sword, with a spear, and with a javelin. But I come to you in the name of the LORD of hosts, the God of the armies of Israel, whom you have defied. The LORD does not save with sword and spear; for the battle is the LORD's, and He will give you into our hands."

And as we know, God rewarded David's faith and enabled him to defeat Goliath in perhaps one of the most personally humiliating and unlikely acts ever recorded in history – David killed this huge, mighty, heavily armed enemy warrior using a simple catapult and a stone.

The Battle is the Lord's

For me, one of the key phrases in that mighty statement of defiance by the young David was… *'For the battle is the Lord's.'* Once we realise that truth, then we can all move in faith and win the battle! We have to be courageous enough to physically go to the enemy and fight as David did, knowing the battle is the Lord's. The battle is in the spirit realm. It is against the powers of darkness; Satan and his demons.

The battle may concern a sin in your life, an aspect of your behaviour over which the enemy has a stronghold or it may concern your church. It may concern your business, the neighbourhood in which you live, your country, or your government. It may be a battle concerning whatever God has laid on your heart that concerns Him, in particular, a battle that could <u>prevent the plan God has for your life.</u>

If you have declared your faith in Jesus Christ and therefore become a child of God, you are now a threat to Satan, and a battle has begun in the spirit realm. But you are not alone, because that battle is between God's people (every brother and sister in Christ) and the enemy's demons.

And the encouraging thing is, your ability to win the battle has nothing to do with your own physical strength. You can be a ten and a half stone 'physical weakling' like me and still overcome the enemy! And this is because *'The battle is the Lord's'* and it is always won by God's **spiritual power,** not your physical power. As it says in Zechariah 4 verse 6:

'Not by might, nor by power, but by My Spirit,' says the LORD of hosts'.

So, your part is to go into the battle, and if you do, God's promise is to turn up! And when He turns up, *anything* can happen!

You cannot win the battle without adequate preparation.

Now, one thing you mustn't do is just turn up on the battlefield. That's God's role. Your role, like any warrior or serviceman going into battle against their enemy is to first spend some time in the barracks; not drinking tea or coffee, not reading some seedy glossy magazine, but putting on your **'armour'.** In days of old, armour would include chain mail, helmets, swords, shields and the like. In modern day warfare, it would include special helmets, rifles or machine guns, grenades, bulletproof vests etc.

So, let's now take a look at the armour we are told to put on and use according to the Bible, in Ephesians chapter 6.

The first thing I note is, before telling us to put our armour on,

Paul, the writer says in verse 10, *'In conclusion, be strong in the Lord and in the power of His [boundless] might.'*

What does he mean *'In Conclusion'*...

Well, in a nutshell, in this letter he has been telling the believers in the church in Ephesus a number of facts about themselves. It's so easy to listen to Satan's lies, so Paul, who understands this, is reminding these children of God of some truths about themselves. That they are **redeemed**, that they are **'in Christ'**, he is telling them about **God's grace**, the **unity of the Spirit**, about the **need to turn from their sin** and to **imitate God**, and also **how wives, husbands and children are to behave** towards each other.

Now he is concluding and warning us all of the need to be strong in Christ. Why? Because the enemy's lies are subtle and it is easy to believe them, especially lies concerning the important points Paul has laid out in his letter - our redemption, our standing in Christ, God's grace, the beautiful Holy Spirit, relationships and sin.

So we should expect attacks from the enemy in these areas because from time to time, we will hear lies whispered into our ears.

Examples of Satan's Lies:

'You're not really saved'.

'I can destroy you easily - anybody can see that you're not in Christ because of the things you do, you say and you think!'

'You don't deserve God's grace, why should He extend it to you? You're not even right with Him. In any case, that sin you love to do won't do you any harm. God's just a kill-joy, He doesn't want you to have a good time'.

'You could find yourself a much better looking wife. Look around you at all those beautiful younger women. They'd love to have a workaholic husband like you who would shower them with

everything they need to make them happy.'

'Your kids are in such a mess, why don't you make them leave home. They're such an embarrassment when they turn up at church… Life would be so much easier if you stopped trying to change them and just let them get on with their own lives.'

These are all examples of the kind of lies that Satan and his demons will keep telling you and will become believable, if you do not know who you are in Christ. This powerful sixth chapter in Ephesians gives us insight into how to avoid listening to them or believing them.

So let's begin our battle plans by *'being strong in the Lord and in the power of His [boundless] might.'*

Moving to verse 11, we learn two things, first that God's precepts (or commands) *'are like the splendid armour of a heavily-armed soldier.'*

I love the Amplified Bible translation. Here we learn that if we obey God's precepts (or commands), then in effect we wear His armour! Amazing! Remember, God says: *'Obedience is better than sacrifice'* (1 Samuel chapter 15 verse 22, NLT).

And second, that by putting on *'the FULL armour of God'* then we will *'be able to stand up against ALL the schemes, strategies and the deceits of the devil.'*

But note the very first phrase of verse 11. *'Put on the full armour'*.

FULL armour! Why? Because if you only put on <u>some</u> of the armour instead of <u>all of it</u> you will be vulnerable to your enemy. And it's easy to see why. Supposing you've got all your armour in place except your helmet. How then will you defend yourself from an arrow that has been shot so fast at your head that by the time you see it you've no time to move out of its way? Likewise, if you've forgotten your shield, how then will you extinguish all the flaming arrows of the evil *one*?

The other thing I noticed, is that the last phrase in verse 11 says: *'stand up against all the schemes and the strategies and the deceits of the devil.'*

What are we to stand up against? <u>**ALL**</u> the **schemes, strategies** and **deceits** of the devil. So, notice Satan has an arsenal of weapons and ammunition that he plans to use against you.

What comes to your mind when you think of 'schemes, strategies and deceits'? As I typed this sentence in my manuscript on my PC, I felt God say to me "Check out the meaning of those words" and I thought I would choose one meaning of each to list here for you. But I was amazed at how relevant each meaning was just for the word 'scheme', and I could see that I needed to list them all here for you. I found my mind running away with itself as I read the list! This was literally what I read at 'dictionary.com' (I have genuinely not edited any of these – the date of the search was 29th January 2018). As you read the following definitions of the three words, *schemes, strategy* and *deceit*, think of each sentence and phrase in relation to Satan's potential plans against you and other followers of Christ…

<u>**'Scheme'**</u> noun

1. A plan, design, or program of action to be followed; project.

2. An underhand plot; intrigue.

3. A visionary or impractical project.

4. A body or system of related doctrines, theories, etc., e.g., a scheme of philosophy.

5. Any system of correlated things, parts, etc., or the manner of its arrangement.

6. A plan, program, or policy officially adopted and followed, as by a government or business. E.g., The Company's pension scheme is very successful.

7. An analytical or tabular statement.

Next came strategy…

'Strategy' noun, plural 'strategies'.

1. Also, strategics, the science or art of combining and employing the means of war in planning and directing large military movements and operations.

2. The use or an instance of using this science or art.

3. Skilful use of a stratagem. E.g., the salesperson's strategy was to seem always to agree with the customer *(author's note, for 'salesperson' read 'devil' who gives you the thought "I'm no good." He will then say "You're right you'll never be any good!")*.

4. A plan, method, or series of manoeuvres or stratagems for obtaining a specific goal or result: a strategy for getting ahead in the world.

And finally, deceit:

'Deceit' - noun

1. The act or practice of deceiving; concealment or distortion of the truth, for the purpose of misleading; duplicity; fraud; cheating. E.g., *once she exposed their deceit, no one ever trusted them again.*

2. An act or device intended to deceive; trick; stratagem.

3. The quality of being deceitful; duplicity; falseness: *a man full of deceit.*

That very last phrase sums up the devil – *A man full of deceit!*

By the way, the devil never goes away, he is always looking for another chance to attack you, which is why the Bible warns us in 1 Peter chapter 5 verse 8 to **'Be sober [well balanced and self-disciplined], be alert and cautious at <u>all times</u>. That enemy of yours, the devil, prowls around like a roaring lion [fiercely hungry], seeking someone to devour.'**

James similarly warns us (James chapter 4 verse 7), *'So submit to [the authority of] God. Resist the devil [stand firm against him] and he will flee from you.'*

So, if the devil can't 'eat you for dinner' today (because you have your FULL armour in place), he may come back next time he is hungry, which could be tomorrow, next week, next month, next year – whenever he finds you tired, weary, lazy and walking about on the battlefield 'undressed'! So, keep on **all** your armour, **all** of the time! In this regard, let me encourage you to read chapter 4 of the Old Testament Book of Nehemiah. Nehemiah and the people of Israel are rebuilding the walls of Jerusalem, against fierce enemy opposition. Pay special attention to verses 21 to 23….

Next, what for me is the **key verse** (verse 12) of Ephesians chapter 6. It tells us *'our struggle is not against flesh and blood [contending only with physical opponents], but against the rulers, against the powers, against the world forces of this [present] darkness, against the spiritual forces of wickedness in the heavenly (supernatural) places.'*

The New King James Version of the Bible renders the verse this way:

'For we do not wrestle against flesh and blood, but against principalities, against powers, against the rulers of the darkness of this age, against spiritual hosts of wickedness in the heavenly places.' (NKJV).

Many scholars have tried to explain what is meant by, and whether there is a difference between, 'principalities', 'powers', 'rulers of this age' and 'spiritual wickedness in the heavenly places'. I do not want to enter into conjecture here, but suffice to say we are in a battle against sinister forces in the spiritual realm. Paul is clear that our battle is not against 'people' but our action is to be directed at these demonic forces that are behind the wrongful behaviour of humankind.

So what does all this mean in terms of your day-to-day struggles? Well, for example, it might have been a young 'boy racer' that cut you up in his car the other day causing you to get angry, but the struggle relating to that incident is in *the spirit realm,* it is not against that young man. What made you angry was the person's **actions** (his behaviour) which itself may have simply been caused by the difficulties or sin that that man struggles with - which in turn has been brought upon him by the sin of the world, the flesh or the devil. Or the cause of his behaviour may go further back to when he was much younger, e.g., it could have been caused by a lack of Christian teaching at school, or growing up in an anti-Christian society or perhaps he experienced some uncaring parental treatment - any one of these kind of things might have resulted in him behaving in an anti-social way.

Likewise, a person or group of people may come against you, your family or the Church in some way, but there is usually a spiritual reason why that has happened, in which case we need to discern *the reason* and pray about it to reveal whether it originates in the spiritual realm. We can then come against the demon in Jesus' Name, because **He** has given us power to do that.

If you are sceptical about the truth of verse 12 of Ephesians chapter 6, then once again I recommend you find a good book like the one I referred to earlier by David Diga Hernandez.[3] If you read and study the subject more deeply, I promise you this whole concept will become so much more believable and understandable.

Don't worry, GOD IS IN CONTROL – NOT Satan!

As we discover more about the reality of spiritual warfare it is important to remember that *'He who is in you is greater than he who is in the world.'* (1 John chapter 4 verse 4b, NKJV). Paul explains this fact to us all in Colossians chapter 2 where he tells us that:

'Christ is the head over <u>all rule and authority</u> [of every angelic and earthly power]. He has disarmed the rulers and authorities

[those supernatural forces of evil operating against us], He made a public example of them [exhibiting them as captives in His triumphal procession], having triumphed over them through the cross.'

The devil **HAS** <u>lost the war,</u> but what we are contending with in our lives daily, is the fact that the battles rage on until Christ returns in triumph. Whilst we wait patiently for Him, we need to understand and apply chapter 6 of Ephesians in order to overcome the devil's schemes against us.

So let's return to it. In verse 13 we are encouraged to *'put on the complete armour of God, so that we will be able to [successfully] resist and stand our ground in the evil day [of danger], and having done everything [that the crisis demands], to stand firm [in your place, fully prepared, immovable, victorious]'.*

Here we see the analogy of the battlefield.

I've never taken up boxing but to me the description here is a bit like a boxer when he is on the receiving end of some good punches. If he waivers, he goes down. But if he stands his ground, stands *'firm in his place, fully prepared* (to return the punches), and *immovable',* then fear can set into his opponent and the boxer may have a good chance of winning the fight (being *'victorious'*).

Once again, this verse urges us to *'put on the <u>complete</u> armour of God.'*

With our full armour in place, Paul tells us to do *'everything [that the crisis demands].'*

What is demanded, of course, depends on the nature of the crisis. However, it doesn't mean putting on all the armour, because that should be in place on our body <u>all the time</u>. So, if our armour is in place, what does it mean to *do everything that the crisis demands?* I believe it's more to do with keeping calm, drawing upon the strength and peace of God, and also remaining immovable and steadfast against whatever the specific crisis is.

I also believe it means applying some of the principles of 'Crisis Management.'

Remarkably, and very unlike me, my youngest son is extremely calm in a crisis. In the natural, I am prone to panic and impulse. Philip is able to separate out the panic, and think logically and calmly.

On a website *nextavenue.org* I found a secular piece entitled *'How to stay calm in any crisis. These 3 easy yet powerful practices can restore clarity and focus'.*

Before I tell you what the 3 easy yet powerful practices are, please don't judge me for using, on this occasion, a secular piece to illustrate a biblical principle, (particularly in the case of practice number 1). I believe you will see what I am getting at as you read on!

So, here we go… What are those three powerful practices?

Mindfulness meditation, gratitude and self-compassion. So let's try applying these 'powerful practices' to the subject matter…

1. **Mindfulness meditation.** Apparently this is to focus on the specific 'here and now'. So, you might say "I've encountered an attack of the devil; what's going on, what do I need to do right now?" Answer? Talk to God (pray).

2. **Gratitude.** How might you show gratitude? "Father, thank you so much that the battle is yours and not mine. I'm here in this awful unexpected situation, what do I need to do? Please speak to me and help me overcome". In other words, talk to God (pray!).

3. **Self-compassion.** Don't beat yourself up. All the great men of God fouled up along the way of achieving great things for God. Instead ask for forgiveness. "Lord forgive me I slipped up this time, help me to move on and overcome next time". Yes, point three also means talk to God (pray).

I could be completely wrong, but it seems to me that the most important thing to do when a spiritual crisis comes is **to pray.**

Remember I am focussing here on doing *'everything [that the crisis demands].'*

There are also some practical things that we must all do to avoid getting into a crisis in the first place.

First of all, have an accountability partner. By far the best accountability partner if you are married, is your wife! Get into the habit of confessing your sins to your accountability partner. To be motivated to do that, you must of course be confident the partner is completely honest and will keep entirely to themselves whatever confidence you share with them.

Practical ways to avoid sin.

Here are some practical ways to avoid falling into your sins or bad habits. For example if you are, or have been, caught up in pornography, don't watch TV alone or use a PC alone. Be careful what newspapers or magazines you read.

If you are attracted to the opposite sex in an inappropriate way, don't go to places where you will come across them 'unhelpfully attired' e.g., the beach, swimming pools, discos etc.

Ask your accountability partner to check with you regularly how you are coping with your area of weakness. Be honest with him (or her if your accountability partner is your wife); if you are still struggling, confess it to your partner and ask God to forgive you. I and others can testify that something of the enemy's stranglehold is broken when sinful behaviour kept in the dark is brought out into the light through confession and repentance.

If, after confession, you struggle again, remember you are not a failure; that is a lie of Satan. You are human like every man who has, or will ever walk the face of the earth. But don't be complacent and just accept that weakness. God loves you so much He doesn't want to leave you where you are but is determined to help you to get to where He is taking you, which is always a much better place.

Whilst on the subject of doing *'everything [that the crisis demands]'* I want to digress for a few moments into holiness. I believe this is an important aspect of spiritual warfare because Satan will do everything he can to stop you and me from living a holy life.

The Bible says,

'But like the Holy One who called you, be holy yourselves in all your conduct [be set apart from the world by your godly character and moral courage]; because it is written, "YOU SHALL BE HOLY (set apart), FOR I AM HOLY." ' (1 Peter chapter 1 verses 15 and 16).

What does that mean?

Anything that is holy, including you and me, is **'set apart'.** It doesn't mean perfect, but set apart. We are set apart from our old life-style and dedicated to God's holy work and a new, better, lifestyle in Christ.

If your marriage is under attack, seek help from spiritually mature Christian friends; attend the Marriage Course (I refer to this in Volume Two Chapter One) - learn how to deal with relational conflict (we will study that in Volume Two). Don't bury your head in the sand, as many men find it easier to do. Pride is the original sin and caused Satan to rebel against God (read *'MERE CHRISTIANITY'* by CS Lewis).

My dear brother-in-Christ, you have to realise the battle in which you are engaged is ongoing every minute of every day, even though at many times you won't realise it. This too is intentional on the devil's part because that is one way he can catch you off guard. If I think I am not on the battlefield today, then I won't be attacked… will I? I'm afraid to tell you *"Yes you will."*

You must remember to put on your God-given armour, not just

every time you wake up, but also to keep it on every time you go to bed. The next attack just might come in the middle of the night!

Returning now to Ephesians chapter 6. Verse 13 concludes, *'having done everything [that the crisis demands], to stand firm [in your place, fully prepared, immovable, victorious].'*

At this point, if you are applying what this Holy Scripture has told you, you have prayed in the midst of the crisis, God has been true to Himself and enabled you to overcome, you are still standing firm, fully prepared for the next tactic of the enemy and so far immovable and victorious. Well done you! Victory is yours, in Jesus Name, Amen!!

It's now time to read verse 14:

'So stand firm and hold your ground, HAVING TIGHTENED THE WIDE BAND OF TRUTH (personal integrity, moral courage) AROUND YOUR WAIST and HAVING PUT ON THE BREASTPLATE OF RIGHTEOUSNESS (an upright heart).'

I find this verse so powerful. I don't know about you, but I am currently at a place where some Scriptures have the power of causing me to literally burst forth with tears, as I read them. I don't know why. I don't know if it's spiritual but I believe it is. What I experience isn't solely the emotion of joy, it's something deeper. At other times, the reason for crying after reading God's Word is because of the conviction of sin.

If you have experienced this kind of emotion – crying at the power of God's Word – you will know what I am talking about. Oswald Chambers talks about *'Bringing back the ministry of tears.'* It was Charles Spurgeon who first talked about a **'Ministry of Tears'** and he defined it as **'Liquid prayers'.**

Having digressed momentarily into the subject of holiness, let's get back to Ephesians chapter 6 verse 14…

'Stand firm and hold your ground, HAVING TIGHTENED

THE WIDE BAND OF TRUTH (personal integrity, moral courage) AROUND YOUR WAIST and HAVING PUT ON THE BREASTPLATE OF RIGHTEOUSNESS (an upright heart).'

As I said earlier in this book, I love the Amplified translation of the Bible, because when a phrase isn't clear, it tells us what those phrases mean...

'Band of truth' (or 'belt of truth' in other translations) = personal integrity, moral courage.

'Breastplate of righteousness' = an upright heart.

But I discovered something new, and to find this out I had to take time to check the Amplified Bible text note and look at the bottom of the page. Most of us men aren't good at that are we? You know, spending an extra two minutes to check understanding! Oh no, we're far too busy to do that aren't we?

Anyway, let's look at the Band of Truth.

Where it says *'tighten the band of truth around your waist'*, it literally means 'girded your loins (with the band or belt)'. The Amplified Bible footnote says this:

'Girded your loins, (is) a phrase often found in the Bible. (It) is an urgent call to get ready for immediate action or a coming event. The phrase is related to the type of clothing worn in ancient times. Before any vigorous activity, the loose ends of clothing (tunics, cloaks, mantles, etc.) had to be gathered up and tucked into the wide band worn around the midsection of the body. The band (usually about six inches wide) also served as a kind of pocket or pouch to carry personal items such as a dagger, money or other necessary things. Gird up your mind or gird up your heart are examples of variants of this phrase and call for mental or spiritual preparation for a coming challenge.'

So, it turns out that this 'band of truth' is what Paul was thinking of when he wrote this letter to the Ephesians. We discover here that it was a band (not a belt). And a band wasn't used to hold up your trousers! It was much more important than that.

Here in verse 14 Paul is saying that when you come under attack, you are to stand firm, hold your ground, and act with personal integrity, moral courage and an upright heart.

Now I put it to you that unless you are born again and Spirit-filled, to do those things in the natural when the enemy is causing you grief is impossible. To respond in such a way requires you and I to act like Jesus, which requires us to be full of His Spirit.

The truth that Paul is referring to (encompassing personal integrity and moral courage), is the truth of God revealed in The Gospel which has its outworking in the believer's life. The outward sign that you have put in place the band of truth (as part of your armour) is that you will display the characteristics of Jesus in all aspects of your everyday life.

The Breastplate of Righteousness.

Being armed with the Breastplate of Righteousness (displaying a heart that is upright) means you will respond against the blows and the arrows of your various spiritual enemies with God's righteousness, which again works itself out in an ethical sense, i.e. be an imitator of God.

Now let me ask you a serious question. Would you or your spouse, mother, father, closest friend or whoever knows you best, describe you as *'totally honest, full of integrity, morally courageous and with an upright heart'*?

If the answer is yes, then you probably already have these two items of armour in place (that is the band of truth and the breastplate of righteousness). If as you reflect upon this question you are uneasy or wavering - even slightly - about the answer, then there is at least a chink in that armour. If you know the answer is 'no', 'not really', or 'there is room for improvement', then you may have forgotten to put this piece of armour on altogether. If your armour is missing or damaged, you need help - either in putting it on or in repairing the damage - because demons will find ways to get through any missing and damaged piece of armour.

You see, if you haven't remembered to put on your band of truth, then when you need to run or fight, you will trip over your girdle or your tunic.

Having no band of truth around your loins, means you've nowhere to keep your dagger to protect yourself. When the enemy confronts you, he will see you are inadequately protected and powerless, and so he will find it easy to defeat you.

What is 'integrity'?

I said above that the 'band of truth' is synonymous with personal integrity and moral courage.

A website called 'Thefreedictionary.com' is a sound site to visit to check on the meaning of words. There you will find three definitions of the noun 'Integrity'.

1. *Steadfast adherence to a strict moral or ethical code: e.g. a leader of great integrity.*

2. *The state of being unimpaired; soundness: e.g. The building's integrity remained intact following the mild earthquake.*

3. *The quality or condition of being whole or undivided; completeness: e.g. replaced a lost book to restore the integrity of his collection.*

What moral or ethical code do you adhere to?

Do you adhere steadfastly to *'The Gospel of Peace'?* Do you accept God's Word as your ultimate authority on truth? Is your 'yes', yes and your 'no', no? Are you a man of your word? Do you compromise your integrity by telling 'little white lies', or similarly, are you 'economical with the truth'?

If there were a mild 'earthquake' in your life, would your integrity remain intact?

Are you 'whole and undivided' in your allegiance to God? Or have you lost something in your walk with Him and become lazy, complacent, and perhaps even decided not to restore that which you have lost?

Jesus is expecting you and me not to waiver. If you and I want to be a disciple of His, then He has some no-nonsense, uncompromising words of warning to us. Remember Jesus is in no way controlling. He gently asks us *if* we want to do something, or *if* we want to follow Him. But if we say "Yes we do…" then He says this in reply: 'If anyone comes to me and does not …….. He cannot be my disciple!' see Luke chapter 9 verses 21 to 26 and Luke chapter 14 verses 26 and 27.

So, if you are wavering, let the words of King Solomon (David's son) give you some free wise counsel. He points out in Song of Solomon chapter 2 verse 15 that it's the **little things** that spoil our walk with God. Actually His words are these; *"Catch the foxes for us, the little foxes that spoil and ruin the vineyards [of love], while our vineyards are in blossom."*

Oswald Chambers' daily devotional book is called 'My *Utmost* for His Highest' because he knew and taught that our _good_ acts of service aren't good enough for God. God expects our _best_ says Chambers.

And despite warnings like these from King Solomon and Oswald Chambers, we find ourselves listening to the enemy's lies, such as…

"God won't mind if you don't address that little sin in your life, after all, you spend practically all your time serving Him - He loves you and He wants you to *'enjoy life, and have it in abundance [to the full, till it overflows].'* He tells you this in His Word." (John chapter 10 verse 10).

Satan is subtle, he knows Holy Scripture better than we do, and delights in taking a truth and twisting it ever so slightly so that you believe his subtle lies and deception.

This is confirmed right at the beginning of human creation in Genesis chapter 3 verse 1 (NIV) where Satan (in the form of a serpent) said to Eve, *"Did God really say.........?"* And that little expression inevitably raises doubts in a person's mind. We have to be on our guard and reply "YES HE DID!"

Now, back to verse 14. The second phrase used in the Amplified translation to explain the band of truth is 'moral courage'.

What is Moral Courage?

Dictionary.com defines courage as:

'The quality of mind or spirit that enables a person to face difficulty, danger, pain, etc., without fear; bravery.'

It also quotes this somewhat appropriate idiom:

'To have the courage of one's convictions, to act in accordance with one's beliefs, especially in spite of criticism.'

In the Scripture, Paul is talking about *'moral courage'* and since the context is spiritual warfare I think the question is 'Do we, do you, believe you are strong enough spiritually to venture where God is sending you (ministry wise)? Do you persevere when the attack of the enemy is relentless, and are you able to withstand *difficulty, danger, pain etc* on the battleground of spiritual warfare 'without fear'? Do you demonstrate, in difficult situations, your *'bravery'* and courage to speak out the Word of God not only when people do not want to hear it, but also and especially *'in spite of criticism'?'*

Paul says you will be able to, if you have put on your wide *'band of truth'* and tightened it in place.

What is Truth?

At His trial, ahead of our Lord's crucifixion, Pilate asked Jesus the age-old question: **'What is truth?'** As followers of Jesus, we have to tell the world we have the answer. In these times of 'relative truth', and 'what's truth for you isn't necessarily truth for me', we have to courageously proclaim 'there is *absolute* truth' and it has been established for eternity in God's 'Instruction Manual' – The Holy Bible.

In recent times you may have noticed that a subtle change in the meaning of words has gradually been accepted by the modern world. So for example 'gay' until recently meant 'carefree, cheerful, bright and showy', but today it is used to describe somebody who is attracted to a member of the same sex, and this latter meaning has taken over as the primary meaning in most modern on-line dictionaries. 'Wicked' used to mean 'evil, morally bad' etc., but many of today's young people use this word when referring to something that is wonderful and lovely! 'Marriage' now means a sort of social contract no longer confined to a man and a woman; 'faith' has come to mean 'religion' (as opposed to belief in our Saviour Jesus Christ), and to most unbelievers all religions are now considered equal and meaningless. The redefining of words is another subtle work of the enemy to distort absolute truth. Equality and political correctness have become more important than truth. Human rights have become sacrosanct too and that's a good thing, but why do we only apply these rights to human beings <u>after</u> they have left the 'safety' of their mother's womb?

Whilst it is not the remit of this book to discuss in any depth such a fragile subject, I could spend a lot of time talking about the unborn child and abortion, and that could easily form the basis of an entire book. But I would like to take a small digression on this subject of redefining words and the twisting and distorting of God's absolute truth, in order to share with you just one insight from God's Holy Word about the unborn child. This makes it as clear as it can possibly be, that a child in the womb is a LIVING HUMAN BEING; and as such, the pro-abortion agenda of this world is a distortion of God's absolute truth, and is in direct opposition to the value that God places on the human life of every unborn child.

Let me encourage you to take a look at the first chapter of the Gospel of Luke. It is a beautiful account of two women: Mary, the mother of Jesus, and Elizabeth (Mary's cousin), who was the mother of John the Baptist.

As we know, Mary conceived Jesus supernaturally, in fulfilment of the Word of God, and by the power of the Holy Spirit. Elizabeth, who was barren, also conceived her son John in fulfilment of God's promise to her husband Zechariah.

Let me ask you to read Luke Chapter 1 (the whole chapter), and then go back and highlight verses 26, 36, 41, 44, 56 and 57. Do you notice anything?

Now take a second read of the chapter, but this time just read verses 26 to 57. You will discover that the unborn child of six month's gestation, in Elizabeth's womb, was actually able to sense that something very special was occurring outside its mother's womb, and as a result, the child leapt in its mother's womb. What Elizabeth's unborn baby (John the Baptist) sensed was the fact that inside the womb of Mary, (who had just entered Elizabeth's house), was the Saviour of the world – the Son of God, Jesus Christ!

So, how could Elizabeth's unborn child sense the presence of the Messiah, if the child was 'not a living human being' in the womb, but merely a 'blob of cells' or a 'foetus' as is often referred to by the medical institution and by abortion activists?

Having given this example from Holy Scripture, please know that I empathise with any woman who may have to make a very difficult choice concerning the future of her unborn child, particularly when complications arise. I also realise and appreciate that, throughout our lives, we all have to make choices, some good and some not so good. However, I do not believe that it can be God's will for abortion to be used as a form of birth control under the label of 'Women's Health Care' after a woman discovers that she is pregnant, since abortion brings to an end the life of an unborn baby.

Coming back now to the subject of truth… There is a biblical reason why many often intelligent people, (like Pontius Pilate of old, and modern day national leaders, whether kings, queens, presidents or prime ministers, businessmen and the like) simply do not understand or believe God's truth. This is what we discover in 2 Corinthians chapter 4 verses 3 and 4:

'But even if our gospel is [in some sense] hidden [behind a veil], it is hidden [only] to those who are perishing; among them the god of this world [Satan] has <u>blinded the minds of the unbelieving</u> to prevent them from seeing the illuminating light of the gospel of the glory of Christ, who is the image of God.' (Author's emphasis).

Satan has blinded the **minds** of the unbelieving to the truth of the Gospel. And so, not for the first time, I wish to remind you that…

The Battle is for the mind.

Joyce Meyer has written a great book about this subject, called 'Battlefield of the Mind'. [4] I strongly recommend it!

Returning to the second part of verse 14…

'Stand firm and hold your ground, HAVING TIGHTENED THE WIDE BAND OF TRUTH (personal integrity, moral courage) AROUND YOUR WAIST and HAVING PUT ON THE BREASTPLATE OF RIGHTEOUSNESS (an upright heart).'

We've dealt with the first part of this verse in detail. Let me more quickly cover the second part *'PUT ON THE BREASTPLATE OF RIGHTEOUSNESS (an upright heart).'*

What, then, is an *'upright heart'*?

Dictionary.com gives us (in the context of a person being

upright), these two meanings for the adjective 'upright':

'Adhering to rectitude; righteous, honest, or just: e.g., an upright person.

'Being in accord with what is right: e.g., upright dealings.'

As regards the noun 'rectitude', we are given two definitions, both of which I believe are spiritually appropriate (it is a quality or a state):

'Rightness of principle or conduct; moral virtue: e.g., the rectitude of her motives.

Correctness: e.g., rectitude of judgment.'

So then, putting on the breastplate of righteousness, surely means, being straight (honest and *correct*) with people (like Jesus was, and He included many words of 'tough love', especially towards those in authority, whom He rebuked, challenged and corrected).

It also means being morally *righteous, honest, and just* - full of integrity.

It means having excellent *judgement*, judging things correctly, showing no favouritism or bias. Ensuring our day-to-day dealings with others are *upright*.

Being correct and *in accord with what is right* implies <u>doing things right</u>, but I was always taught it is better to do <u>the right thing</u> (there is a big difference between the two!). I'll leave you to decide.

'The breastplate of righteousness' – put it on, have faith in God, and He will supernaturally help you to have an upright heart and behave in a righteous way.

Verse 15 is next:

'And having strapped on YOUR FEET THE GOSPEL OF PEACE IN PREPARATION [to face the enemy with firm-footed stability and the readiness produced by the good news].

The Gospel of peace – 'The Good News'.

Many years ago, after I became born again, I would have read this verse in the NIV Translation of the Bible. My NIV Study Bible is well thumbed and very dog-eared now because after being Spirit-filled I hungered and thirsted for the Word of God, and I couldn't get enough of it! It's the same today, but I prefer to study the Amplified Bible translation because, for me, it makes the text easier to understand. Prior to that time, I never really read the Bible at all, but it was read to me by others in church services, often in the King James or New King James Versions. Verse 15 is rendered in the NKJV, *'and having shod your feet with the preparation of the gospel of peace'*. That didn't really speak to me; it made little sense. And until you are born again, the KJV or NKJV can be difficult to understand.

From 1991 until recently, I went through a long phase in my life when I more or less only ever read the NIV translation of the Bible. The NIV renders this verse as follows:

'And with your feet fitted with the readiness that comes from the gospel of peace'.

So I imagined that what this Scripture was telling me to do was to walk around with some sandals on my feet, appearing 'holy' and being at peace with everybody.

But when I read the Amplified translation, a light switched on in my mind. It suddenly dawned on me - particularly after reading the footnote assigned to this verse - that I have an incredibly powerful weapon available to help me stand upright when under attack. This translation is powerful:

'And having strapped on YOUR FEET THE GOSPEL OF PEACE IN PREPARATION *[to face the enemy with firm-footed stability and the readiness produced by the good news].*

Aha, I thought, sandals are not exactly going to offer me *firm-footed stability.* Then the light in my mind got brighter as I read the Amplified Bible footnote, which explained that this verse is a reference to shoes worn by the Roman soldiers of that time, which in fact were **studded with hobnails to give them stability on the battlefield.**

What dawned upon me after first reading this verse in the Amplified translation was this: If you or I wore flimsy sandals onto the filthy, slimy, or rocky battlefield, we would slip over before we even made it to the front line. But hobnailed boots? Wow, now if 'push came to shove' I can stand more firmly – AND I can even run if required!

So, what **are** these hobnailed boots that God has put in the arsenal for us? The Scripture tells us exactly what they are. They are, of course, The Good News of the Gospel, our great Gospel of Peace. We must at all times stand on the Gospel; without it we have nothing to offer the world and nothing with which to repel the enemy. ALL of our armour is based on Christ!

Because of what Jesus did on the Cross for you and for me, we have new life, by the power of His Holy Spirit living in us - and when the battle in the natural is over, as believers (and overcomers) we are promised a victor's crown to wear in the eternal Kingdom of Heaven! As you share the Good News of the Gospel, as you evangelise your neighbour, your friends, even strangers, **you** are taking ground for God. You are claiming back what the devil has stolen; the lives of people loved by God. And as you recall the truth of this Gospel of peace, it gives you more courage and faith so that as you go into battle for God, this faith and courage will help you overcome **all** the schemes of the enemy.

This Gospel of Peace is related to the very next piece of armour Paul describes to us –

The Shield of Faith.

'Above all, lift up the [protective] shield of faith with which you

can extinguish all the flaming arrows of the evil one.' (Verse 16).

Our faith in God protects us from the schemes of the evil one. You may have watched films involving medieval armies on the battlefield attacking each other, with cavalrymen or warriors on horseback wielding their shields to deflect the approaching sword or spear.

But, apparently, the imagery Paul had in mind (once again according to the Amplified translators' footnote) is that of *'the large Roman soldiers' shield designed to protect the entire body. It had an iron frame and was covered in several layers of leather. When soaked in water before a battle, the shield could put out the fiery missiles thrown at them by the enemy'.*

So when you hold out *'The Shield of Faith',* you can know that it protects your entire body. It may be heavy, but your God-given supernatural strength will enable you to hold it in place. It's dripping in water so as to protect you by extinguishing the flames of fiery missiles coming at you from natural - as well as supernatural - foes. Perhaps you would prefer to imagine your shield of faith dripping instead with the blood of your Saviour, wiping all your sins away in your moment of need. So, hold tightly on to your faith. It will help you overcome all the lies that the enemy whispers into your ears.

There is one last item of armour you need to put on to protect you. This item is to be placed on your head. It is a helmet; **The Helmet of Salvation.** Then - interestingly last of all - you have **a weapon** that God has given you with which to strike out against your foe. This is a sword, **The Sword of the Spirit,** and you will wield it in your hand, but it's no ordinary sword! We find this helmet and sword referred to in verse 17…

'And take THE HELMET OF SALVATION, and the sword of the Spirit, which is the Word of God.'

Let's start with:

The Helmet of Salvation.

This Scripture tells you that your helmet, represents your salvation.

The enemy hates the fact that if you are a confessing, repentant, overcoming believer in Jesus Christ, you are saved from eternal damnation in Hell. Satan's constant unrelenting plan is focussed on trying to make you lose your faith in Christ Jesus as your Saviour. It is very clear from Scripture that Hell is the final place for Satan and his demons; but this also includes anyone who refuses to believe in Jesus Christ, and also those who once followed Jesus, but have since rejected Him and remain unrepentant. In that last sentence, I nearly wrote 'Hell is the final *resting* place for Satan', but Jesus is emphatic – there is no rest in that place; there is only eternal torment and suffering there!

Many 'liberal Christians' do not believe in Hell or eternal damnation. To those of you who think like this, I would remind you that no less than five times in the New King James Version of Matthew's Gospel, Jesus describes Hell either as *'outer darkness'* or a *'furnace of fire* – and in all five cases, He says that in this place there will be either *'weeping'* or *'wailing'* and also *'gnashing of teeth'*. I am not asking you to believe me, but for your own sake, believe the Word of God: Hell is real! It is an appalling truth that few churches these days teach or preach about the reality of Hell and the consequences of sin. Jesus is more vocal about this than any other person in the Bible, so clearly Satan is working overtime in suppressing this truth within the Church. Come on Church WAKE UP!

Satan's ongoing battle plan is to attempt to scupper your salvation, and because of this God has given every believer the **Helmet of Salvation** to protect you from the devil's cunning and mischievous lies which he whispers into your mind in an attempt to derail you from your God-ordained destiny.

Being given armour is one thing, but we have to *use* the armour. We have to put it on. If you work in a factory, your employer may be duty bound to provide you with PPE (personal protective equipment) to wear to keep you safe, but it's of no use until you put it on!

Often is the time, in the past, I have left my spiritual armour 'in the cupboard' and regretted it greatly. Don't make *my* mistake!

'**Take**' the helmet – it means pick it up and put the helmet on. We all have these separate pieces of armour available to us, but are you putting them to use, or are you leaving them at home in the closet?

If your helmet is on your head, then it is where it should be. You are *wearing* it. Having the helmet of salvation in place implies that you are *aware* of the **certainty** of your salvation through the biblical truth that the blood of Jesus Christ, your personal Saviour, has redeemed you from your deserved fate – which is spending eternity in Hell with Satan and his minions. When it comes to a surety concerning salvation, I believe that one of the reasons so many Christians, when asked, cannot say with certainty that they know they are going to Heaven when they die, is because their helmet (of salvation) is not in place. Consequently the lies of Satan are able to speak to them louder than the truth of God's Word.

Interestingly, for years, when I heard born again Christians saying they were going to Heaven when they died, I thought that was an arrogant, self-righteous thing to say. But God has shown me this truth that when you know who you are in Christ, you will be able to say with certainty (by God's grace) 'I *am* going to heaven when I die'. That is the undeniable truth of God's Word for those who believe. Acts chapter 16 verse 31 is unambiguous. The Amplified translation is one of the clearest renderings *"Believe in the Lord Jesus [as your personal Saviour and entrust yourself to Him] and you will be saved, you and your household [if they also believe]."*

If you need reassurance about this truth, Romans chapters 5 and 10 are two excellent chapters to check out on this subject, but there are many other Scriptures if you do a search for them.

Now let's look at:

'The Sword of the Spirit, which is the Word of God.'

This is the only piece of 'armour' that we don't actually put on to protect ourselves. The sword of the Spirit is a weapon that we pick up and use forcefully to attack an enemy as well as to defend ourselves.

Without the Word of God to reassure you of absolute truth, it is easy to believe the half-truths and lies of Satan and the people of the world.

Once again though, you have to **'take'** the sword – it means take it out of its scabbard and thrust it into the enemy! It's useless just to know about it, you MUST use it each time you are attacked!

This spiritual sword of the Spirit is a **most powerful weapon** and I want to ask you to bear with me while I take a few extra paragraphs to enlighten you further.

A sword has two sides and two sharp edges. Likewise there are two aspects to what the sword of the Spirit represents, which is the Word of God. The first aspect of the sword of the Spirit is Holy Scripture, which has been _written_ down for us in the form of The Holy Bible, and the second aspect of the sword of the Spirit is the Word of God _spoken_ into our spirit at appropriate times of need by God's Holy Spirit. Putting it simply; I am talking about **The Written Word and The Spoken Word.**

The Written Word of God.

When tempted three times in the wilderness by the devil, Jesus responded with the sword of the Spirit – the Written Word of God

- "It is written….. It is written….. It is written." Jesus corrected Satan's lies with God's eternal truths (See Luke chapter 4 verses 1 to 13). And Jesus tells us that *'the truth will set you free.'* (John chapter 8 verse 32).

Probably my most favourite Scripture in the Bible is the opening verse in John's Gospel. The version I remember most is the one I used to sit in awe of at every Anglican candlelit carol service I have ever attended. It is one of God's eternal mysteries but I believe one of the most important foundational truths. It was usually read from either the King James or New King James Version as follows. You may know it well:

'In the beginning was the Word, and the Word was with God, and the Word was God'. (NKJV).

We then discover in the verses that follow the above opening verse of John chapter 1, that this *'Word'* is a person. Because in verse 14 we learn this: *'And the Word became flesh and dwelt among us, and we beheld His glory, the glory as of the only begotten of the Father, full of grace and truth.'* (NKJV).

John, the Gospel writer, is referring to Jesus Christ, the only begotten Son of the Father. Jesus Christ is the Word made flesh. If He is the <u>Word of God made flesh</u> then for me that literally means (and I personally believe) Jesus is 'the Bible made flesh'. I believe God gave me this revelation several years ago. As I said in Chapter Two, it is, and will remain an eternal mystery. But I believe it to be an eternal supernatural truth. It needs a step of faith to believe it. But if you can take that step of faith and believe this revelation, then you too will recognise why 'the sword of the Spirit' which is the Word of God is so powerful. It is the most important offensive weapon God has given you. We don't need fighter jets, machine guns, nuclear missiles and the like to win each battle, because 'the sword of the Spirit' is **<u>all powerful</u>** and will guarantee success against the attacks of Satan and his demons.

Theologians have written many pages about the meaning of the original Greek word 'logos' that John used to describe Jesus when he wrote his Gospel, and you can research that for yourself if you want to study this further, but for me, as I have said, there are two key aspects. The first aspect is to know and to quote appropriate words of Holy Scripture to the enemy when he speaks lying, deceptive or slightly twisted words into your mind. The devil's words often sound like truth, so as a warrior, you need to do your homework by knowing in depth the Word of God. Remember Jesus overcame the devil in the wilderness by quoting Holy Scripture (truth) to the devil. The truth of Holy Scripture will counteract the subtle untruths of the enemy.

The Spoken Word of God.

In the context of spiritual warfare, the second aspect to the 'Word of God' is God speaking to you by His Spirit. We can see examples throughout Scripture of God speaking to people in order to inspire and direct them, encourage them, protect them, etc. For example, in Mark chapter 13 verse 11, talking to His disciples, Jesus says:

'When they take you and turn you over [to the court], do not worry beforehand about what to say, but say whatever is given to you [by God] in that hour; for it is not you who speak, but it is the Holy Spirit [who will speak through you].' (Author's emphasis).

In Acts chapter 4 verse 8, addressing the Sanhedrin (The Jewish High Court) we read:

'Then Peter, filled with [the power of] the Holy Spirit, said to them, "Rulers and elders of the people [members of the Sanhedrin, the Jewish High Court]…' (Author's emphasis).

The early Church came under immense persecution, and many was the time God spoke through His gallant faithful warriors to ward off their enemies, many of whom were from within their own camp! It is the same today, so listen to God and speak out

His precious mighty truths, especially to the enemy because we know that *'Satan himself masquerades as an angel of light.'* (2 Corinthians chapter 11 verse 14).

Often God will give you His Words to speak in many different settings. Simply ask Him. He does it by His Spirit speaking directly into your mind. I particularly believe He will do this for you when you need to testify to others about the Gospel. Sometimes, He will give you words of knowledge, to speak into others' lives to encourage and build them up or to warn them about something. By mentioning this I am now getting into the subject of the gifts of the Spirit so I will return to the matter in hand – the sword of the Spirit.

The sword of the Spirit (The Word of God) <u>**will**</u> guarantee you success against the enemy, but only PROVIDED you have already put firmly in place all the armour that protects you from body blows, arrows and the like, while you are striking out at the enemy with your *sword of the Spirit.*

The following two Scriptures will give you an insight into how much power the sword of the Spirit carries. These two verses are written in Revelation chapter 19 where the writer, John, is sharing a God-given word of knowledge (or prophecy) concerning the End Times War between God's heavenly army and the powers of darkness. The context is that God is judging the world, and Christ the Conqueror is coming to put a final end to the devil and his followers. In both of the following verses, John is describing the actions of Jesus, who in this final battle scene, has these Words written on His robe and on His thigh *"KING OF KINGS, AND LORD OF LORDS."* (Verse 16).

These are the verses:

'From His mouth comes a sharp sword (His word) with which He may <u>strike down the nations,</u> and He will rule them with a rod of iron; and He will tread the wine press of the fierce wrath of God, the Almighty [in judgment of the rebellious world]. (Verse 15).

And…

'The rest <u>were killed with the sword which came from the mouth of Him who sat on the horse,</u> and all the birds fed ravenously and gorged themselves with their flesh.' (Verse 21).

Did you know that Satan is so in fear and trepidation at the truth of God's Holy Word, that he will do *anything* to stop you and me from taking time to read it and discover its power, not only to set us free, but also to break down his strongholds?

No wonder the great majority of humankind was prevented from reading the Word of God for some 1600 years after Christ's ascension – that is until the invention of the printing press and the subsequent publishing and availability of the King James Version of the Bible.

I am also not surprised that today, many 'Christians' never read their Bibles, despite having several of them collecting dust on their book shelves. Many – I would suggest the vast majority of people - have been blinded by Satan to its powerful, liberating truth!

So, the chief offensive weapon God has given you to succeed in your daily battle to overcome the world, the flesh and the devil, is the mighty powerful sword – The Holy Bible. If you do not read God's Holy Word on a daily basis, why not make a commitment before Almighty God right now that you will make a habit of reading it regularly? He will help you to do that because He wants you to use His Mighty Word in all your daily battles!

Does God give us any other spiritual weapons?

Well, God does give us one other offensive weapon, but Paul doesn't use the weapon imagery of Roman soldiers to describe it to us, and perhaps it is the reason some teachers forget about it or ignore it when discussing 'The Armour of God'.

Perhaps Paul felt it was so important that he didn't want to introduce any potential for misunderstanding…

Here it is in Ephesians chapter 6, verses 18 to 20:

'With <u>all prayer and petition pray</u> [with specific requests] at all times [on every occasion and in every season] in the Spirit, and with this in view, stay alert with all perseverance and petition [interceding in prayer] for all God's people (literally the saints). And pray for me, that words may be given to me when I open my mouth, to proclaim boldly the mystery of the good news [of salvation], for which I am an ambassador in chains. And pray that in proclaiming it I may speak boldly and courageously, as I should.' (Author's emphasis).

Paul is reminding us of the power of prayer. I guess I could have written a whole chapter on the power of prayer for men and maybe I will one day. But for now I want to stay specifically with these verses and succinctly pull out the following eight key points that I see concerning the power of prayer in the spiritual battle against the enemy:

<u>**Our prayers should be specific.**</u> Believe it or not, God actually wants to know precisely what it is you want Him to do for you, or for whomever or whatever it is you are praying to Him about!

<u>**We should pray and offer petition at all times, on every occasion and in every season.**</u> According to thefreedictionary. com, a petition means *'A solemn supplication or request, especially to a superior authority; an entreaty'*. So this Scripture is telling us to pray and make our requests of God - essentially as often as we possibly can.

<u>**We should pray in the Spirit.**</u>

Some will read this as an instruction to pray 'in tongues'. Apparently, the Greek word translated *"pray in"* can have several different meanings. It can mean "by means of," "with the help of," "in the sphere of," and "in connection to." Praying in the Spirit does not refer to the words we are saying. Rather, it refers to how we are praying.

It therefore seems more likely to me that what Paul is saying here is pray according to <u>the Holy Spirit's leading</u> i.e., pray for things the Spirit leads you to pray for. After all, Jesus told His disciples including you and me, to pray *'Thy will be done…'* So if we pray for things the Spirit leads us to pray for, they will be in God's will, and He can, and wants to answer them!

For those who take this verse to mean pray in tongues, that is also an excellent thing to do. God has given Spirit-filled believers the gift of speaking in tongues (see Acts chapter 2 verses 1 to 4), and Paul encourages us in other Scripture passages to pray in tongues. If that is what Paul intended in this specific Scripture then we are to do this, but also, as he says, to pray for specific things, which requires us to speak in our natural language (e.g., *'pray that in proclaiming it I may speak boldly and courageously, as I should').*

We must stay alert

Stay open to, and alert to, the leading of God's Spirit, and when you hear His voice, pray as His Spirit directs. So, as well as praying according to the leading of the Holy Spirit, stay alert so you can hear His leading. Also, stay <u>alert</u> because *'Your enemy the devil prowls around like a roaring lion looking for someone to devour.'* (1 Peter chapter 5 verse 8 NIV).

We must persevere

Keep on keeping on. God's timing isn't usually our timing, and if you persevere in prayer, then at the right moment, you **will** get your breakthrough so long as you are praying in God's will. Perseverance is the ability to wait with patience, hope and trust in God, for something to happen or to change, whilst we carry on with our daily life.

We must intercede

There are many books written about intercessory prayer. For now I would just comment that intercessory prayer doesn't simply mean asking God to do what you think He should do for a loved one or friend who is going through a difficult time. It means seeking God's will for that person, which may actually involve more pain for the individual or situation before a breakthrough comes! *'"For my thoughts are not your thoughts, neither are your ways my ways", declares the Lord'* (Isaiah chapter 55 verse 8 NIV).

Intercessory prayer can also mean you - the person praying - does something practical directly for the person concerned. To give a simple example, often is the time I have felt the Lord say to me, words to the affect, *'I want you to go and visit the person you are asking me to comfort in their loneliness.'*

We must pray for all God's people – that is our brothers and sisters in Christ, even those we may struggle to get along with in the natural!

We must proclaim the Gospel boldly (even if, like Paul, we are in chains!).

Whilst some feel called to the specific ministry of evangelism, Paul is reminding us that we are <u>all</u> expected to tell those within our circle of influence (family, friends or colleagues) about the Gospel.

You may be thinking, 'That's all very well, but how can I pray *all the time* like Paul suggests when I have a full time job to do and I have a wife and children who expect me to help them and spend quality time with them? I have to find time to buy the groceries, wash the car, relax over a game of golf etc, etc.'

Well, I'm copping out of answering that question by responding *"I am writing this book as God's messenger. Don't shoot the messenger!"*

To be serious, I'm a human being too, and at times I struggle with some of God's instructions! But what I do know is that there are many things each of us will have to pray about and seek God for the answers. I could say it's about balance, but when I read the story of Mary and Martha, Jesus didn't say it was about 'balance', did He? No, He told Martha that her sister, Mary - who was hanging off His every word while Martha was busy cooking - had chosen what was best...

"Martha, Martha, you are worried and bothered and anxious about so many things; but only one thing is necessary, for Mary has chosen the good part [that which is to her advantage], which will not be taken away from her." (Luke chapter 10 verses 41 and 42).

Jesus told Martha - in love - that her priorities were wrong. Maybe He wants to tell us the same thing.

There are many helpful books that give us pointers about how to spend more time in prayer, but every helpful idea will mean each of us having to make sacrifices. I heard R.T. Kendall teach his audience at a 'Spring Harvest' Conference in the UK, to set their alarm one hour earlier every morning and spend that time quietly with God, praying and studying His Word. Good, but challenging advice! It helped me; and trying to apply it forced me to change my priorities.

An accountability partner and I, one day agreed we both needed to 'put God first'. I still have the little somewhat faded yellow 'Post It' sticker on the top of my computer monitor saying 'GOD FIRST!' It reminds me to pray before switching on the PC, and make some time to do God's work *before* attending to my own.

Well, I've now completed what I wanted to say about this incredible passage of Scripture concerning the Armour of God, and I just want to conclude by saying I find it interesting that the Book of Ephesians has nothing to say about protecting our back. After all, many is the time that somebody (especially a coward) will 'stick the knife in your back'.

And so I find great comfort from the words of the prophet Isaiah, who, speaking to God's people in Isaiah chapter 52 verse 12 says:

'For the LORD will go before you, and the God of Israel will be your rear guard.'

Not only does God go ahead of us, if we are His, and we use His armour to protect ourselves, but most importantly, He protects our back from attack too. Praise God!

I also want to recommend that those of you who have been inspired by God to look more deeply into this incredibly important spiritual teaching, consider getting hold of a copy of David Diga Hernandez's book entitled *'25 Truths about Demons and Spiritual Warfare'* (See Recommended Reading Section at the end of this book).

In chapter 23 of his book [5] (chapter entitled 'Demons can't penetrate the Armour of God'), Hernandez talks us through the life changing piece of Scripture I have been addressing in this chapter.

Interestingly, he also regards two of our items of armour as *offensive.*

But, whereas I have added Prayer to the list of defensive and offensive armour and weapons, and I see Prayer as offensive, Hernandez sees the Shoes of Peace as an offensive weapon.

I would like to summarise his comments about our armour:

First our Defensive Pieces of armour. These, he says, are to *fight and resist deception.*

The Belt of Truth.

He says this represents your **readiness** to go into battle. The sheath helping you to keep your sword at hand (God's Word).

The Breastplate of Righteousness.

This, he believes, represents *righteous living* and is the antidote to sin.

The Shield of Faith.

This brings about *right believing.* You trust God and you believe His Word. It is the antidote to the lies of Satan. If your life is not saturated in God's Word, how can you recognise the subtle lies of the devil?

The Helmet of Salvation.

This is your **renewed mind** and your renewed mind protects against doubt (the lies of Satan). Your salvation brings confidence, trust and reassurance. You have to know and believe that your salvation is a done deal. If you doubt this, then there is a chink in your armour through which Satan and his demons can easily penetrate.

These four defensive postures ensure personal victory. The next two which are offensive, help you to ensure victory for others in your life:

The Shoes of Peace.

These, he says, are for preaching the Gospel message.

The Sword of the Spirit.

Our sword strikes down the evil archer. Declaring **the truth** (of God's Word) **pierces the source of deception.**

I have made the point, not just during this chapter, but at the beginning of this book, that our belief that the Word of God is absolute truth is <u>foundational</u> to our walk with God and defeating the lies of the enemy. Hernandez agrees with me, and the following paragraph from his book is an excellent way of explaining to you why this is so important. Here is what he says – and it comes from page 180 of his key chapter 23 concerning the power of the armour of God [6].

'*So-called experts scream self-contradicting rhetoric and have become useful puppets of hell. The big lie they're peddling? There is no truth.*

The world is being persuaded to reject the idea of absolute truth. "To each his own," they say. "What might be right for you is not necessarily right for all!" Speaking what to them sounds like love and tolerance, they naively fail to see the destructive and hateful origins of their demon-authored fiction.

Call it whatever you want to call it – tolerance, hedonism, moral relativism, acceptance, understanding. The evil idea is that no one has the truth, and, therefore, no one can ever really be wrong. The world will applaud your efforts to search for truth yet hypocritically condemn you if you say you have found it. The reason people do not like the idea of absolute truth is because if there is an absolute truth, then there is an absolute standard of morality. If there is an absolute standard of morality, there is a definite right and a definite wrong.

'This is the verdict, that light has come into the world, and men loved darkness rather than light, because their deeds were evil'. - John 3:19.

The one who stands for truth is, therefore, treated as a bigot and considered to be hateful. Nonetheless, as Christ's soldiers we must be ready with the truth, for Jesus boldly declared, "I am the way, the truth and the life. No-one comes to the Father except through me." (John 14:6)'

There are two final Scriptures I would like to lay before you for you to reflect upon, concerning this important topic of spiritual warfare…

'For the word of God is living and active and full of power [making it operative, energizing, and effective]. It is sharper than any two-edged sword, penetrating as far as the division of the soul and spirit [the completeness of a person], and of both joints and marrow [the deepest parts of our nature], exposing and judging the very thoughts and intentions of the heart.' (Hebrews chapter 4 verse 12).

The Second Scripture comes from the NIV translation of 2

Corinthians chapter 10 verse 3 to 5…

'For though we live in the world, we do not wage war as the world does. The weapons we fight with are not the weapons of the world. On the contrary, they have divine power to demolish strongholds. We demolish arguments and every pretension that sets itself up against the knowledge of God, and we take captive every thought to make it obedient to Christ.'

Before I close this important chapter I want to encourage you to obtain a copy of another book that I believe will help you greatly to discover many things about yourself and your soul. It is written by John Eldredge and this book is a best-seller. It is called *Wild at Heart*[7]. In it, he touches on the Armour of God and he has his own 21st century personal translation of the wonderful words of Paul in chapter 6, of his epistle to the Ephesians. I particularly like Eldredge's words…

This is what he says…

'Lord I put on the belt of truth. I choose a lifestyle of honesty and integrity. Show me the truths I so desperately need today. Expose the lies I am not even aware that I'm believing. Lord, I wear your righteousness today against all condemnation and corruption. Fit me with your holiness and purity – defend me from all assaults against my heart. I do choose to live for the Gospel at any moment. Show me where the larger story is unfolding and keep me from being so lax that I think the most important thing today is the soap operas of this world. Jesus, I lift against every lie and every assault the confidence that you are good, and that you have good in store for me. Nothing is coming today that can overcome me because you are with me. Thank you Lord for my salvation. I receive it in a new and fresh way from you and I declare that nothing can separate me now from the love of Christ and the place I shall ever have in your kingdom. Holy Spirit, show me specifically today the truths of the Word of God that I will need to counter the assaults and the snares of the enemy. Bring them to

mind throughout the day. Finally, Holy Spirit, I agree to walk in step with you in everything – in all prayer as my spirit communes with you throughout the day.'

So, men of God, let us put all our armour on, and keep it on 24/7! We must not risk taking it off to have a rest. Our enemy is snapping at our heels relentlessly, looking for someone to devour! If you grow weary and discard your spiritual armour, you do so at your peril, and I suggest that is the reason the devil has caused so many men of God to go astray and be taken out of ministry. Jesus Christ is imploring you and me to be overcomers. When we do overcome, He looks forward one day to saying to you and to me, 'Well done My good and faithful Servant.'

Chapter 4

OVERCOMING AND ERADICATING
SIN FROM YOUR LIFE

'For this is the will of God, that you be sanctified [separated and set apart from sin]: that you abstain and back away from sexual immorality; that each of you know how to control his own body in holiness and honour [being available for God's purpose and separated from things profane], not [to be used] in lustful passion, like the Gentiles who do not know God and are ignorant of His will; and that [in this matter of sexual misconduct] no man shall transgress and defraud his brother because the Lord is the avenger in all these things, just as we have told you before and solemnly warned you. For God has not called us to impurity, but to holiness [to be dedicated, and set apart by behaviour that pleases Him, whether in public or in private]. So whoever rejects and disregards this is not [merely] rejecting man but the God who gives His Holy Spirit to you [to dwell in you and empower you to overcome temptation].' (1 Thessalonians Chapter 4 verses 3 to 8).

God has laid on my heart a deep, deep desire to see men saved from the ravages of sin caused by Satan and his evil forces. All too often, I have found myself standing by while good men, godly men even, are taken out by Satan. What do I mean by men 'being taken out'?

I mean *destruction*! Marriages ending, businesses folding, sons' and daughters' lives turned upside down, murder, rape, suicide, broken hearts. The list goes on. You name it, it is going on every day somewhere in the world. And it's happening to Christian men as well as unbelieving men. What's more, it can happen to you.

It starts in the mind…. Subtle lies whispered into your mind by Satan and his demons. You believe the lie, you act upon it, and by doing so, you lose the battle. You know the kind of thing he whispers….

"That woman down the street is far more beautiful than your wife. She would bring the fun back into your life."

"Why don't you get divorced, you'll be free then. You'll have your life back again – the children will understand."

"Try these porn sites, no-one will know and it's so much fun."

"Just borrow a little more money to expand your business; your accountant will be happy to 'cook the books'. Put your staff on short time, profits will soar and your family will be so pleased with you as they see the fruits of your labour."

"You'll never get out of the mess you're in. Your integrity is shot. Best solution? If I were you, I'd take my own life. No more bills to pay, no more worry, peace at last."

These and countless others, are **<u>lies</u>** of Satan, and we need to see them for what they are.

Referring to Satan, Jesus said this (John chapter 10 verse 10)…

"The thief comes only in order to steal and kill and destroy. I came that they may have and enjoy life, and have it in abundance [to the full, till it overflows]."

There are many lies that Satan wants you to believe. The first one is that he doesn't exist; that he is just a figment of your imagination. The second is this: 'You can indulge in sin and have and enjoy life <u>and</u> have it to the full'.

At this point, and indeed throughout this book, I want to be honest with you. I do not want you to believe that because I am writing about how to overcome sin, that somehow I have managed to overcome it all, and that I no longer sin. I wish that were the case. The fact is I sin unknowingly and sometimes knowingly, just like most men. But it doesn't mean God can't or won't use me to help others sin less than they do. We are human and therefore not perfect, but we can all resolve to sin less if we choose to. And my prayer, as you progress through this long chapter, is that God will convict you to WANT to sin less, and eventually not to sin at all! After all, doing or saying something sinful is a choice, and to choose to do sinful things also demonstrates a lack of self-control.

So let me begin by defining what sin is.

1. WHAT IS SIN?

Sinning may be a choice, but what is sin?

Charles Price [1] is an excellent Bible teacher, and I remember listening to him at a Spring Harvest event in Skegness in the 1990's. He taught that the word 'sin' originated as a term used in the sport of archery. Sin meant 'missing the mark'. If you aimed at the target and missed, you committed sin, or you sinned. It meant your arrow missed the mark. Our 'mark' is, at all times, to do the will of God. When we don't do that, then we sin.

The definition of 'sin' according to thefreedictionary.com is as follows.

Sin (noun).

1. *A transgression of a religious or moral law, especially when deliberate.*

2. *(Theological definition):*

a. *Deliberate disobedience to the known will of God.*

b. *A condition of estrangement from God resulting from such disobedience.*

3. *Something regarded as being shameful, deplorable, or utterly wrong.*

The dictionary also gives us two idioms:

1. *'Live in sin'* – *To cohabit in a sexual relationship without being married.*

2. *'As sin'* – *meaning 'Completely or extremely': e.g.* **He is** *guilty* **as** *sin.*

Note that according to this website (as of 18th February 2018), the idiom is still true – to 'live in sin' means to cohabit in a sexual relationship without being married. I wonder, in this politically correct society, for how much longer that truth will continue to be accepted as truth, and how long it will be before that definition is eradicated from our dictionaries?

So far then, 'sin' means missing the mark, transgressing a religious or moral law, deliberately disobeying the known will of God, a condition of estrangement from God resulting from such disobedience, and something regarded as being shameful, deplorable, or utterly wrong.

You are probably thinking, 'No great surprises there then.'

In fact, I believe most Christians would say, "Yeah, those are good definitions of sin." Probably most unbelievers would say the final phrase in the above sentence *'something regarded as being shameful, deplorable, or utterly wrong'* was a good definition.

The point is, if sin is 'missing the mark' and 'deliberate disobedience of God's will' then that likely includes a lot of things that some might **not** consider to be sin. Why?... Because in order to know for sure whether what you do or say is 'sin' – in the eyes of God - then you need to know **God's Word** and **God's will**. And that is because God's Word **is His truth**, and from it, you learn His will.

God is a God of grace and because He longs for you to know His truth, He will often reveal it to you by His Holy Spirit.

When you know God's will then you can know that, for example, carelessly leaving a plastic drinking bottle on the beach is a sin. Why? Because we know that plastics in rivers and seas are causing massive pollution and death of marine life. Moreover, God said in the first chapter of the book of Genesis that we are to take care of His creation, which includes this beautiful world we live in. He actually said (verse 28) *"have dominion over the fish of the sea, over the birds of the air, and over every living thing that moves on the earth."* (NKJV).

Later in Scripture (e.g., in Micah chapter 6 verse 8), God explains how He expects His people to behave. Amongst other things He tells us we are to act justly and mercifully, as He promises to do for those living in His kingdom.

But, throughout the Bible, we see countless examples of God's chosen people not ruling or acting justly or mercifully. Instead, we see many examples of behaviour that exemplifies sin.

To name but a few, Paul lists the following as sins, in 2 Corinthians chapter 12…

'Strife, jealousy, angry tempers, disputes, slander, gossip, arrogance and disorder.'

Do you find yourself gossiping in the office or down the pub? It's an easy trap to fall into.

In reference to how we should talk, Jesus tells us in Matthew chapter 5 verse 37 (NKJV):

'Let your 'Yes' be 'Yes,' and your 'No,' 'No.' For whatever is more than these is from the evil one.'

So a little distortion of the truth or a 'little white lie', as my mother would call it, is not only a sin, but Jesus tells us it is 'of the devil'.

If you are not sure if something is sin, then Paul warns us in Romans chapter 14 verse 23 not to do it. He says this:

"But if you have doubts about whether or not you should eat something, you are sinning if you go ahead and do it. For you are not following your convictions. <u>If you do anything you believe is not right, you are sinning.</u>" (NLT, author's emphasis).

To help people avoid falling into the enemy's traps, which he sets for the unsuspecting Christian to fall into, Jerry Bridges has written a very helpful book called 'Respectable Sins' [2]. I mentioned this in Chapter 1. In his book, we learn of eighteen not-so-obvious sins of which we need to be aware. It is a humbling read and guaranteed to make you realise just how much we all fall short. Here is a list of those sins that Bridges believes we ignore or tolerate; some are grouped together but there are 18 below in all:

Ungodliness
Anxiety and frustration
Discontentment
Unthankfulness
Pride
Selfishness
Lack of self-control
Impatience and irritability
Anger
Judgmentalism
Envy, jealousy, competitiveness, controlling others
Sins of the tongue
Worldliness

Oswald Chambers makes a cutting observation about sin and what it isn't, as well as what it is. He says

'Sin is a fundamental relationship – it is not wrong doing, but <u>wrong being</u> – it is deliberate and determined independence from God'. [3] (Author's emphasis).

If you deliberately believe you are independent from God, this is rebellion. To believe you are independent from God is a bit like saying *"I am going to ignore the will of God for my life. I know better. I will do **my** thing and 'stuff everyone else'. If you don't like what I do or say that's your problem"*. This attitude and behaviour is one characteristic of not only many people of the world, but also of some people who claim to be Christians but who are **NOT** born again, and even some who are born again!

I said earlier that in order to help you know if you are 'transgressing a religious or moral law, or deliberately disobeying the known will of God' you will need to have a good knowledge of God's Holy Word, the Bible.

Apparently, listed in the Old Testament alone are a total of 613 of God's laws, beginning with those recorded by Moses at the time he was given the Ten Commandments by God on Mount Sinai.

A brother-in-Christ, the late Revd Norman Vivian, told the congregation while preaching one day at the church I attend, that instead of trying to remember 613 laws, if we add up 6, 1 and 3 we get 10. Therefore it's best that we just concentrate on the 10! By that, of course, he meant the Ten Commandments. And if, like mine, your memory is not that good any more, Jesus, thoughtfully summed up those Ten Commandments with just two (Mark chapter 12 verses 29 to 31; see following Scripture), and if we live by them, we keep all the law.

I will call these two Great Commandments… **The Antidote to Sin:**

"The first and most important (commandment) is: 'HEAR, O ISRAEL, THE LORD OUR GOD IS ONE LORD; AND YOU SHALL LOVE THE LORD YOUR GOD WITH ALL YOUR HEART, AND WITH ALL YOUR SOUL (life), AND WITH ALL YOUR MIND (thought, understanding), AND WITH ALL YOUR STRENGTH.' This is the second: 'YOU SHALL [unselfishly] LOVE YOUR NEIGHBOUR AS YOURSELF.' There is no other commandment greater than these."

I truly believe if you and I could obey those two Commandments

24/7/365 we would not sin! I have written this Chapter because in my experience, at times, obeying those two Commandments, is difficult!

When Jesus referred to 'loving your neighbour as yourself', the kind of love He was talking about was *agape* love (from the Greek word). We see from the Amplified Bible notes that this type of love is not so much a matter of emotion as it is of doing things for the benefit of another person - that is having an unselfish concern for another and a willingness to seek the best for another. Our feelings about doing things for others should not actually play any part in the matter!

Can you imagine living in a world where everybody showed that kind of respect for God and that kind of love for his or her fellow human beings?

In the past, I have personally printed off the Ten Commandments and stuck the piece of paper on my wall so I can easily and quickly refer to them. There are books available that help explain the Ten Commandments, and assist us in seeing where we are missing the mark. I would need to write another Chapter to cover that topic, but for now, in the context of defining sin, I believe the simplest definition of sin is… **Deliberately not obeying Jesus' summary of the Ten Commandments.**

As I said, Jesus' summary is to *'LOVE THE LORD YOUR GOD WITH ALL YOUR HEART, AND WITH ALL YOUR SOUL (life), AND WITH ALL YOUR MIND (thought, understanding), AND WITH ALL YOUR STRENGTH and to [unselfishly] LOVE YOUR NEIGHBOUR AS YOURSELF.'*

The issue for many of us is that these things do not come naturally. If we have a spirit of rebellion, then we will struggle to love God. Frank Sinatra's famous song "I Did It My Way" may be well loved by the masses, but it is not in any way a reflection of how God intends us to act.

One of the ways of showing God your deepest love and respect is by obeying His commands and fulfilling His will for your life. In today's culture, the word *'obedience'* has negative connotations but when God commands you to obey His Word, it is because He knows what is best for you. Throughout the Old Testament, we read that when His people **obey** His commands, God blesses them. But when they do **not** obey, all manner of evil and hardship come upon them. Sin has its consequences.

In the New Testament, we see in Matthew chapter 28 and the Great Commission that, according to the Amplified translation, one of the duties placed upon all those who are called to disciple people, is to implore others to obey Jesus' commands:

'Go therefore and make disciples of all the nations [help the people to learn of Me, believe in Me, and obey My words].' (Verse 19a).

In Mark chapter 9 and Luke chapter 9, God the Father says this to us concerning His Son Jesus Christ:

"This is My beloved Son. Listen to Him and obey Him!" (Author's emphasis).

John tells us in chapters 14 and 15 of his Gospel, that Jesus said, *"If you [really] love Me, you will keep and obey My commandments."*

And in John chapter 8 Jesus said, *"If you abide in My word [continually obeying My teachings and living in accordance with them, then] you are truly My disciples.* (Verse 31, author's emphasis).

I hope you are getting the message that the key to not living a life of sin, and to being a true disciple, is to obey God's Word!

Jesus and the apostle Paul help us to better understand what it means to love our neighbour as our self. Jesus explains this to us with the well-known parable of the Good Samaritan in Luke chapter 10. Paul goes into great detail about how to love others in

1 Corinthians chapter 13. I will leave you to look at those passages of Scripture for yourself.

One of my most common sins, which I struggle weekly to correct, is the sin of interrupting my wife. Michele suffers with a genetic condition called Gilbert's Syndrome which, among other symptoms, causes chronic fatigue. Basically, many things for her are a struggle each day, and that includes holding an extensive conversation, particularly in the mornings when her body is at its weakest. When I interrupt her, she rightly feels upset. And almost always, my interruption (which is for the purpose of clarification) would not have been necessary if I had simply been patient and allowed her to finish what she was saying. 1 Corinthians chapter 13 says (amongst many other invaluable pieces of advice) *'Love endures with patience and serenity, (love) is not rude.'* Knowing the Scriptures enables us to realise whether or not certain behaviour is sinful. It is clear from this Scripture that interrupting my wife – or anyone else come to that - is rude, and so it is therefore a sin.

Another way you can know if you are disobeying the known will of God is this: when He speaks His will for your life, into your mind, and you ignore Him or say "No way Lord, you must be kidding", that is a sin. Often God's will for your life isn't necessarily written in the Bible; God will tell you, either directly by His Holy Spirit or through a word God has given to another person (a word of knowledge) which they (hopefully!) then speak to you.

Two primary Greek words are used in the New Testament to describe Scripture and are translated 'word'. One is *'logos'* and the other is *'rhema'*.

The following information is from the Christian website iblp. org,

'logos, refers principally to the total inspired Word of God and to Jesus, Who is the living Logos.

Biblical Examples of Logos

The following passages of Scripture give examples of the logos of God:

"In the beginning was the Word [logos], and the Word [logos] was with God, and the Word [logos] was God" (John 1:1).

"The seed is the word [logos] of God" (Luke 8:11).

"Holding forth the word [logos] of life" (Philippians 2:16).

"Study to show thyself approved unto God, a workman that needeth not to be ashamed, rightly dividing the word [logos] of truth" (II Timothy 2:15).

"For the word [logos] of God is quick, and powerful" (Hebrews 4:12).

"Being born again, not of corruptible seed, but of incorruptible, by the word [logos] of God, which liveth and abideth forever" (I Peter 1:23).

Rhema—The Spoken Word

The second primary Greek word that describes Scripture is rhema, which refers to a word that is spoken and means "an utterance." A rhema is a verse or portion of Scripture that the Holy Spirit brings to our attention with application to a current situation or need for direction.

Every word of God is inspired, and "all Scripture is given by inspiration of God, and is profitable for doctrine, for reproof, for correction, for instruction in righteousness." (II Timothy 3:16). It is the Holy Spirit Who illuminates particular Scriptures for application in a daily walk with the Lord.

The words of Jesus are significant on this point. "Man shall not live by bread alone, but by every word [rhema] that proceedeth out of the mouth of God" (Matthew 4:4). Jesus also stated, "The words [rhema] that I speak unto you, they are spirit, and they are life" (John 6:63).

When God gives a rhema for us to act upon, He often confirms it by a second rhema, that "in the mouth of two or three witnesses shall every word [rhema] be established" (II Corinthians 13:1).'

iblp.org quote Scriptures from the King James Version of the Bible.

My own personal experience of this is that I believe with a certainty that is unshakeable, but which I cannot logically prove, that God asked me to write this book as a direct result of a rhema word He spoke into my mind during the winter of 2017. He subsequently confirmed this on a number of occasions.

Moving on… first then, we need to know God's Written Word (logos) in order to have an awareness of whether any of our actions and behaviour are sinful, and second we need to be listening out for His rhema Word – which is described as His *'gentle whisper'* (1 Kings chapter 19 verse 12) or His *'still small voice'* (NKJV), either directly into our mind, or spoken to us by others (and in both cases subsequently confirmed by Scripture or other Christians).

Sometimes we know a word is of God without consulting God's Word or Scripture for confirmation, but we must be careful to test any word that we 'hear', and ensure that it is in line with Scripture lest that word has come from the enemy, to lead us astray. 2 Corinthians chapter 11 verses 13 to 15 warns us of listening to wrong voices with these words, *'For such men are counterfeit apostles, deceitful workers, masquerading as apostles of Christ. And no wonder, since Satan himself masquerades as an angel of light. So it is no great surprise if his servants also masquerade as servants of righteousness'.*

I have spoken a lot about what sin is, and want to draw this to a close by briefly commenting on the final two definitions of sin according to thefreedictionary.com.

2b. A condition of estrangement from God resulting from such disobedience.

3. Something regarded as being shameful, deplorable, or utterly wrong.

The Bible warns us that we can grieve the Holy Spirit (see 1 Thessalonians chapter 5 verse 19 and Ephesians chapter 4 verse 30). The following Scripture from the Old Testament is a warning not to grieve Him. Isaiah reports, *'But they rebelled and grieved His Holy Spirit; Therefore He changed into their enemy, And He fought against them.'* (Isaiah chapter 63 verse 10).

What is meant by grieving the Holy Spirit? In Ephesians chapter 4, verse 29 to 31, Paul is talking about sin. So, we can deduce that, for example, whenever we do not love our neighbours as ourselves, we are grieving the Holy Spirit. Many Christian teachers agree that when we grieve the Holy Spirit, He withdraws from us for a season.

I believe that this is what brings about *'A condition of estrangement from God resulting from such disobedience'* - one of the definitions I listed for sin.

I think the final definition *'Something regarded as being shameful, deplorable, or utterly wrong'* is a useful definition for both believers and unbelievers, but its problem is that it is completely subjective. What one man regards as acceptable behaviour, another may regard as deplorable. It's only when we have a reference to absolute truth that we can determine what is and isn't sin. For the believer, that absolute truth is God's Word and God's will.

2: WHAT MAKES US SIN?

So having discussed what sin is, let's now ask our self this question:

"Why do we sin?"

Why don't we simply obey God's commands and His will for our lives all the time? After all, most of us know that God's will is perfect, and all He ever wants is what is best for us.

Many of us will find we can obey God for much of the time, but not all of the time. Let's be clear: no man can achieve what would amount to perfection by claiming to be sinless! Indeed the Bible tells us only Jesus was sinless (Hebrews chapter 4 verse 15).

So why do we fail to obey God so often? The answer lies in what's known as 'The Fall of man'.

The 'Fall of Man' is recorded in Genesis chapter 3. In essence, what we learn about humankind, is that when God created the first man - Adam - and later created for Adam a wife Eve (not Steve by the way, but Eve!) these two people enjoyed a perfect relationship with God. At the point of their creation, they were without sin. But as a result of them being confronted by the devil and his subtle lies, they yielded to temptation and fell into sin. They rebelled against God's rhema Word (His spoken Word to them) and did something **expressly forbidden** by God. In fact, they chose to do the _only thing_ God commanded them **not** to do. They were completely free to walk around the Garden and commune with Almighty God and do whatever they wanted EXCEPT eat from *'the tree of the knowledge of good and evil.'* (Genesis chapter 2 verse 9 NKJV).

By disobeying God, they both discovered for the first time what sin was. The knowledge they gained from eating 'the forbidden fruit' opened up to them a previously unknown experience…. SIN. God punished them for their sin (their rebellion) in two ways. He banished them from the Garden, causing them to experience pain – something that they had been free from until their sin - and He also made them have to endure hard work.

As a result of their sin, the human disposition altered for all time. Rather than our originally created default disposition being to do what is right - as it was before The Fall – from that point onwards, when sin entered the human race, the human default disposition became to do what is wrong in the sight of God.

In the beginning, in the Garden of Eden, man only knew how to be like God; being perfect and behaving in a sinless way. When sin 'entered the camp' humankind's disposition was changed by their rebellion - and we have been in rebellion ever since. King David was only too aware of this. In Psalm 51 verse 5 he tells us

"I was brought forth in [a state of] wickedness; In sin my mother conceived me [and from my beginning I, too, was sinful]."

We see this when we observe our young children. When they are weaned and begin to walk and talk, they get into mischief straight away. We don't have to teach them to be naughty; we have to teach them how and why NOT to be naughty, and instead to be good!

Young children always seem to want their own way, don't they? They usually want what their brother or sister has, or what their friends have. They instinctively know how to lie when they think they are going to get into trouble and their mother or father might 'tell them off'.

Rebellion means saying or thinking 'I know best' or (when we are young) 'I know better than my parents'. And later, as we grow up, we say or think 'I know better than God.' Believing that we know better than God, is the original sin of rebellion or pride, which began in *humans* when Adam and Eve listened to and acted upon the subtle lies of the original *spiritual* rebel... SATAN.

The question is then, how do we stop rebelling? How do we stop sinning against God, and against our fellow men and women? We will come to that shortly, but first of all I want to consider...

3. WHAT ARE THE KEY SINS MEN STRUGGLE WITH?

Before listing some of these specifically, I wanted to revisit Jesus' summary of the Ten Commandments:

"The first and most important (commandment) is: 'HEAR, O ISRAEL, THE LORD OUR GOD IS ONE LORD; AND YOU SHALL LOVE THE LORD YOUR GOD WITH ALL YOUR HEART, AND WITH ALL YOUR SOUL (life), AND WITH ALL YOUR MIND (thought, understanding), AND WITH ALL YOUR STRENGTH.' This is the second: 'YOU SHALL [unselfishly] LOVE YOUR NEIGHBOUR AS YOURSELF.' There is no other commandment greater than these."

Let me ask you, can you honestly say you love God with all of your heart, all your soul, all your mind and all your strength? If the answer to that one is "Yes", then question number two is, do you really love your neighbour(s) as yourself?

I feel that when I take time to reflect upon who my neighbour is and how I treat him and her, I begin to realise some of my faults, some of the sins that I and other men that I know, struggle with.

I have listed below some sins, either that I have been guilty of, or which I have observed from time to time in other men, in the home, in the workplace or in a social setting:

Mistreating our loved ones, e.g., verbal, physical or psychological abuse, control, manipulation, general neglect.

Lying.

Envy.

Anger.

Use of pornography.

Alcohol abuse.

Workaholism.

Bad language.

Road rage.

Bullying.

I thought of these in a single minute! I am sure you could think of many more very quickly.

CS Lewis in his classic book 'MERE CHRISTIANITY' explains what he believes is man's **greatest** sin.

Interestingly it is none of the above. You may have read the following passage from his book for yourself. He articulates it brilliantly:

'There is one vice of which no man in the world is free; which everyone in the world loathes when he sees it in someone else; and

of which hardly any people, except Christians, ever imagine that they are guilty themselves. I have heard people admit that they are bad-tempered, or that they cannot keep their heads about girls or drink, or even that they are cowards. I do not think I have ever heard anyone who was not a Christian accuse himself of this vice. And at the same time I have very seldom met anyone, who was not a Christian, who showed the slightest mercy to it in others. There is no fault which makes a man more unpopular, and no fault which we are more unconscious of in ourselves. And the more we have it ourselves, the more we dislike it in others.

The vice I am talking of is Pride or Self-Conceit: and the virtue opposite to it, in Christian morals, is called Humility. You may remember, when I was talking about sexual morality, I warned you that the centre of Christian morals did not lie there. Well, now, we have come to the centre. According to Christian teachers, the essential vice, the utmost evil, is Pride. Unchastity, anger, greed, drunkenness, and all that, are mere fleabites in comparison: it was through Pride that the devil became the devil: Pride leads to every other vice: it is the complete anti-God state of mind. [4]

So there you have it – from one of Britain's 'Christian heavyweights'! Pride is man's worst sin.

Keynote:

The next section of this chapter I believe may be the most important part of this book that you will read. I have not pulled any punches. I believe this is the subject matter that God most wants to bring to men's attention in this 21st century; and for those men who are affected, God is desperate to set you free.

In this section I am going to deal with a specific battle many men struggle with in one form or another, and I am going to refer to it as **'secret sin'**. This is quite a large topic – I cannot deal with it quickly so please bear with me, as I truly believe this is something from which God is *particularly anxious* to set us all free.

4. DEALING WITH SECRET SINS

"You have placed our wickedness before you, our secret sins [which we tried to conceal, You have placed] in the [revealing] light of Your presence." (A prayer of Moses - Psalm 90 verse 8).

'Then He said to me, "Son of man, do you see what the elders of the house of Israel do in the dark, each man in his [secret] room of carved images? For they say, 'The LORD does not see us; the LORD has abandoned the land.'" He also said to me, "Yet again you will see even greater repulsive acts which they are committing."' (Ezekiel chapter 8 verses 12 and 13).

'So don't make judgments about anyone ahead of time—before the Lord returns. For he will bring our darkest secrets to light and will reveal our private motives. Then God will give to each one whatever praise is due.' (1 Corinthians chapter 4 verse 5 – NLT).

What do I mean by secret sins?

'Secret sins' are those that Satan will, <u>at all costs,</u> persuade you to keep hidden in darkness. After all, if nobody knows about them, then we can believe that our little sin(s) does not matter, as no-one is being hurt. That is a lie of Satan. **All** sin leads to death (See Romans chapter 6 verse 16). Secret sin not only harms the perpetrator, but is a sin against God. King David tells us that in Psalm 51.

I have chosen the phrase 'secret sins' because I do not want to limit them to those committed *in private*. Secret sins include those also done with somebody or in the presence of others, but NOT in the presence of friends or family members who know the perpetrator.

In this category, I am intentionally including sins like being at the pub drinking when you have told your loved one that you are still at the office, or with a friend. I am including having an affair, or using a prostitute, without anybody's knowledge. It might even be something as 'relatively minor' as being insincere, dishonest or deceptive with others. For example, when you say something you don't mean, it is a sin, but you have kept the sin to yourself (**made a secret of it**) because the other person thought you meant what you said. For example, saying "I will pay you what I owe you tomorrow" when you know you are not in a position to do that and have no intention of doing that. You will get found out tomorrow when you don't make the payment, so why lie in the first place? Why not just tell the person the truth?

I have succumbed to secret sins in the past, and from time to time even now. In the past I had a complacent attitude about it, but now, if I *'regard sin in my heart'* (see Psalm 66), God brings conviction upon me pretty quickly, enabling me to confess it.

God wants to help His sons (and daughters come to that) confess their secret sins and bring them out of the darkness and into the light in order to set us completely free. Jesus tells us in John's Gospel (chapter 12 verse 46) that one of the reasons He came to earth was to set us free from the pain of having to *'live in darkness',* or put in today's English... living with sin.

In my personal experience, it is only when any of our sins (whether secret or not) have been brought into the light through confession and repentance, that we can experience the deep peace, the joy, and fullness of life that Christ came to give us (see John chapter 10 verse 10).

Oswald Chambers says, *'If a man cannot get through to God, it is because there is a secret thing he does not intend to give up – I will admit I have done wrong, but I no more intend to give up that thing than fly.'* [5]

Let me ask you a question…. Are you struggling to get through to God? Are you enjoying your secret sin so much that it has got a complete hold of you? The particular sin may even make you feel like you are possessed by a demon. If so, please let me encourage you to confess it to God right away. If you have already done that in the past – perhaps countless times – but still continue in that sin, please ask another man that you know and trust to pray for you. He may need to pray with you regularly until you are set free. In Christ Jesus there IS the power to enable you to overcome. Today really **can** be the first day of your liberation; your deliverance.

If by God's grace, you have been set free from your secret sins in the past, praise His Holy Name! But watch out, as Peter reminds us (1 Peter chapter 5 verse 8), *'Be sober [well balanced and self-disciplined], be alert and cautious at all times. That enemy of yours, the devil, prowls around like a roaring lion [fiercely hungry], seeking someone to devour.'*

If, on the other hand, you are wondering why I have even raised this subject, because you have **never** succumbed to doing things in private that you know would not be pleasing to God, then praise the Lord for this, because, it is only by His grace that you have not yet fallen. Praise God too, because you are very likely in a small minority group amongst those who profess to be followers of Jesus Christ. But again, a word of warning! In 1 Corinthians chapter 10 verse 12 it says *'So, if you think you are standing firm, be careful that you don't fall!'* (NIV).

Be on your guard against your enemy – that prowling lion, called Satan. He may simply be waiting for an opportune time to tempt you.

If you think I am exaggerating the issue of secret sin, please let me share with you a magazine article God used to open my eyes to the magnitude of the problem Christian men experience with two particular 'secret sins': that of viewing pornography, and masturbation.

The front cover of 'Christianity' magazine, February 2009, had as its main headline:

'INTERNET PORN – The unspoken problem in your Church' [6]

In the article, written by Martin Saunders, it says *'According to a 2007 survey by website ChristaNet.com, around 50 per cent of men and 20 per cent of women – all of them Christians – admitted to an 'addiction' to Internet-based pornography. In separate research by American ministry xxxchurch, 37% of pastors said that porn addiction was a daily struggle for them.'* The article also states that whilst the article did not attempt to address the rights and wrongs of masturbation *'most pornography consumption is accompanied by masturbation'*.

The magazine dedicated five pages to this article and many facts were discussed which even today are never addressed in any UK church setting of which I have been made aware. I do not intend to go through the article in detail. My motivation in bringing this subject up is to make more church leaders <u>aware of the seriousness of the issue</u> and the urgent need to address it in the Church today. I pray that God will raise up many church leaders and men's ministry workers who will be brave enough to confront this problem head-on, by admitting that this problem is real, discussing it openly, praying with men who struggle, and watching as God sets men free.

<u>Is there a specific setting for sex that is acceptable to God?</u>

Absolutely. God gave us the gift of sexual intercourse to cherish in one setting only – conventional marriage. I am talking about God's definition of marriage, not the world's. God's intention has always been that marriage is the union of one biological man with one biological woman to the exclusion of all others, and that exclusion includes inappropriate images and photographs of other women. As I look around and read news headlines, I can't help believing that the devil, in these End Times - whilst using every weapon at his disposal to tempt and destroy us - is particularly using sexual sin to bring down countless men of God.

Over the course of the last several years, there has been a significant increase in the number of men (and occasionally women), whose sexual misdemeanours have made mainstream headline news.

Amongst the first group of such people to be brought to our

notice in recent times by the secular news media, were *priests*. As a result, the Church came under so much attack from critics that before long, the view of much of the general public became that priests are all 'sexual perverts or paedophiles.' It was as if God began to bring into the light, the secret sins of those in high positions who professed to be followers of Christ; those of whom the world would have rightly expected to have behaved better.

Sadly, in both the Roman Catholic and Anglican Churches, sexual sin by those in authority, particularly against the young – boys and girls – was almost monthly news for some time, and is still being exposed even now as I type this paragraph in early 2018.

In 2011, in the UK, a paedophile scandal began to break out within the **secular world**. My wife sensed and shared with me that it was as if God was saying to all the unbelievers who love to point their finger at His beloved Church, that *"this sin is even more rampant in your domain"* (in the world of the unsaved).

Little do the people of the world know or believe 'their domain' is the realm of Satan and his demons.

The beginning of the uncovering and exposing of secret sexual sins in the secular, unbelieving world of well-known celebrities being brought out of darkness into the light, began with the shaming of a man the British public loved. He was a famous DJ, TV and radio personality, and a prolific charity fundraiser. He was even awarded an OBE in 1971 for his charity work, and later knighted by the Queen. It came to light, soon after his death in 2011, that this man – Jimmy Savile - abused his various positions of trust over decades, and was actually a predatory paedophile.

Then in quick succession, the secret lives of four other well-known UK celebrities were brought into the light.

The publicist Max Clifford, pop star Gary Glitter, entertainer Stuart Hall, singer, artist and TV personality Rolf Harris; slowly but surely one after another, well known respected men were exposed for their dark deeds involving sexual sin. These once highly respected men were tried, convicted and sent to prison for their offences.

Just a few years later, the US Film industry was exposed for some of the 'secret sins' perpetrated by high-profile people upon unsuspecting female celebrities. It now seems sexual harassment by men against women was an accepted 'secret sin' in Hollywood and the film industry for decades.

Next to appear in the UK news was the predatory sexual harassment of young English teenage boy footballers by professional football coach Barry Bennell. He was convicted of 43 child sex offences in February 2018.

Then the world discovered secret sexual sins were being carried out by some of the employees of International Relief Charities - against famine victims. The first to be mentioned was Oxfam, but since then other agencies and charities have also been named.

At the time of writing (February 2018) the TV news was reporting a new kind of sexual sickness. A 29 year old University Lecturer Matthew Falder – a so called 'Dark Web' paedophile – was jailed for 32 years for admitting 137 charges - including rape - against 46 people over ten years. He was described in court as 'warped and sadistic' – he tormented and blackmailed his victims and shared indecent and degrading images on the so-called 'Dark Web'. Two of the user names he created for his 'dark web' site activities included 'evilmind' and '666devil'.

I believe that since it is God's people who understand that the war on sin is against spiritual forces and demonic beings rather than human beings, we need to recognise that we, as God's chosen people, are best placed to enable - through prayer and deliverance - those under Satan's influence to be set free. I pray for an army of God's men to rise up to overcome the enemy's power, particularly in this area of sexual depravity and sin.

I have personally met many Christian men who – praise God – have courageously given their testimonies about how God has set them free from addictions to pornography, alcohol, gambling and drugs. Those whom God has set free from these sins are often the ones He will use to help other men be set free. The enemy knows God is in the business of doing this; no wonder Satan works hard to keep our secret sins in darkness.

Sexual 'self-gratification.'

The last thing I will include in this section is a more detailed mention of a topic I have referred to in earlier parts of this book, in the context of sin. It is a widespread occurrence amongst men, and is something I have talked about to a number of church leaders over the decades and I have never been offered a satisfactory answer as to whether or not this is a sin. This is the act of *masturbation*. Not once have I heard the word mentioned, let alone discussed, in a formal church setting or 'House Group.'

Perhaps this is because the word 'masturbation' is not mentioned in the Bible. We can see from Old and New Testament Scriptures that some sexual acts are clearly wrong in the eyes of God. For example, to have sex outside of marriage, to have sex with a member of the same sex, and to have sex with animals; all these acts are wrong and explicitly condemned by God. Masturbation, is in effect committing a sexual act with yourself, or as I have stated above, an act of 'sexual self-gratification.' The Bible appears to remain silent about this, and, no doubt, that is why I have struggled to find a consensus of views about this subject from church leaders.

Let's be serious about this. How can masturbation - committing a sexual act with our own body - be acceptable to a righteous, Holy God who clearly commands that the act of sexual intercourse is reserved for the marriage bed? I read somewhere that Orthodox Jewish men will not even so much as touch their genitals when showering because they do not want to be tempted to sin.

But if masturbation is sinful, why doesn't there seem to be a clear biblical Scripture to confirm this?

My wife, Michele, brought the following New Testament Scripture to my notice in this context…

1 Corinthians chapter 7 verse 5

"Do not deprive each other [of marital rights], except perhaps by mutual consent for a time, so that you may devote yourselves [unhindered] to prayer, but come together again so that Satan will not tempt you [to sin] because of your lack of self-control."

There are two things in this verse I wish to bring to your attention. The first is not connected directly with the subject of masturbation, but Michele emphasised something to me which I found really interesting. It was one of those moments like a lightbulb being switched on in my mind by the Holy Spirit, and so I will share it with you. What Michele pointed out to me from the passage of Scripture above is that God expects married couples to *devote* themselves **to prayer** in those periods of time when they are not engaged in sexual intimacy. Wow, what a revelation!

The Bible clearly makes the point that abstaining from sex for a period of time, to devote ourselves to prayer, should be a priority for married couples.

Now, returning to my main point, that of masturbation and what the Bible has to say about it.

In verse 2 of Chapter 7, Paul finds it necessary to point out to the Corinthian believers, that because we are a fallen people, we are tempted to participate in sexual immorality. As a result of this, he says, let each man have his own wife, and each woman her own husband. He goes on to say in verses 3 and 4 that we are to share our bodies with each other as a married couple.

Having set the context, let us return to verse 5. He tells us of the importance of not depriving each other (of sexual fulfilment), but also to abstain from sexual activity from time to time in order to focus on prayer. He then says this:

"...come together again so that Satan will not tempt you [to sin] because of your lack of self-control."

'Come together again' – spend an *intimate* time with your wife satisfying each other's sexual needs, so that Satan will not tempt you to sin because of your lack of self-control.

In what kind of sin does a man indulge if he gets sexually frustrated and lacks self-control? I will tell you in blunt terms.

If the desire for sexual intimacy or specifically orgasm is very strong, or if he is listening to the voice of Satan and not the voice of God, this is what a man will consider: He will seek out an alternative method of satisfaction (due to *'lack of self-control'*) and he will justify this alternative action for all manner of reasons including *"too much testosterone"* and *"Well, God created me to need to have my sexual needs satisfied regularly"* - either of which may be true; but these are common excuses for satisfying **in the wrong way** a God-given desire to create children, as well as the God-given gift of enjoying sexual intimacy with his wife.

What is the first alternative method of sexual satisfaction that a man will resort to? *Masturbation.*

Some men reading this part of the book will be shocked that I am being so explicit about this. The reason for my focussing on this behaviour is about to unfold. Please read on.

Christian men will know, without any doubt, that *looking at pornography* whilst masturbating, in order to meet their sexual urges, is a sin. However, it is my intuitive belief that most men will believe **Satan's lie** that simply masturbating *without* looking at graphic sexual images, or having thoughts of inappropriate images, is NOT sinful. They **will justify** this in their minds by telling themselves that as their masturbation is WITHIN the confines of their marriage, then surely it is not an act of sin?

Let's be clear about this; if our marriage is struggling and our sex life is not what we hoped it would be, once a man starts masturbating, at some point in time his thoughts will undoubtedly turn to looking at sexually explicit images in order to satisfy his urges further, and when that fails to quench the cravings of his flesh, it can lead to him seeking to have an affair and committing adultery.

I believe that since the potential for all of this is high, then this *clearly* shows that the initial act of masturbating, without sexual images, in order to stimulate and fulfil ones sexual urges, is a sin.

'Rather, clothe yourselves with the Lord Jesus Christ, and do not think about how to gratify the desires of the flesh.' (Romans chapter 13 verse 14, NIV).

The solution to all sin is to obey God's Word, confess it to God and repent of it, turn away from it. God is the God of mercy and if you are caught up in this, or *any sin*, God is waiting to hear your sincere confession and repentance so that He can forgive you totally.

This chapter is about overcoming and eradicating all types of sin from our life. Why is this important? Aren't we living under grace in these New Testament times? It is to this question that I will now turn.

5. WHY SHOULD WE STOP SINNING?

This might seem a strange question in the context of Christian teaching. The reason I have included this section is because many of us struggle with certain sins either for a short season or for extended periods of time, and we can find ourselves believing the lie that it 'doesn't matter' because 'we all sin anyway'.

As I said at the beginning, we have a choice – to sin or not to sin. We have to **want** to stop sinning. Our core desire should be to 'crucify the flesh.'

I want to look at **why** we should want to stop sinning before we look at **how** to stop. I have actually met some believers who seem to think along these lines… "We are living under grace, and so sin is not such a big issue because God will forgive a little sin here and there won't He? Nobody's perfect and God is the God of love, surely He expects us to trip up and so it's no big deal…"

My response is "Well it is a big deal actually!"

This kind of logic is running rampant in some sections of the global Church. I do not subscribe to it and I would like to take some time from Scripture to explain why I do not subscribe to it. What's more, I believe an increasingly liberal approach within the Church towards sin is outright rebellion against God's Word, and surely rebellion from those who profess to be God's children must be breaking His Heart!

Let me ask you to read the following New Testament Scripture by the disciple of whom it is said walked <u>closest to Jesus</u>. He was described in John chapter 13 verse 23 as the disciple *'whom Jesus loved (esteemed)'*:

'Everyone who practices sin also practices lawlessness; and sin is lawlessness [ignoring God's law by action or neglect or by tolerating wrongdoing—being unrestrained by His commands and His will]. You know that He appeared [in visible form as a man] in order to take away sins; and in Him there is [absolutely] no sin [for He has neither the sin nature nor has He committed sin or acts worthy of blame]. No one who abides in Him [who remains united in fellowship with Him—deliberately, knowingly, and habitually] practices sin. No one who habitually sins has seen Him or known Him. Little children (believers, dear ones), do not let anyone lead you astray. The one who practices righteousness [the one who strives to live a consistently honourable life—in private as well as in public—and to conform to God's precepts] is righteous, just as He is righteous. The one who practices sin [separating himself from God, and offending Him by acts of disobedience, indifference, or rebellion] is of the devil [and takes

his inner character and moral values from him, not God]; for the devil has sinned and violated God's law from the beginning. The Son of God appeared for this purpose, to destroy the works of the devil. No one who is born of God [deliberately, knowingly, and habitually] practices sin, because God's seed [His principle of life, the essence of His righteous character] remains [permanently] in him [who is born again—who is reborn from above—spiritually transformed, renewed, and set apart for His purpose]; and he [who is born again] cannot habitually [live a life characterized by] sin, because he is born of God and longs to please Him. By this the children of God and the children of the devil are clearly identified: anyone who does not practice righteousness [who does not seek God's will in thought, action, and purpose] is not of God, nor is the one who does not [unselfishly] love his [believing] brother.' 1 John Chapter 3 verses 4 to 10.

That is a powerful, sobering Scripture to read, and on certain days when I read it I can feel heavily convicted by the Holy Spirit of a particular sin or sins. The good news, however, is that the same disciple who wrote that stern passage also wrote this message, two chapters earlier:

'If we say we have no sin [refusing to admit that we are sinners], we delude ourselves and the truth is not in us. [His word does not live in our hearts.] If we [freely] admit that we have sinned and confess our sins, He is faithful and just [true to His own nature and promises], and will forgive our sins and cleanse us continually from all unrighteousness [our wrongdoing, everything not in conformity with His will and purpose]. If we say that we have not sinned [refusing to admit acts of sin], we make Him [out to be] a liar [by contradicting Him] and His word is not in us'. (1 John chapter 1 verses 8 to 10).

It therefore appears clear to me that John is saying this: if we profess to be followers of Jesus Christ we **must not sin**; but if and when we do sin, we must **confess** it quickly to God and turn from that sin (**<u>repent</u>**) and we will receive God's gracious cleansing and **<u>forgiveness.</u>**

Oswald Chambers gives a helpful insight into 1 John chapter 3 verse 9 where it says *'No one who is born of God [deliberately, knowingly, and habitually] practices sin.'*

Chambers says this:

'Do I seek to stop sinning or have I stopped sinning? To be born of God means that I have the supernatural power of God to stop sinning. In the Bible it is never – Should a Christian sin? The Bible puts it emphatically – A Christian must not sin. The effective working of the new birth life in us is that we do not commit sin, not merely that we have the power not to sin, but that we have stopped sinning. 1 John 3 v 9 does not mean we cannot sin; it means that if we obey the life of God in us, we need not sin.' [7]

In Chapter One, I referred to the fact that somebody once said *'too many Christians treat sin like a strawberry milkshake, instead of like a deadly rattlesnake'.* The fact is that some people just like a particular sin too much to want to give it up.

Would you agree that the sins you most struggle to stop doing are those things you realise are sin but you either enjoy doing them, or they are things you are addicted to?

And isn't it the case that in circumstances where you believe those sins are not affecting the lives of others, then it becomes even more 'believable' to you that God is OK about your sins because you are living under grace, and so He will forgive you? Such sins that spring to my mind include pornography, masturbation, sinful thoughts about others - anything in fact that we do, or think, that is done in secret.

Let me assure you that this thinking is nothing other than the result of hearing in your mind **<u>a lie of Satan</u>**; and God wants to <u>convict us</u> of this fact, not condemn us. So concerned is God to expose to you and me the lies of Satan concerning sin, that no less than 26 of the 27 books comprising the New Testament warn us against the dangers of sin!   With that in mind, I would like to show you some more Scriptures on this subject, beginning with one of the key Scriptures in the New Testament *concerning grace* (Ephesians chapter 2 verses 8 and 9)….

'For it is by grace [God's remarkable compassion and favour drawing you to Christ] that you have been saved [actually delivered from judgment and given eternal life] through faith. And this [salvation] is not of yourselves [not through your own effort], but it is the [undeserved, gracious] gift of God; not as a result of [your] works [nor your attempts to keep the Law], so that no one will [be able to] boast or take credit in any way [for his salvation].'

As you read the next well-known Scripture (John chapter 3 verse 16) and understand it in the light of the above Scripture, you may see why many Christians believe they are going to Heaven when they die, regardless of sin.

"For God so [greatly] loved and dearly prized the world, that He [even] gave His [One and] only begotten Son, so that whoever believes and trusts in Him [as Saviour] shall not perish, but have eternal life."

The problem with drawing a logical conclusion from just these two biblical verses about sin and salvation is that we make 2+2=6.

Let me explain. The same writer who penned Ephesians chapter 2 verses 8 and 9 also penned this:

"What shall we say [to all this]? Should we continue in sin and practice sin as a habit so that [God's gift of] grace may increase and overflow? Certainly not!..." (Romans chapter 6 verses 1 and 2).

To make the point even more strongly, just twenty verses after writing John chapter 3 verse 16, John also wrote this:

'And anyone who believes in God's Son has eternal life. Anyone

who doesn't obey the Son will never experience eternal life but remains under God's angry judgment." (NLT).

So, *"Should we continue in sin? Certainly not!"*

What is the consequence of **disobeying** Jesus? We will *'NEVER experience eternal life but we remain under God's angry judgement!'*

If you disobey Jesus, you sin. Why, because in John chapter 8 and verse 11, after forgiving the sins of the woman caught in adultery, He then *commanded* her to *"Go, and sin no more"*. (NKJV). Likewise, in John chapter 5 verse 14 Jesus tells a man whom He has just healed *"See, you are well! Stop sinning or something worse may happen to you."*

Why am I labouring this point?

Because, if you read either or both of the two Scriptures, Ephesians chapter 2 verses 8 to 9 and John chapter 3 verse 16, <u>without looking at the context of the chapter and relevant book,</u> or take the verses - as some do - in isolation, then both of those verses could be seen as a licence to sin. What's more, as I said earlier, I have met a number of 'born again' Christians who, by their behaviour, seem not to have read any other Scriptures than those two, and consequently say to me things like, "Don't worry about such and such a sin Chris, it's Ok, God understands, after all, we are saved by grace and not by works." Or they say the same thing about sins that they are wilfully committing!

Yes **we are saved by grace**, but so that we do not misunderstand Paul's teaching and the rest of the New Testament teaching about being saved by grace, we have to compare these two verses in Ephesians with other Scriptures, not only written by other Apostles but also by **Paul himself**.

It goes without saying that this applies to the use of any Scripture out of context; indeed many strands of Christianity – cults, in particular – begin out of a person's desire to make a Scripture or unrelated series of random Scriptures match up with their own pre-determined personal, and not biblical, beliefs.

Regarding the scriptural truth that we are saved by grace, we find in the Book of James the complementary truth that faith without deeds cannot save us, and so there is a requirement for good deeds in the offer of salvation. By 'deeds', this does not just mean doing good towards others, it means doing the good deeds of living in obedience to God's Holy Word, e.g., deeds of righteous, godly behaviour and conduct. No doubt, this statement of mine will be construed by some as heresy, so please before you persecute me, check ALL of the Chapter of James, put it into the context of his Epistle and also in the context of Jesus' teachings and ALL of the writings of the New Testament. Thank you!

"What is the benefit, my fellow believers, if someone claims to have faith but has no [good] works [as evidence]? Can that [kind of] faith save him? [No, a mere claim of faith is not sufficient— genuine faith produces good works.]" (James chapter 2 verse 14).

James is not talking about the condition of a mild change in the flesh that causes us to seek to be seen by others to be engaged in nice social acts that make us appear like godly and faithful people, e.g. arranging the church flowers, feeding the homeless, cleaning the church building, editing the Parish Magazine.

Whilst activities like these are important acts of grace in their own right, James is talking about good works that flow out of a faith based on our love for God. Such a deep love of God originates from the knowledge of His amazing gift of salvation, which prompts us to become born again and as a result, we determine to 'crucify our flesh', which results in obeying what His Word teaches us in every aspect of our lives.

The good deeds we then willingly undertake are works of obedience, bringing all our thoughts into captivity and our flesh into subjection, to obey Christ. This is a daily and even hourly responsibility in order to remain faithful followers of Christ. It is dangerous and wrong to undertake outward acts of visible good works for our church and community, if we are engaged in unrepentant secret sins. Sooner or later God will expose them, to our shame.

I mentioned above, just two verses of Romans chapter 6. If you need convincing of what I have said, or if you would like a full explanation of what it means to 'crucify the flesh' you may find it helpful to read the whole Chapter, and so here is the amazing passage in full. In this Chapter we also learn that the 'wages of sin is death!' (Verse 23)…

"What shall we say [to all this]? Should we continue in sin and practice sin as a habit so that [God's gift of] grace may increase and overflow? Certainly not! How can we, the very ones who died to sin, continue to live in it any longer? Or are you ignorant of the fact that all of us who have been baptized into Christ Jesus were baptized into His death? We have therefore been buried with Him through baptism into death, so that just as Christ was raised from the dead through the glory and power of the Father, we too might walk habitually in newness of life [abandoning our old ways]. For if we have become one with Him [permanently united] in the likeness of His death, we will also certainly be [one with Him and share fully] in the likeness of His resurrection. We know that our old self [our human nature without the Holy Spirit] was nailed to the cross with Him, in order that our body of sin might be done away with, so that we would no longer be slaves to sin. For the person who has died [with Christ] has been freed from [the power of] sin.

Now if we have died with Christ, we believe that we will also live [together] with Him, because we know [the self-evident truth] that Christ, having been raised from the dead, will never die again; death no longer has power over Him. For the death that He died, He died to sin [ending its power and paying the sinner's debt] once and for all; and the life that He lives, He lives to [glorify] God [in unbroken fellowship with Him]. Even so, consider yourselves to be dead to sin [and your relationship to it broken], but alive to God [in unbroken fellowship with Him] in Christ Jesus.

Therefore do not let sin reign in your mortal body so that you obey its lusts and passions. Do not go on offering members of your body to sin as instruments of wickedness. But offer yourselves to God [in a decisive act] as those alive [raised] from the dead [to a new life], and your members [all of your abilities—sanctified, set apart] as instruments of righteousness [yielded] to God. For sin will no longer be a master over you, since you are not under Law [as slaves], but under [unmerited] grace [as recipients of God's favour and mercy].

What then [are we to conclude]? Shall we sin because we are not under Law, but under [God's] grace? Certainly not! Do you not know that when you continually offer yourselves to someone to do his will, you are the slaves of the one whom you obey, either [slaves] of sin, which leads to death, or of obedience, which leads to righteousness (right standing with God)? But thank God that though you were slaves of sin, you became obedient with all your heart to the standard of teaching in which you were instructed and to which you were committed. And having been set free from sin, you have become the slaves of righteousness [of conformity to God's will and purpose]. I am speaking in [familiar] human terms because of your natural limitations [your spiritual immaturity]. For just as you presented your bodily members as slaves to impurity and to [moral] lawlessness, leading to further lawlessness, so now offer your members [your abilities, your talents] as slaves to righteousness, leading to sanctification [that is, being set apart for God's purpose].

When you were slaves of sin, you were free in regard to righteousness [you had no desire to conform to God's will]. So what benefit did you get at that time from the things of which you are now ashamed? [None!] For the outcome of those things is death! But now since you have been set free from sin and have become [willing] slaves to God, you have your benefit, resulting in sanctification [being made holy and set apart for God's purpose], and the outcome [of this] is eternal life. For the wages of sin is death, but the free gift of God [that is, His remarkable, overwhelming gift of grace to believers] is eternal life in Christ Jesus our Lord." (Romans Chapter 6, author's emphasis).

I hope by now, you are convinced if you weren't already, that Scripture makes it very clear indeed that we really **do** need to want to **stop sinning**. So finally, I will address the question 'How do we do that?'

6. HOW DO WE STOP SINNING?

Author Michael L Brown wrote an excellent book on this subject. His book is entitled 'Go and Sin No More.' [8]

In view of the size of his book, how can I attempt to answer the question 'How to stop sinning' in just a few paragraphs? I will try!

Brown begins his book by giving us sixty reasons not to sin!

He then tells us what the Bible says about sin; he goes on to talk about God's grace and ends by telling us of the need to be Holy.

I believe that, in order for you and I, as human beings, to be able to change from our default condition - which is that of committing sin - to being able to say 'No' to sin, we need **God's intervention**. His chosen method of intervention is what Jesus describes as our need to be 'born again'.

What does it mean to be born again?

I include in the definition of born again, being Spirit-filled, which as you will likely know, is clearly stated and discussed in Acts chapter 2 verses 1 to 21. If you have not received the baptism of the Holy Spirit, please can I encourage you to read that passage and pray earnestly to God to be filled with the Holy Spirit.

What does it mean then to be born again and Spirit-filled? As I mentioned earlier, this teaching of being born again requires us to 'crucify the flesh.' It means to be transformed by God by the power of the Holy Spirit. Before we look into what the Holy Scriptures tell us about being born again, I want to share with you the thoughts of Oswald Chambers once again.

Chambers has a lot to say about being 'born again and crucifying the flesh'.

'No-one is ever united with Jesus Christ until he is willing to relinquish not sin only, but his whole way of looking at things. To be born from above of the Spirit of God means that we must let go before we lay hold, and in the first stages, it is the relinquishing of all pretence. What our Lord wants us to present to Him is not goodness, nor honesty, nor endeavour but real solid sin; that is all He can take from us. And what does He give in exchange for our sin? Real solid righteousness. But we must relinquish all pretence of being anything, all claim of being worthy of God's consideration.'

If you are *'willing to relinquish* (your) *hold on all* (you) *possess,* (your) *hold on your affections, and on everything, and to be identified with the death of Jesus Christ',* then Chambers says *'go through the crisis, relinquish all, and God will make you fit for all that He requires of you.'* [9]

And in his March 16th entry (An Updated Edition in Today's Language) he says this,

'One of the penalties of sin is our acceptance of it. It is not only God who punishes for sin, but sin establishes itself in the sinner and takes its toll. No struggling or praying will enable you to stop doing certain things, and the penalty of sin is that you gradually get used to it, until you finally come to the place where you no longer even realise that it is sin. No power, except the power that comes from being filled with the Holy Spirit, can change or prevent the inherent consequences of sin.' [10]

Many men have discovered for themselves the eternal truth that being filled with the Holy Spirit is the only way they can overcome the default condition to sin that we inherited from our forefathers, Adam and Eve when **they** decided to rebel against God's Word and chose sin instead of <u>obedience to God</u> in the Garden of Eden.

Before we can meaningfully invite the Holy Spirit to enter and rule our lives we must make a conscious decision to give up our right to ourselves, that is our God-given right to choose self (and what we want), ahead of choosing God and what **His Word commands.** Choosing 'self' results from following the ways of our previous disposition; that is before we became born again. In fact, choosing 'self' ahead of God and others, comes from the devil.

And so the challenge is this. If you haven't already, will you give up totally this right to yourself, a right that most of us like too much to give up? Will you turn back to God and follow *only* His ways? Perhaps Chambers' assertion that this old right we all have is of the *devil* might encourage you to give it up once and for all! I believe that this is the crunch question, and many of us struggle in our commitment to God and His command to be Holy, because we cannot, or will not, give up our right to follow our own desires.

What can we learn from Jesus about being born again?

The teaching of being born again, is introduced to us by Jesus, in Chapter 3 of John's Gospel....

'Now there was a certain man among the Pharisees named Nicodemus, a ruler (member of the Sanhedrin) among the Jews, who came to Jesus at night and said to Him, "Rabbi (Teacher), we know [without any doubt] that You have come from God as a teacher; for no one can do these signs [these wonders, these attesting miracles] that You do unless God is with him." Jesus answered him, "I assure you and most solemnly say to you, unless a person is born again [reborn from above—spiritually transformed, renewed, sanctified], he cannot [ever] see and experience the kingdom of God."

Nicodemus said to Him, "How can a man be born when he is old? He cannot enter his mother's womb a second time and be born, can he?" Jesus answered, "I assure you and most solemnly say to you, unless one is born of water and the Spirit he cannot [ever] enter the kingdom of God. That which is born of the flesh is flesh [the physical is merely physical], and that which is born of the Spirit is spirit. Do not be surprised that I have told you, 'You must be born again [reborn from above—spiritually transformed, renewed, sanctified].' The wind blows where it wishes and you hear its sound, but you do not know where it is coming from and where it is going; so it is with everyone who is born of the Spirit."' (John chapter 3 verses 1 to 8).

One day, while I was working on this book, after I had already drafted this paragraph, I was spending my quiet time with God, and my morning Bible reading devotional included John Chapter 1. It was then that I realised for the first time that the Gospel writer John actually introduces us to the teaching of being born again (being transformed by God), not in John chapter 3, but earlier, in John chapter 1 and verse 13. Here he says - of those who believe in the Name of Christ - that we are born... *'...not of blood [natural conception], nor of the will of the flesh [physical impulse], nor of the will of man [that of a natural father], but of God [that is, a divine and supernatural birth—they are <u>born of God—spiritually transformed, renewed, sanctified</u>].'* (Author's emphasis).

The Bible is telling you here that if you believe in the Name of Jesus Christ, you are born of God, which causes you to be spiritually transformed, renewed and sanctified – that is, set apart for God's purposes. Bear with me as I explain the following.

It is clear from both this Scripture and the John chapter 3 Scripture that it is our **spirit alone** that is transformed. If you and I believe in Jesus Christ and we have made Him Lord of our lives, we have God's Spirit living in us and **our spirit is made perfect**.

Why then, even when we are born again of God, do we still sin?

The answer is because our flesh (our body) and our mind battle against our spirit (See Romans chapters 7 and 8). Our **body and our thoughts have not been transformed** and sanctified. We have to make our flesh SUBMIT to the will of our transformed spirit and God's Spirit in us. Paul tells us in Romans chapter 12 verses 1 and 2 that we are to present our bodies as a *'living sacrifice'* and be transformed by *the 'renewing of our minds.'*

Remember you are a *'Temple of the Holy Spirit'* (1 Corinthians chapter 6 verse 19). God dwells inside every believer's body by His Spirit, but the way some of us use and abuse our bodies to gratify our sinful nature, is it any wonder that the Holy Spirit flees away from us for a time. He cannot bear to dwell in a body dominated by sin. Often is the time that some of us grieve the Holy Spirit by our fleshly thoughts and actions.

I also want to say that in order not to sin, we must not yield to temptation. To understand how not to succumb to temptation, we need to look at the example of Jesus and how He responded when He was tempted in the wilderness. Each time the devil tempted Jesus with something Jesus knew to be sinful, He countered Satan with Holy Scripture by saying to Satan, *"It is written....."* (See Luke chapter 4). So as I said previously in both Chapter One and Chapter Three, we need to know the Scriptures – the Word of God - in order to overcome the enemy's lies. If we don't know our Scriptures we won't even know that Satan is telling us a lie, let alone how to counter his lies!

Overcoming sin, even if you are born again, Spirit-filled and know your Bible really well, can still be difficult. This is where the principle laid down in James chapter 5 verse 16 can be extremely helpful. James tells us to *'confess your sins to one another [your false steps, your offenses], and pray for one another, that you may be healed and restored. The heartfelt and persistent prayer of a righteous man (believer) can accomplish much [when put into action and made effective by God—it is dynamic and can have tremendous power].'*

Accountability groups of two or maximum three men can be really helpful. The idea is that you ideally meet (or at least talk on the phone) regularly (weekly if possible) to explain what it is you are specifically struggling with, and give a regular update of how you are dealing with the sin. Is it recurring or have you overcome? Have you slipped back? It requires absolute trust and confidentiality between the group members in order that you can be completely open and vulnerable with each other. All such group discussions must be completely confidential. When a 'secret sin' is spoken out from the darkness into the light, that is a particularly powerful act of obedience and seems to more rapidly break the grip of the devil over that sin and enable God to set you free.

Proverbs chapter 28 verse 13 says *'He who conceals his transgressions will not prosper, But whoever confesses and turns away from his sins will find compassion and mercy.'*

Mark chapter 4 verse 22 says *'For nothing is hidden, except to be revealed; nor has anything been kept secret, but that it would come to light [that is, things are hidden only temporarily, until the appropriate time comes for them to be known].'*

As I mentioned earlier, we are seeing more and more that God is exposing the hidden and secret sins of those in the Church and also those in the world of unbelievers. I believe this is going to escalate as we move towards the time of the return of Jesus Christ.

I'd like to close this chapter with this summary:

When we give our lives to Christ, when we are born again, when we are Spirit-filled, our own spirit is renewed, transformed and sanctified. God's bit is done. He alone is able to transform our spirit. However, we have a part to play. Our part is to crucify our flesh and say to our flesh, and to the world and to the devil, *"No more will I satisfy you and your ways, I am sold out for God, everything I think, say and do, will bring glory to God from this day henceforth."* God has made you and I responsible for transforming our sinful body of flesh. God will not do this for us, although many of us may wish He would.

Having said that, Jesus is keen to help us in every way that we will let Him, and one way is to let Him live in us, the life we cannot live for ourselves.

Oswald Chambers puts it like this:

'The weakest saint who transacts business with Jesus Christ is liberated the second he acts and God's almighty power is available on his behalf. We come up to the truth of God, confess we are wrong, but go back again. Then we approach it again and turn back, until we finally learn we have no business going back. When we are confronted with such a word of truth from our redeeming Lord, we must move directly to transact business with Him. 'Come to Me...' (Matt 11 v28). His word come means to act. Yet the last thing we want to do is come. But everyone who does come knows that, at that very moment, the supernatural power of the life of God invades him. The dominating power of the world, the flesh, and the devil is now paralyzed; not by your act, but because your act has joined you to God and tapped you into His redemptive power.' [11]

The spiritual battle is for your mind, and so we must change the way we think, talk and act, and make all these things line up with the Word of God, and obey the Word of God.

To conclude then; how - in one phrase – can we overcome sin? How do we stop sinning?

The answer is in **'crucifying the flesh'.** That means <u>stop 'feeding'</u> the desires of your flesh – it means **starve** your sinful cravings to death!

Finally, a word of warning. Once you make the deliberate, conscious decision not to pander to your flesh or the ways of the world, or to the schemes of the devil, Satan will be on your case like he has never been on it before.

Not only that, but your unbelieving associates, friends and family members will all think (from their perspective) that you have 'lost the plot'. However, the rewards - both in this life and the next - will be extraordinary. Why? Because God is looking for overcomers, and a crown awaits every one of us who overcomes the flesh, the world and the devil (1 Corinthians chapter 9 verse 25, 1 Peter chapter 5 verse 4, 2 Timothy chapter 4 verse 8, James chapter 1 verse 12, Revelation chapter 2 verse 10 and Revelation chapter 3 verse 11).

Jesus Christ was the greatest overcomer of all, and when He hung on the Cross, He gained the Victory, and the war was won. The problem is that battles between our flesh and our spirit rage on, and they will continue to do so until Jesus returns to rule this world and banish Satan and his foes to an eternity where they belong - in the Lake of Fire.

In the meantime, *do not fret* (Psalm 37), my brother-in-Christ! Instead, put on the whole armour of God which I outlined for you in Chapter Three and you will be protected by the King of all kings and the Lord of all lords as you battle against the powers of darkness.

VOLUME ONE - Notes

Chapter One

1. *COME ON CHURCH! WAKE UP! - Sin Within the Church and What Jesus Has to Say About It* by Michele Neal. ISBN 978-1-62136-316-3. Used by permission.

2. Source: World report on violence and health, World Health Organisation 2000.

3. *Respectable Sins* by Jerry Bridges. ISBN 978-1-60006-140-0 Used by permission.

Chapter Two

1. *Bible Prophecy for Everyone* by Tim LaHaye. ISBN 978-0736965224. Copyright © 2002/2009 by Tim LaHaye. Published by Harvest House Publishers, Eugene, Oregon 97402, www.harvesthousepublishers.com Used by Permission.

Chapter Three

1. David Diga Hernandez, *25 Truths About Demons and Spiritual Warfare* (Lake Mary, FL: Charisma House, 2016), Used by permission.

2. Ibid

3. Ibid

4. *Battlefield of the Mind* by Joyce Meyer. ISBN 0-446-69214-X

5. David Diga Hernandez, *25 Truths About Demons and Spiritual Warfare* (Lake Mary, FL: Charisma House, 2016), Used by permission.

6. Ibid

7. Taken from *'Wild at Heart: Discovering The Secret of A Man's Soul'* by John Eldredge. ISBN 0-7852-6694-1. © Copyright 2001 by John Eldredge. Used by permission of Thomas Nelson. www.thomasnelson.com

Chapter Four

1. Charles Price – see www.livingtruth.co.uk

2. *Respectable Sins* by Jerry Bridges. ISBN 978-1-60006-140-0 Used by permission.

3. *My Utmost For His Highest* by Oswald Chambers, Entry for 7th October. ISBN 0-916441-83-0. Used by permission.

4. *MERE CHRISTIANITY* by CS Lewis. ISBN 978-0-00-746121-9 © copyright CS Lewis Pte Ltd 1942, 1943, 1944, 1952. Used by permission.

5. *My Utmost For His Highest* by Oswald Chambers. ISBN 0-916441-83-0. Used by permission.

6. Christianity Magazine February 2009 issue. Used by permission. www.premierchristianity.com

7. *My Utmost For His Highest* by Oswald Chambers. ISBN 0-916441-83-0. Entry for August 15th. Used by permission.

8. *Go and Sin No More – A call to holiness* by Michael L. Brown. ISBN 978-0-615-73019-6. Used by permission.

9. *My Utmost For His Highest* by Oswald Chambers. ISBN 0-916441-83-0. Entry for March 8th   Used by permission.

10. *My Utmost For His Highest* – An Updated Edition In Today's Language by Oswald Chambers, edited by James Reimann. Entry for March 16th. ISBN 0-929239-57-1. Used by permission.

11. *My Utmost For His Highest* by Oswald Chambers, Entry for November 4th ISBN 0-916441-83-0. Used by permission.

VOLUME TWO

OVERCOMING
BEHAVIOUR BATTLES

CONTENTS

INTRODUCTION

In Volume One, I wrote about four different areas of our walk with God that can be constant battles for us men. Those areas are broad and can be applied to *all aspects* of our Christian walk. Those are battles for our very soul.

In Volume Two, I will cover five very *specific battles* facing men and how we can overcome them. These battles concern our behaviour towards other people…

Chapter One

BECOMING A BETTER HUSBAND

'In the same way, you husbands, live with your wives in an understanding way [with great gentleness and tact, and with an intelligent regard for the marriage relationship], as with someone physically weaker, since she is a woman. Show her honour and respect as a fellow heir of the grace of life, so that your prayers will not be hindered or ineffective'. (1 Peter chapter 3 verse 7).

'Husbands, love your wives [with an affectionate, sympathetic, selfless love that always seeks the best for them] and do not be embittered or resentful toward them [because of the responsibilities of marriage]'. (Colossians chapter 3 verse 19).

On 6th September 2017, I read with horror the following statistic in my Tearfund prayer diary [1]:

'In the UK, two women die each week due to violence inflicted by their partners. In El Salvador, the figure is one woman every day. In Russia it's <u>one every hour whilst in the Ukraine one woman dies every 35 minutes due to violence inflicted by an intimate partner'.</u> (Author's emphasis).

This got me thinking… *why are some men so violent towards those they love?*

I am not a marriage guidance councillor, although my wife and I have helped couples with relational issues. I am not a psychologist or a psychiatrist so I have no answer based on any appropriate professional qualifications or training, but I have over 45 years of adult life experiences and a knowledge of the Bible, which has helped me understand why *some* people can resort to violence when they have relational difficulties.

The purpose of this chapter is to share with you what you can do to ensure you do **not** resort to violence, but learn the secrets of how to love your wife (if you are married) in a way that will enhance and fulfil your relationship to your mutual benefit.

I have discovered seven things which have not only helped improve my marriage, but actually kept Michele and I together when it might have seemed easier for one of us to walk away from the marriage. And before you fall into the trap of believing walking away is a good option, let me tell you it is NOT God's option. God's Word tells us that marriage is *'a mystery* (Ephesians chapter 5 verses 31 and 32) *of two people becoming one flesh'* (See also Mark chapter 10 verse 8 and Matthew chapter 19 verse 5). How can you walk away from your 'other half' if God's view is that you have become one flesh?

Furthermore, in Matthew chapter 19 verse 6 Jesus adds, *"Therefore, what God has joined together, let no one separate."*

Doubtless, God knew that married men and women would not find it easy (in the natural), to stay together for life and so God's Holy Word has some things to say to husbands about how God expects us to treat our wives. Now, because His ways are designed to be perfect for us, if we choose to follow God's instructions, then it follows that obedience over these matters will inevitably lead to a better marriage. However, before we look at what Scripture says to help us, I want to begin by sharing with you the thoughts of three Christian men – Bob Gass, Paul Tripp and Gary Chapman.

The Cry of Every Soul

In The Word for Today [2], Bob Gass wrote back in 2010, *'When people visit our church what they want to know is "Will you love me as I am, even if I don't fit your mould and change as quickly as you'd like me to?" '*

I believe that is the cry of every living soul. I believe your wife, your children, and all your family members, want to know you will be **patient** and **love them as they are** – whilst God is working on them, in His own timing, to change them for the better.

The first thing I learned about how to be a better husband, and how to experience a better marriage, was to learn to love my wife as God loves me (and you) and that is - UNCONDITIONALLY.

So in my view, the first step in making for a great marriage is…

1 – LOVE YOUR WIFE *UNCONDITIONALLY.*

When my wife and I were redecorating my father's house in June 2010, I unscrewed a bedside cupboard from the wall and found underneath it a hand written note, old and fading, written by somebody who lived in the house before my father. In neat hand-writing was a short note written on an envelope, from a man presumably to his wife, saying he was sorry how *'he didn't measure up to the man'* that she wanted. According to the letter, he was leaving home, walking away from a relationship where he felt unloved. How tragic…

Will you still love your wife if she doesn't fit your mould and doesn't change as quickly as you'd like - or will you, like this seemingly unloved man, choose to walk away?

Pastor Paul Tripp, in his book on this difficult issue, aptly entitled 'What Did You Expect?' [3] says that *'when we experience difficulties in our relationship with our wife, men usually tackle the issue in one of two ways. The first type of man would shy away from dealing with it directly – so he might go quiet, walk away, or compile a mental list of wrongs committed against him by his wife, or he might yell at her in anger or even level a threat. The second type of man would confront the issue, confess and forgive.'*

Not confronting the wrong behaviour is the easy option and I guess is the response of the majority. It was certainly my way of dealing with issues for the first fifty years of my life.

The trouble is, says Tripp, this is a *"comfortable but relationally destructive pattern. Meanwhile, the affection between* [the couple] *is weakening, and the distance between them is widening."* [4]

I don't really know why I found it easier to 'brush issues under the carpet' when I was younger. Sometimes, I still find it easier to act in this way today. I'm certainly not risk-averse, but as I grew up I became 'confrontation–averse'. Even now at the age of 65, I try to avoid confrontation at all costs. Maybe it's just that I find this type of 'avoidance-behaviour' more comfortable. During my first marriage, this was the only way I knew how to deal with issues. In that relationship, I wasn't even aware that our *'affection (for each other) was weakening'* or that *'the distance between us was widening'*. But after 28 years, my first marriage ended in divorce; it was a total shock to me – I did not see it coming.

Confronting the other party is much harder work, but Tripp explains in his book why this is the only approach to take - for those people who want their marriage to flourish.

I have now discovered Tripp is right. Peace-keeping can work in the short term, but in my experience it <u>does not</u> work in the long-term. Interestingly, Jesus never said 'Blessed are the peace-keepers', He said *'Blessed are the <u>peace-makers</u>'* (Matthew chapter 5 verse 9 NIV, Author's emphasis).

Keeping the peace means remaining silent when there are issues that need dealing with. When we don't deal with them, it can lead to us harbouring a grudge; whereas *making peace* involves the hard work of resolving conflict, and I have dedicated an entire chapter, later in the book, to this important topic.

So, the next step for keeping the marriage on an even-keel is this:

2 - BECOME A PEACE-MAKER, NOT A PEACE-KEEPER

Tripp goes on to point out that many of us find it hard to forgive, even though it is the easier and more beneficial option. In his experience, people prefer to go down the route of *"self-righteousness (convincing ourselves that we are not the problem) and accusation (telling our spouse that he or she is the problem).* He says this behaviour *"precludes relationship."* Instead of *"defending our marriage against attack, we are viewing each other as adversaries and throwing up walls of defence against one another."* [5]

He gives a useful insight into why people don't like to forgive – choosing not to forgive gives the aggrieved party destructive power, it makes them feel superior; such people can use it against the other person and it allows the unforgiving party to become the judge (which is actually the role of God alone).

He defines forgiveness as meaning *"you do not carry the wrong with you (bitterness) and you do not treat the other in light of the wrong (judgement)."* [6] Instead, you give the matter to God. The attitude is grace and the goal is reconciliation.

Jesus said *"But if you do not forgive others [nurturing your hurt and anger with the result that it interferes with your relationship with God], then your Father will not forgive your trespasses."* (Matthew chapter 6 verse 15 and Mark chapter 11 verse 26). Furthermore in Matthew chapter 18 verses 21 to 35, Jesus gives a graphic illustration of how God will treat us if we do not forgive. I urge you to read it.

So, Step 3 is…

3 - EMBRACE THE LIBERATING POWER OF FORGIVENESS.

Our ability to forgive others seems to be strongly linked to how deeply we love God. I am grateful to Tripp for letting me into this secret. He says *'it is only when I love God above all else that I will ever love my neighbour as myself'.* [7]

Married man of God, do you not know that your wife is your closest and dearest neighbour?

Do you love God above all else? Do you love God more than your wife? If you don't, it's likely your love for your wife will be lacking in some way.

Tripp says: *'At the foundational level, the difficulties in our marriages do not first come because we don't love one another enough. They happen because we don't love God enough; and because we don't love God enough we don't treat one another with the kind of love that makes marriages work'.* He says *'lasting, persevering, other-centred living does not flow out of romantic attraction, personality coalescence, or lifestyle similarity. It is only when I live in a celebratory and restful worship of God that I am able not to take myself too seriously and I am free to serve and celebrate another'.* [8]

He shows from his counselling experience and from his own life experience that a marriage of love, unity, and understanding will flow out of a daily worship of God as Creator, as Sovereign and as Saviour. I believe Tripp's book is a 'must-read' for those of us who know deep down that our marriages could be better.

Step 4 for a better marriage….

4 - LEARN TO LOVE ONE ANOTHER MORE DEEPLY!

There is one more book I want to refer to, before we look at what the Bible has to say about our role as husbands. The book I have in mind was written for both men and women and, other than the Bible, is one of the most helpful books my wife Michele and I have ever read on the subject of how to live in harmony with one another. It is a true classic and is entitled **'The 5 Love Languages'** by Gary Chapman. He later wrote an edition just for men [9].

In Chapman's book, I learned what for me was the most life-changing fact about relationships. I hadn't learned this anywhere else before. If I had known this revelation from my early adulthood, I am confident my first marriage would not have ended in divorce.

That divorce plays on my mind to this day. Although I wish I could have avoided it, I am nevertheless so grateful to God for the daily grace He pours into my life. At first, I was angry with God, and if the truth be known I blamed Him for the end of my first marriage. I'm glad to report it didn't take me too long to realise it wasn't *God's fault*; and once I had come to terms with things, forgiven both myself, my wife and others for various mistakes, God led me to a wonderful new godly wife in 2005.

Fortunately, due to the relationship of honesty and trust that God has enabled Michele and I to develop, I am still able to meet up with my ex-wife when visiting my two grown-up sons from time to time to enjoy a family meal together, and Michele joins us occasionally. Tragically, however, this is not always the case for divorced individuals, and even worse is the damage that can be caused to many members of the family as a result of the separation.

As I said earlier, Scripture tells us clearly that God's perfect plan for our life is that the marriage of a man to a woman, at the exclusion of all others, should be for life. The fact that this is rarely the case today is evidence to me of the devil's hatred of this Holy Institution.

By now you will be wondering what it was I discovered from Chapman's book that has proven to be life-changing? Let me tell you.

Chapman discovered, after a lifetime of counselling couples, that basically every person feels loved to a greater or lesser degree depending upon five common factors, which he calls 'Love Languages', and these are:

Words of Affirmation
Quality Time Together

Acts of Service
Physical Touch
Gifts

After reading the book, I discovered that my primary love languages are ***physical touch and words of affirmation.*** I then realised that one of the key mistakes I made in my first marriage (and also that I was making in <u>all</u> relationships whether amongst family members, people at church, or at work) was that I subconsciously thought that everybody I met would feel valued and loved, so long as I gave them a friendly hug and told them how wonderful they were.

It turns out that nothing could be further from the truth, unless of course the other person has the same two primary love languages as me, namely physical touch and words of affirmation!

With hindsight, and the knowledge I learned from Chapman's book, I realised my first wife's primary love language was quality time. Whereas she yearned for me to spend more time with her and give her my undivided attention, I was often away on business trips doing everything I could to be 'successful' (to feed my own love language of needing affirmation from others), and to show my first wife how much I 'loved her' by providing a beautiful marital home, together with the income that enabled us to finance our middle-class life style.

I now believe this to be a serious error made by a great number of men. Instead of putting the important emotional needs of our wife first, many of us think it more important to do whatever it takes to be a successful breadwinner.

God obviously knew I would take this same mistaken thinking into my new marriage and I am so grateful to Him that soon after I married Michele, we discovered Chapman's life-changing book.

I found that Michele's primary love languages are *acts of service and quality time,* which means that in order for her to feel loved, she doesn't need lots of hand-holding or to be told ten times a day that she is brilliant at everything and that I love her. Rather, Michele feels loved by me when I put out the rubbish (trash) and occasionally help her by vacuuming the carpets, mopping the floors, helping with gardening, doing the shopping together, or taking her out to a café for some quality time together.

Also, when she asks me to drive her to the beach for a walk (not something that comes easy to me – I want to drive to the beach to lay in the warm sunshine!), it means I need to try to focus on HER needs and fulfil those. It means I have to 'crucify my flesh' and walk with her, sit down with her and have a cup of tea and cake and let her talk to me WITHOUT interrupting her or trying to 'fix things' – which is not easy for me! Men are naturally programmed to 'fix' problems while most women simply want their husband to listen to them as they talk about their problems. I used to hate it when Michele would say to me *"If I wanted you to solve my problem I would have asked you!"* Now I laugh when she says this because I realise what she means is *'I simply wanted to share my struggle with you and be reassured that you are there with me to support me whilst I resolve the problem.'*

The benefit that results, when both people in the relationship learn each other's love languages and feed them, is that they both **feel** loved. For example, although Michele doesn't feel a personal need to hold my arm as we walk along the street together, or to be thanked for everything she does for me, she holds my arm anyway and tries hard to speak positive words to me because she has learned that my love languages are physical touch and words of affirmation. It takes hard work from both parties to do or say things to each other that don't come naturally, but always remember that the prerequisite to a strong loving marriage is that we keep working at it! I'm afraid to have to tell you there is **NO** quick fix!

I remember saying to my ex-wife some time during the separation/divorce "You will never know how much I love you; I love you so much" and that, I believe, was the heart of the problem – **she actually never knew!** Why? Because I didn't know how to show my love for her in the way that she needed because I didn't know her love language. In fact I didn't even realise there was such a thing.

Step 5 for a great marriage, then, is:

5 - LEARN YOUR SPOUSE'S PRIMARY LOVE LANGUAGES AND 'FEED' THEM APPROPRIATELY.

I stated earlier that Gary Chapman's **'The 5 Love Languages'** was one of the most helpful books my wife and I found on this subject. One of the most helpful Christian 'training courses' we attended was **'The Marriage Course',** by Nicky and Sila Lee. [10]

Marrying each other was to prove to be a challenge, not only for me but also for Michele. We are two very different people with two very different love languages. But God is good! In fact God is amazing!

We are both so grateful to Him not only for leading us to **The 5 Love Languages** book but also to **The Marriage Course.** The course was so helpful, that we attended it twice within two years. We did this because we wanted to demonstrate to each other our mutual commitment to making our marriage work right from the start. In fact we first attended the course just one week after our honeymoon, and we re-visited the course two years later to confirm what improvements we had made, and also what relational areas we still had to work on. Second marriages are notoriously difficult to make work for so many reasons, not the least of which is the baggage that each party can carry into the new relationship. The statistics on the number of second marriages that succeed are sadly quite low, and some of our friends (who knew us both well) didn't give us much chance of our marriage lasting more than a few years. We would both admit those first years were indeed very difficult, but by God's grace and with much patience and commitment to the principles we learned from **The Marriage Course** we are still together and still doing the hard work of making our marriage successful some twelve years later.

What is it that makes 'The Marriage Course' so helpful?

Well, first it has been put together by a mature, married Christian couple and secondly, much of it is based on biblical principles. Churches all across the UK host the teaching and so the format naturally varies slightly according to the local resources available and the preferences of the individual leaders.

However, it usually consists of seven evening sessions where a group of couples meet together in a large room, hall or other meeting place, and church volunteers serve a meal to each couple prior to a DVD teaching. The couples then watch and listen to the series of DVD teaching modules, one each week. After that, each couple spend a little time doing some exercises together from a workbook to learn about some of the principles taught. They then speak candidly to each other about what they have learned, as well as having an opportunity to validate each other's feelings about their issues, and resolve to improve areas of difficulty according to the teaching of the course. Let me reassure you, if you haven't already attended the course, that this is done out of earshot of the other couples or the leaders, although the leaders are available to listen and encourage if asked.

The subject matter includes, **1 - Building Strong Relationships, 2 - The Art of Communication, 3 - Resolving Conflict, 4 - The Power of Forgiveness, 5 - Parents and In-laws, 6 - Good Sex** and **7 - Love in Action.**

Michele and I were so impressed with this course that we genuinely would go as far as to say it should be compulsory teaching for **every** married couple. Your marriage does not have to be in a mess – you will benefit from this course even if your marriage is *already* on a good foundation.

There are also courses for courting/engaged couples to attend. One such course, widely respected in the UK, is **THE MARRIAGE PREPARATION COURSE** [11].

What could be better than starting your married life with such a valuable, godly teaching under your belt, BEFORE you walk down the aisle and say 'I do'!?

Step 6 to help you be a better husband and have an amazing marriage is…

<u>**6 - ATTEND THE MARRIAGE COURSE**</u>
<u>**(or similar Christian training course for married couples).**</u>

I will say here and now, it is usually the man in the relationship who is reluctant to participate in such a course - and if that is you, my message to you is this…. 'Get over your pride, get off your butt and show your wife how much you love her by inviting her to attend the very next course in your district!' Trust me, you will not regret it, and the likelihood is you will actually learn something that will greatly benefit your relationship!

If you live outside the UK, and the course run by Holy Trinity Brompton is not available, why not get hold of the teaching material on-line and host a course in your neighbourhood or try finding a similar Christian course to attend. Michele and I actually ran the course in the privacy of our own home to help one Christian couple who were struggling at the time. They found it very rewarding, just as we did. Believe me, no matter whether you have been married for five weeks or fifty years, there is always something you can learn that will help make your marriage more fulfilling, and attending this course is an excellent way of achieving that end.

Ok, I've introduced you to two great books and a training course (all compiled by Christians) to help improve not just your marriage, but your relationships with others generally. Now I want to turn to what we can learn from God's Holy Word on the subject of how to be the husband your wife will honour, respect, and be proud of.

What does the Bible have to say to help us?   That brings me to the final step in becoming a better husband….

7 - APPLY WHAT GOD'S HOLY WORD INSTRUCTS HUSBANDS TO DO.

There are three biblical texts I want to explore. **1 Corinthians chapter 13** - which deals with love and is often read during a church marriage ceremony - **1 Corinthians chapter 7** - which talks about marriage, but I want to begin by exploring **Ephesians chapter 5.**

The writer, Paul, begins the chapter by telling us (both men and women) that we should spend time becoming: *'imitators of God [copy Him and follow His example], as well-beloved children [imitate their father]; and walk continually in love [that is, value one another—practice empathy and compassion, unselfishly seeking the best for others], just as Christ also loved you and gave Himself up for us, an offering and sacrifice to God [slain for you, so that it became] a sweet fragrance.'*

Paul goes on to talk about the dangers of God's wrath coming upon those who habitually sin, and he is setting the scene for something he wants to specifically say to husbands (and wives) about the purity, holiness and special godly intentions for marriage, which is this:

Ephesians Chapter 5 Verses 22 to 33

'Wives, be subject to your own husbands, as [a service] to the Lord. For the husband is head of the wife, as Christ is head of the church, Himself being the Saviour of the body. But as the church is subject to Christ, so also wives should be subject to their husbands in everything [respecting both their position as protector and their responsibility to God as head of the house].

Husbands, love your wives [seek the highest good for her and surround her with a caring, unselfish love], just as Christ also loved the church and gave Himself up for her, so that He might sanctify the church, having cleansed her by the washing of water with the word [of God], so that [in turn] He might present the church to Himself in glorious splendour, without spot or wrinkle or any such thing; but that she would be holy [set apart for God] and blameless. Even so husbands should and are morally obligated to love their own wives as [being in a sense] their own bodies. He who loves his own wife loves himself. For no one ever hated his own body, but [instead] he nourishes and protects and cherishes it, just as Christ does the church, because we are members (parts) of His body. FOR THIS REASON A MAN SHALL LEAVE HIS FATHER AND HIS MOTHER AND SHALL BE JOINED [and be faithfully devoted] TO HIS WIFE, AND THE TWO SHALL BECOME ONE FLESH. This mystery [of two becoming one] is great; but I am speaking with reference to [the relationship of] Christ and the church. However, each man among you [without exception] is to love his wife as his very own self [with behaviour worthy of respect and esteem, always seeking the best for her with an attitude of lovingkindness], and the wife [must see to it] that she respects and delights in her husband [that she notices him and prefers him and treats him with loving concern, treasuring him, honouring him, and holding him dear]'.

I do not intend here to do an in-depth Bible study of this passage but I want to highlight what I believe to be the critical biblical aspects of this passage for husbands today, in these times of political correctness, equality and liberal and/or the self-centred interpretation of God's Holy Word.

I want to begin by saying unequivocally that the Bible is very clear (as I have stated elsewhere) that the word 'Marriage' refers exclusively to a relationship between a biological man and a biological woman. In the Bible, a husband is male and a wife female. This is the Word of God. Only a <u>minority of Governments</u> around the world (approx. 10% at the time of writing, March 2018) have taken it upon themselves to announce that they 'know better than God' and have declared a different definition of this Holy Institution, and sadly the UK Government is one of those. Any Government that redefines marriage is **in rebellion** against God and the Holy Bible, and will be accountable to Almighty God on judgement day, whether they are believers or not.

The first thing I want to say in respect of this Scripture (Ephesians chapter 5) is that, shockingly, some men use verses 22 and 23 to justify all manner of ungodly behaviour towards their wife. Not only that, but they either have never read verses 25 to 33 or have simply torn them out of their Bible.

Verses 22 and 23 are misquoted by some men to justify that, 'wives are to be subject to their husbands because the husband is the head of the wife'. Such an interpretation gives a husband a licence to make his wife do anything that he wants her to do. A quick check of the footnote in the Amplified Bible clarifies the original meaning of verse 22 as follows:

'Wives, be subject to your own husbands, as [a service] to the Lord.'

Footnote:

'The wife to her husband, not to men in general; not as inferior to him, nor in violation of her Christian ethics, but honouring her husband as protector and head of the home, respecting the responsibility of his position and his accountability to God.'

So, first, it is clear that the only man that a woman is to be subject to is her husband. Second, that subjection is to do with the God-ordained fact that the *man* is the spiritual head of the home (and also the church by the way, but that is a whole different topic and beyond the scope of this book). She is in no way *inferior* to him nor is she expected to do anything in violation of her Christian ethics, and she is submitting to her husband's headship purely out of respect to God and God's laws as pertaining to the husband.

The Husband is the Spiritual Head

If you are a husband, how are you to behave as spiritual head of your wife? The first thing we learn is that we husbands are to behave towards our wife in the same way that Christ does as head of the Church (verse 22b).

In Matthew chapter 20 verse 28, the Bible says of Jesus, *"the Son of Man did not come to be served, but to serve, and to give His life as a ransom for many."* Jesus came to serve, not to be served. Therefore, husbands are to do as Jesus did, which is to serve their wife. Yes, that's right; husbands are to be a servant to their wife! How many of us men can truly say this is the way we treat our wife?

Now working through the text from verse 25, we see we are to seek the highest good for our wife and surround her with a caring, unselfish love, just as Christ also loved the Church and gave Himself up for her. If Christ gave Himself up for the Church, it means husbands are to be prepared to sacrifice their life for their wife's wellbeing.

We are to *'wash our wife'* with the Word of God; that means we are to regularly read God's Word to her, sharing our faith and the Holy Scriptures together. In so doing, we make our wife holy (set apart for God, and blameless). How are you doing with this aspect of your role as a husband?

We are to love our own wives as we love ourselves.

Jesus' command was to love our neighbour as our self. If we are to do that for our neighbour, how much more should we love our wife as we love our self! That love is to encompass nourishing, protecting, and cherishing her. One of the things my wife regularly reminds me of, is how much a woman wants above all else to feel **CHERISHED** by her husband.

What does it mean to cherish somebody – it means *'to treat with affection and tenderness; hold dear. To keep fondly in mind; to treasure.* [12]

My wife just popped her head over my shoulder as I wrote this, and said this to me:

"What wives want is for their husbands to realise how blessed they are by God, by Him giving them such a special treasure." That's right, your wife is a special treasure; in fact the Bible says your wife is a blessing from the Lord. Proverbs chapter 19 verse 14: *'House and wealth are the inheritance from fathers, but a wise, understanding and sensible wife is a [gift and blessing] from the Lord.'*

Listen very carefully men. Your wife wants to be loved in a very special and sensitive way and treated in such a way that, on the Day of Judgement when you return your wife back to God - a wife who He has 'loaned to you' during your lifetime - God will be able to say to you, *"Well done my good and faithful servant".* Whether or not God will be able to say such a thing to you depends upon whether or not you have put into practice His Holy Word concerning how husbands should treat their wives!

The Bible's definition of marriage

Moving on to verse 31, we find what for Christians is a biblical definition of marriage:

'FOR THIS REASON A MAN SHALL LEAVE HIS FATHER AND HIS MOTHER AND SHALL BE JOINED [and be faithfully devoted] TO HIS WIFE, AND THE TWO SHALL BECOME ONE FLESH.'

With regards to 'one flesh', the Amplified Bible has a note which explains that the bond between husband and wife supersedes **all** other relationships.

That means our relationship with our wife is more important than our relationship with either of our parents, any of our children, our siblings, business colleagues, or friends. In fact the husband/ wife relationship is more important than our relationship with EVERYBODY ELSE, except God.

Paul's final point here for us men is that we are expected by God to love our wife as we love our self. If you do not love yourself, it does not mean that you need not love your wife. Here the assumption in Paul's analogy is that you love yourself **absolutely,** just as this was Jesus' assumption when He told us *'YOU SHALL LOVE YOUR NEIGHBOUR AS YOURSELF [that is, unselfishly seek the best or higher good for others].'* (Matthew chapter 22 verse 39).

Next, I want to turn to a very long passage about the role of the husband, and some of the issues affecting marriage.

1 Corinthians Chapter 7, verses 1 to 16 and 25 to 40.

'Now as to the matters of which you wrote: It is good (beneficial, advantageous) for a man not to touch a woman [outside marriage]. But because of [the temptation to participate in] sexual immorality, let each man have his own wife, and let each woman have her own husband. The husband must fulfil his [marital] duty to his wife [with good will and kindness], and likewise the wife to her husband. The wife does not have [exclusive] authority over her own body, but the husband shares with her; and likewise the husband does not have [exclusive] authority over his body, but the wife shares with him. Do not deprive each other [of marital rights], except perhaps by mutual consent for a time, so that you may devote yourselves [unhindered] to prayer, but come together again so that Satan will not tempt you [to sin] because of your lack of self-control. But I am saying this as a concession, not as a command. I wish that all the people were as I am; but each person has his own gift from God, one of this kind and one of that.

'But I say to the unmarried and to the widows, [that as a practical matter] it is good if they remain [single and entirely devoted to the Lord] as I am. But if they do not have [sufficient] self-control, they should marry; for it is better to marry than to burn with passion.

'But to the married [believers] I give instructions—not I, but the Lord—that the wife is not to separate from her husband, (but even if she does leave him, let her remain single or else be

reconciled to her husband) and that the husband should not leave his wife.

'To the rest I declare—I, not the Lord [since Jesus did not discuss this]—that if any [believing] brother has a wife who does not believe [in Christ], and she consents to live with him, he must not leave her. And if any [believing] woman has an unbelieving husband, and he consents to live with her, she must not leave him. For the unbelieving husband is sanctified [that is, he receives the blessings granted] through his [Christian] wife, and the unbelieving wife is sanctified through her believing husband. Otherwise your children would be [ceremonially] unclean, but as it is they are holy. But if the unbelieving partner leaves, let him leave. In such cases the [remaining] brother or sister is not [spiritually or morally] bound. But God has called us to peace. For how do you know, wife, whether you will save your husband [by leading him to Christ]? Or how do you know, husband, whether you will save your wife [by leading her to Christ]?

'Now concerning the virgins [of marriageable age] I have no command of the Lord, but I give my opinion as one who by the Lord's mercy is trustworthy. I think then that because of the impending distress [that is, the pressure of the current trouble], it is good for a man to remain as he is. Are you bound to a wife? Do not seek to be released. Are you unmarried? Do not seek a wife. But if you do marry, you have not sinned [in doing so]; and if a virgin marries, she has not sinned [in doing so]. Yet those [who marry] will have troubles (special challenges) in this life, and I am trying to spare you that. But I say this, believers: the time has been shortened, so that from now on even those who have wives should be as though they did not; and those who weep, as though they did not weep; and those who rejoice, as though they did not rejoice; and those who buy, as though they did not possess [anything]; and those who use the world [taking advantage of its opportunities], as though they did not make full use of it. For the outward form of this world [its present social and material

nature] is passing away.

'But I want you to be free from concern. The unmarried man is concerned about the things of the Lord, how he may please the Lord; but the married man is concerned about worldly things, how he may please his wife, and his interests are divided. The unmarried woman or the virgin is concerned about the matters of the Lord, how to be holy and set apart both in body and in spirit; but a married woman is concerned about worldly things, how she may please her husband. Now I say this for your own benefit; not to restrict you, but to promote what is appropriate and secure undistracted devotion to the Lord.

'But if any man thinks that he is not acting properly and honourably toward his virgin daughter, [by not permitting her to marry], if she is past her youth, and it must be so, let him do as he wishes, he does not sin; let her marry. But the man who stands firmly committed in his heart, having no compulsion [to yield to his daughter's request], and has authority over his own will, and has decided in his own heart to keep his own virgin [daughter from being married], he will do well. So then both the father who gives his virgin daughter in marriage does well, and he who does not give her in marriage will do better.

'A wife is bound [to her husband by law] as long as he lives. But if her husband dies, she is free to marry whomever she wishes, only [provided that he too is] in the Lord. But in my opinion a widow is happier if she stays as she is. And I think that I also have the Spirit of God [in this matter].'

The first thing we learn from this long passage is that due to the temptation to engage in sexual immorality, men are encouraged to marry a woman. Women too are encouraged to find a husband.

The husband and the wife are both told to fulfil their *'marital duty'* to their spouse with <u>goodwill and kindness.</u> What is our marital duty? From the text it is clear it is talking about sexual relations because, Paul goes on to tell us that in marriage we *'share each other's body'* and that we are not to *'deprive each other'*, except by mutual consent for a time in order to devote our time to prayer. But we are to *'come together again'* so that we are not tempted by the devil to sin due to a lack of self-control.

It is clear to me that Paul is saying we are not to deny each other sexual intercourse, otherwise it could lead us to being tempted to engage in sexual immorality (please see my comments about this in Volume One, Chapter Four page 134, under the heading 'Sexual Self-gratification').

Paul then says he really wishes all Christians were single, so that we can be fully devoted to the Lord rather than having to focus on the needs of a fellow human being i.e., our spouse.

Is it OK to divorce your wife?

To those of us who choose to marry, he says we are not to leave our wife, but if we do leave, he says we are to **be reconciled** to each other, or else become single once again (i.e., not re-marry). This is a command echoed by Jesus in several Scriptures concerning divorce (see Matthew chapter 5 verse 32, Luke chapter 16 verse 18, Matthew chapter 19 verses 1 to 9 and the parallel verses in Mark chapter 10 verses 1 to 12).

As an aside, I would like to point out that the Matthew chapter 19 verse 9 Scripture includes an important 'caveat' from Jesus: *'except for sexual immorality'*. I have listed below some different translations so we can get a feel for a fuller translation from the original Greek.

"I tell you that anyone who divorces his wife, except for sexual immorality, and marries another woman commits adultery." (NIV).

"And I tell you this, whoever divorces his wife and marries someone else commits adultery—unless his wife has been

unfaithful" (NLT).

"And I say to you, whoever divorces his wife, except for sexual immorality, and marries another, commits adultery; and whoever marries her who is divorced commits adultery." (NKJV).

I make this point because some people in the Church feel it is a sin for a divorcee to marry again. It seems clear to me that whilst God's plan for marriage is that it should be life-long, here Jesus is in effect saying that it is acceptable to re-marry where the divorce has been caused as a result <u>of the spouse's adultery</u>, with a subsequent unwillingness of the adulterous spouse to seek reconciliation.

Returning now to the 1 Corinthians passage. What follows are some of Paul's personal views, as distinct from God's will or commands. Paul says if you are married to a non-Christian woman, provided she consents to live with you, you must not leave her. Likewise, in the case of a woman married to an unbelieving husband. However he says if the unbelieving partner leaves the marriage, let them go. The marriage is not binding in such circumstances (since they are an unbeliever).

Paul also makes some difficult to understand comments about being saved, one spouse by the other. The Amplified Bible footnote helpfully clarifies the Scriptural truth here as follows:

'The unbeliever is not saved by marriage to a Christian. Each person, whether spouse or child, must make a personal decision to accept and follow Christ to receive salvation and God's promises.'

Paul points out what married men (and women) know only too well; that marriage will have its problems!

Because the return of the Lord could occur at any moment, Paul states his own opinion that it might be better not to marry since it brings with it the additional concern of worrying about worldly things and also how to please one's wife. Hence, he says, marriage can result in the dividing of our interests. Whilst he acknowledges benefits of remaining single, Paul still upholds marriage. He remains neutral as to whether it is better to protect your daughter from the challenges of marriage or whether to encourage her to marry. Both options are acceptable but he says our conscience about this is what matters. Finally, in this passage, Paul confirms the Lord's teaching that marriage, for believers, is for life. He says a wife is bound to her husband as long as he lives, but if he dies, she is free to re-marry any man she wishes - but only so long as he is a believer – but Paul thinks a widow would be happier living alone.

Finally in this Chapter, I want to take a brief look at what we can learn about loving our wife from the following classic Scripture…

1 Corinthians Chapter 13.

'If I speak with the tongues of men and of angels, but have not love [for others growing out of God's love for me], then I have become only a noisy gong or a clanging cymbal [just an annoying distraction]. And if I have the gift of prophecy [and speak a new message from God to the people], and understand all mysteries, and [possess] all knowledge; and if I have all [sufficient] faith so that I can remove mountains, but do not have love [reaching out to others], I am nothing. If I give all my possessions to feed the poor, and if I surrender my body to be burned, but do not have love, it does me no good at all.

'Love endures with patience and serenity, love is kind and thoughtful, and is not jealous or envious; love does not brag and is not proud or arrogant. It is not rude; it is not self-seeking, it is not provoked [nor overly sensitive and easily angered]; it does not take into account a wrong endured. It does not rejoice at injustice, but rejoices with the truth [when right and truth prevail]. Love bears all things [regardless of what comes], believes all things [looking for the best in each one], hopes all things [remaining steadfast during difficult times], endures all things [without weakening].

'Love never fails [it never fades nor ends]. But as for prophecies, they will pass away; as for tongues, they will cease; as for the gift of special knowledge, it will pass away. For we know in part, and we prophesy in part [for our knowledge is fragmentary and incomplete]. But when that which is complete and perfect comes, that which is incomplete and partial will pass away. When I was a child, I talked like a child, I thought like a child, I reasoned like a child; when I became a man, I did away with childish things. For now [in this time of imperfection] we see in a mirror dimly [a blurred reflection, a riddle, an enigma], but then [when the time of perfection comes we will see reality] face to face. Now I know in part [just in fragments], but then I will know fully, just as I have been fully known [by God]. And now there remain: faith [abiding trust in God and His promises], hope [confident expectation of eternal salvation], love [unselfish love for others growing out of God's love for me], these three [the choicest graces]; but the greatest of these is love.'

Many of God's people fervently seek spiritual gifts from God. Indeed, we are encouraged so to do; in the very last verse before the above passage, (Chapter 12, verse 31a of 1 Corinthians), Paul says *'But earnestly desire and strive for the greater gifts.'*

However, Paul immediately qualifies his comments about seeking spiritual gifts in this chapter by telling us clearly that not one single spiritual gift is of any use to us, unless we have love; in fact we learn that *'I am nothing'* and *'it does me no good at all'* if I don't have love.

We then learn what it really means to love somebody, and throughout this passage, Paul is talking about *'agape'* love. As I explained in Volume One, Chapter Four of this book, agape love is not so much a matter of emotion as it is of doing things for the benefit of another person - that is having *'an unselfish concern for another and a willingness to seek the best for another'*. It's the kind of love Jesus was referring to when He commanded us to love our neighbour as ourselves.

And it is here in this Chapter of 1 Corinthians, that we discover what this love looks like.

A picture of unconditional love

Unconditional love endures with patience and serenity (calmness and tranquillity); it is kind and thoughtful; **not** jealous or envious. It does not brag, is **not** proud or arrogant (i.e., it does not exaggerate one's own worth or importance).

Are you getting the picture? If this is how you are to love your neighbour; how much more so are you to love and cherish your wife, in a similar manner?

The passage continues… love is **not** rude or self-seeking, **not** provoked nor overly sensitive or easily angered. It does not take into account your spouse's wrongdoing!

Is this a picture of the love you express day in, day out, towards your wife?

According to this Scripture, it should be!

It does **not** rejoice at injustice, but rejoices with truth. It bears all things irrespective of the outcome, believes all things, it looks for the best in the other person, remains steadfast and endures irrespective of the rubbish going on in your life.

How about a reality check? Does this describe the way you love your wife, as well as others…?

This Scripture also says love never fails nor ends, whereas spiritual gifts may pass away and/or cease.

It concludes by telling us that at the end of the day, just three things remain, '**faith** [abiding trust in God and His promises], **hope** [confident expectation of eternal salvation], and **love** [unselfish love for others growing out of God's love for us], these three [the choicest graces]; **but the greatest of these is love'.**

Do you, will you, love your wife like this?

In the context of this chapter on loving our wife unconditionally, it is clear to me that God is looking for men who will love their wife as His Holy Word defines right here in 1 Corinthians chapter 13.

Jesus didn't say that loving people in this way would be easy, but the truth is that this is the way that God loves you, me and our wife (and our enemies actually), and out of our love <u>for Him</u>, this is how He wants us to love our wife. As I said in Step 4, if we do not love God **deeply**, it will be very difficult to love our wife unconditionally.

I want to challenge you if you are in ministry. Whether you are a church leader, a worship leader, a prophet, a leader in men's ministry or whatever kind of church ministry, if you are focussing on that ministry to the detriment of your relationship with your wife, you *'have become only a noisy gong or a clanging cymbal'* and as Paul also says, you have become *'nothing'*.

Jesus would say this to you:

"If you are presenting your offering at the altar, and while there you remember that your brother has something [such as a grievance or legitimate complaint] against you, leave your offering there at the altar and go. First make peace with your brother, and then come and present your offering." (Matthew chapter 5 verses 23 and 24).

For the word 'brother' in the above passage, read **'wife'.**

From this passage, it seems clear to me that Jesus is saying if you have to surrender your God-given ministry, giving it back to Him (i.e., putting it on hold) for three weeks or 6 months or however long it takes to put things right concerning your relationship with your wife, then do it! God has called you to love your wife more than any other human being on the planet. He has **never** called you to **ANY** ministry that would compromise your relationship with your wife. So much so, that He would actually instruct you to lay down your Christian calling and would give you permission to not attend church whilst you go and put things right with those with whom you are having relational difficulties.

As a final comment, I would say this to you, men of God: if you put none of this teaching into practise, then do not be surprised if your wife does not respect you, or if your marriage becomes 'stale' or, in the worst case scenario, if a divorce seems imminent. I thought my first marriage was as near perfect as it could get. How wrong I was! I wish I had read a book like this and had the chance to apply what it taught me…

So, how is your marriage? Is it time for a reality check? If so, it's over to you.

If you want your marriage to improve, or if you want an already good marriage to be *even better*; if you want to be a husband your wife will be drawn to, it's time to do the hard part of putting into practise what you've read. I've given you the advice of some experts in the field, I've suggested you sign up with your wife and attend the best UK marriage improvement course there is, and I've shared with you what God expects of you, from His Holy Word.

Will you come through for your wife? Will you obey God in this key area of relationship?

If you will, the rewards will be truly wonderful for you both!

My final words on this subject…..

Marriage is like a marathon, it's not like a sprint. It takes a lot of training and practise. It's hard work, and at times involves much pain - doubt can even set in along the way. It takes a long time to perfect, and you can always learn to do it better. If you give in when the going gets tough, you will fail, but if you keep going through the pain barrier, you've every chance of winning the race. Your spouse will be forever grateful and you both will benefit greatly. Not only that, but at the end, as you pass the winning post,

God will say to you, ***"Well done my good and faithful servant"***.

Don't you long to hear those words?

Chapter Two

BECOMING A BETTER FATHER

'A million UK children are growing up without a father in their lives, says a new report on family breakdown. The Centre for Social Justice report says lone parent families are increasing by more than 20,000 a year, and will top two million by the next general election. In some areas fatherlessness has reached such high levels that they are virtual "men deserts", it adds.' [1]

As I began to think about what to write in this chapter, I felt God prompt me to do a little research into the state of the family in this twenty first century. I was well aware of the havoc and destruction the devil was inflicting upon God's Holy Institution of marriage and the family unit that is the bedrock of civilisation, (particularly in the UK) but until I checked out some on-line reports, I hadn't realised just how much family values were under attack.

The above summary of a recent Centre for Social Justice Report paints a distressing picture. More and more children are growing up in an environment where their father is not there. Sadly, increasing numbers of children do not even know who their dad is.

Assuming you are a caring person, these statistics will be deeply worrying. As you delve deeper into this subject you will see that it is not just absent fathers that cause major problems for their children's wellbeing, it is also what are called 'emotionally unavailable fathers'. This phrase refers to men who are at home some of the time but when they are, they devote almost no time at all to their children. Apparently, the effects of emotionally unavailable fathers on their children are almost identical to those where the father is physically absent.

NINE DEVASTATING EFFECTS OF THE ABSENT FATHER

One on-line report lists nine effects as follows:

1. Five times the average suicide rate.
2. Dramatically increased rates of depression and anxiety.
3. Thirty-two times the average rate of incarceration.
4. Decreased education levels and increased drop-out rates.
5. Consistently lower average income levels.
6. Lower job security.
7. Increased rates of divorce and relationship issues.
8. Substantially increased rates of substance abuse, and
9. Increases in social and mental behavioral issues. [2]

I believe these facts are an indictment of the Western World's postmodern, anti-God, anti-marriage, easy-divorce, self-centred, hedonistic, narcissistic, materialistic way of living. If you are a father, it's time to wake up! As Christians, our role is to reverse this trend! No wonder the God-ordained role of father is so important. No wonder God calls us to be excellent fathers.

The purpose of this chapter is to help you be just that!

Before I go on, I realise that sometimes it is easy to misunderstand words that are written in a book such as this one. I therefore want to make it clear that I am well aware that a whole army of single mothers are bringing up their children exceptionally well, despite there being no man in the home to help them. One of my wife Michele's sisters had to undertake this role alone, and her now grown-up, happily married son values all that his mum single-handedly did for him and loves her deeply as a result. The point I want to make here is simply that neither a mother nor a father singly possess the resources to give a child *everything* that the child needs. Parenting was meant to be a co-operative effort between a team consisting of a male husband and a female wife, each of whom bring unique personal qualities (some of which are gender-related) to the role and hard work of parenting.

WHO THEN IS OUR ROLE MODEL FATHER?

God is our model of how to be a 'perfect father'. God loves you and me unconditionally, He hates sin, but He loves the person. There is **nothing** you and I have done or can do that will stop God from loving us; God *is* love.

We have talked about sin in Volume One - Chapter Four, and discussed how it steals our joy and that it can separate us from the Father, but despite the things we do that grieve God, He loves us deeply, but urges us to repent of our sin.

We have seen how King David was the only man in the Bible described as a man after God's own heart, but he committed adultery and ordered a man to be murdered. There was a consequence to that sin and we discussed it in Volume One - Chapter Two, but God loved David, and David loved God too.

Despite his failings and imperfections, in God's eyes, David was a dearly loved son, because of **his repentant heart concerning his sin.**

Jesus, however, was the only model of a PERFECT Son.

Since none of us is perfect, how are you doing on the *'How to be a better-father'* scale?

Our sons and daughters aren't perfect either. Where might they feature on a *'How to be a better child'* scale?

Well I guess, in order to answer that question, we need a scale to refer to, and to find the scale we need to turn to God's Holy Word, the Bible.

<u>WHAT CAN WE LEARN FROM THE BIBLE?</u>

Where do we start when we look into the Bible and try to discover the 'How to be a perfect father' grading scale from which we can calculate our score?

It's hard to know, because in a sense, most of the 1,189 chapters of the Bible give us some insight into God the perfect Father, Jesus the perfect Son, and the many great men of God.

But, there is part of one chapter of Luke's Gospel that most of us know really well, and this is a good place to start. It is referred to as The Parable of the Prodigal Son. It is a picture of how a perfect father responds to a wayward child. It reads as follows...

'Then (Jesus) *said, "A certain man had two sons. The younger of them [inappropriately] said to his father, 'Father, give me the share of the property that falls to me.' So he divided the estate between them. A few days later, the younger son gathered together everything [that he had] and travelled to a distant country, and there he wasted his fortune in reckless and immoral living. Now when he had spent everything, a severe famine occurred in that country, and he began to do without and be in need. So he went and forced himself on one of the citizens of that country, who sent him into his fields to feed pigs. He would have gladly eaten the [carob] pods that the pigs were eating [but they could not satisfy his hunger], and no one was giving anything to him. But when he [finally] came to his senses, he said, 'How many of my father's hired men have more than enough food, while I am dying here of hunger! I will get up and go to my father, and I will say to him, "Father, I have sinned against heaven and in your sight. I am no longer worthy to be called your son; [just] treat me like one of your hired men."' So he got up and came to his father. But while he was still a long way off, his father saw him and was moved with compassion for him, and ran and embraced him and kissed him. And the son said to him, 'Father, I have sinned against heaven and in your sight; I am no longer worthy to be called your son.' But the*

father said to his servants, 'Quickly bring out the best robe [for the guest of honour] and put it on him; and give him a ring for his hand, and sandals for his feet. And bring the fattened calf and slaughter it, and let us [invite everyone and] feast and celebrate; for this son of mine was [as good as] dead and is alive again; he was lost and has been found.' So they began to celebrate.

"Now his older son was in the field; and when he returned and approached the house, he heard music and dancing. So he summoned one of the servants and began asking what this [celebration] meant. And he said to him, 'Your brother has come, and your father has killed the fattened calf because he has received him back safe and sound.' But the elder brother became angry and deeply resentful and was not willing to go in; and his father came out and began pleading with him. But he said to his father, 'Look! These many years I have served you, and I have never neglected or disobeyed your command. Yet you have never given me [so much as] a young goat, so that I might celebrate with my friends; but when this [other] son of yours arrived, who has devoured your estate with immoral women, you slaughtered that fattened calf for him!' The father said to him, 'Son, you are always with me, and all that is mine is yours. But it was fitting to celebrate and rejoice, for this brother of yours was [as good as] dead and has begun to live. He was lost and has been found.'" (Luke chapter 15 verses 11 to 32).

In Old Testament times, a wayward Jewish child would have been scolded and disciplined with 'the rod of correction' (Proverbs chapter 22 verse 15). It is likely that a son who went to the wild extremes of the son pictured in the above parable, would have been made a family 'outcast.' He certainly would not have been accepted back into the family again, which is why the son in the parable was hoping (perhaps in his mind hoping beyond hope) that if he was really fortunate, his father might be prepared to take him back as a servant.

FATHERS ARE TO BE MERCIFUL

Under the New Covenant of grace ushered in with the arrival of God Incarnate (Jesus Christ), punishment was to change, totally. Mercy was to replace justice. Yes, God is just, but when Jesus died on the Cross for you and me, He paid the price to <u>make it just</u> that God could forgive us for our sins, when we confess and repent of them. The penalty for sin, according to the Bible, is death. If we sin, God's justice demands yours' and my death, but Jesus paid the price to redeem us from the penalty of death. He died in our place.

In this parable, Jesus illustrates a scenario, which was completely unimaginable to the Jewish listeners of His time. There are many gracious acts described by Jesus in this parable that no father of that time would have contemplated doing towards their wayward son. Jesus was making a statement of what the New Covenant between God and humanity (you and me) looked like, and He was teaching us to begin to behave in this 'new way'.

The New Covenant of grace, in a sense, introduces us to unconditional love. It teaches us that we are to love our children regardless of what they do or don't do. Our love for them does not condone their sin – our love for our children continues, despite their failings.

What is it that would have made no sense to the audience who were listening to Jesus at that time?

I have undertaken some research into biblical Jewish culture and discovered the following: first the son should not have asked his father for his share of the estate. It was disrespectful and totally inappropriate, as this share was not due to him until after his father's death.

Second, the son would have known that his father would not have given it to him and that his father would probably have given him a 'thick ear' for daring to ask.

Third, the listeners would have been flabbergasted that a good

Jewish son would frivolously spend his inheritance on 'reckless and wild living' (sexual immorality).

Fourth, within Jewish culture, pigs were ceremonially unclean animals, and no upright Jewish man would even consider working in a field to feed them! The very thought would have disgusted him.

Fifth, after Jesus had done His best to make it clear that this son scored zero out of ten on the scale of a 'perfect son', Jesus tells us that eventually the son came to his senses, meaning he was convicted of his sin and decided to return to his father with a repentant heart. And when he did return home, he hoped to be taken back - albeit as a servant. But Jesus then tells us that *'his father saw him and was moved with compassion for him, and ran and embraced him and kissed him.'*

In that culture, there was no way any father would run after his son, especially a wayward one. Again, this was unthinkable; and the act of embracing and kissing such a son who had brought disgrace on the family would simply not have happened. The listeners must have been dumb-struck!

Finally, what we read in verses 22 to 24 must have had the audience either in fits of hysterical laughter or total disbelief, because, once again, what Jesus describes this father doing is unimaginable in that particular culture: *"'Quickly bring out the best robe [for the guest of honour] and put it on him; and give him a ring for his hand, and sandals for his feet. And bring the fattened calf and slaughter it, and let us [invite everyone and] feast and celebrate; for this son of mine was [as good as] dead and is alive again; he was lost and has been found." So they began to celebrate.'*

The act of giving his son both a robe and a ring was to demonstrate that the son had been given back his authority as the father's son.

Let me ask you a question. If you were that father and your son returned to you, hoping for mercy...

HOW WOULD YOU HAVE RESPONDED?

At those times when your son or daughter is as far out of line as it is possible to be, will you respond like the father in this story? If so, you score ten out of ten!

Or might you respond like an imperfect father? To get an insight into what that looks like, let's see how the elder son reacted when he found out what the noise was all about! I realise the elder son isn't the father, but you will immediately see why I am drawing your attention to his angry thoughts…

The first thing we see is that *'the elder brother became angry and deeply resentful and was not willing to go in.'*

At times, that's a picture of me! If you were to ask Michele, she would tell you that there are times when I respond to something I'm not happy about by having a rant and then sulking. I'm not a man who rants very often. Instead I normally deal with anger by going quiet, and retreating 'into my cave', which isn't very helpful either!

The anger shown by this son was, in reality, how any Jewish person of that time would have reacted to the situation described in Jesus' parable. This son was not obnoxious, just normal. In fact, I would go so far as to suggest he was probably a decent young man, and we can see from the text that he lived in a way that honoured his father. In the next verse of the parable we see how he responded to his father's pleading with him to receive his brother back with love. The elder son reminds his father what a great son he personally is compared to his unworthy brother. *"Look! These many years I have served you, and I have never neglected or disobeyed your command. Yet you have never given me [so much as] a young goat, so that I might celebrate with my friends; but when this [other] son of yours arrived, who has devoured your estate with immoral women, you slaughtered that fattened calf for him!"*

Did his father respond "Aha, point taken son"? Astonishingly, no! On the contrary, the father now makes the key point about how we are to behave towards our disobedient, rebellious, uncaring, sinful children. In the natural, this is **NOT** easy. Once again, we need the Perfect Father's grace <u>and</u> we need a large helping of the indwelling of the Holy Spirit in order to respond as the father in Jesus' parable responded:

"Son, you are always with me, and all that is mine is yours. But it was fitting to celebrate and rejoice, for this brother of yours was [as good as] dead and has begun to live. He was lost and has been found."

As the great hymn writer once wrote…

Amazing Grace, how sweet the sound,
That saved a wretch like me.
I once was lost but now I'm found,
Was blind, but now I see. [3]

The passage of Scripture above is a picture of how our perfect Father in Heaven loves us, and it is God's intention that you and I work as hard as we can to love our children in this perfect way too, despite their failings. So…..

FATHERS ARE TO LOVE UNCONDITIONALLY

What else can we learn from God's Word?

I find it interesting that there is no actual 'Commandment' relating to how fathers are to behave towards their children. But there is a Commandment instructing how children should behave towards their parents – i.e., *"Honour (respect, obey, care for) your father and your mother, so that your days may be prolonged in the land the LORD your God gives you.'* (Exodus chapter 20 verse 12).

Whilst it doesn't say so in God's Word, I can imagine He would expect fathers to think similarly about the way we behave towards our children, but since I am not a theologian, I can't substantiate that. We are not called to obey our children, but we are certainly called to *love and care* for them.

Close to the very beginning of Luke's Gospel, the Gospel writer tells us something about the heart of fathers towards their children. At that time, for some reason, the hearts of fathers were not right. He also tells us that John the Baptist was sent by God to rectify this problem in order that we could be made ready, as it were, to receive the Lord Jesus Christ. I wonder if this is why Luke is the Gospel writer who records Jesus' parable of the Prodigal Son? The teaching of that parable is clearly something that the men of the time found difficult to come to terms with. With regard to Luke's point concerning John the Baptist, I find his Scripture in Luke chapter 1 interesting. Here it is (verse 17)…

"It is he (John the Baptist) *who will go as a forerunner before Him (Jesus) in the spirit and power of Elijah, to <u>turn the hearts of the fathers back to the children,</u> and the disobedient to the attitude of the righteous [which is to seek and submit to the will of God]— in order to make ready a people [perfectly] prepared [spiritually and morally] for the Lord."* (Author's addition and emphasis).

Could it be that fathers have always found it difficult to deal with their children in a merciful way and with unconditional love? Could it be that only men who receive Christ as their Saviour can do this, consistently?

Whatever is the case, we have been called by Jesus to love our children as He loves us.

In Ephesians chapter 6, Paul talks about family relationships, and in connection with the treatment of our children he says this in verse 4…

'Fathers, do not provoke your children to anger [do not exasperate them to the point of resentment with demands that are trivial or unreasonable or humiliating or abusive; nor by showing favouritism or indifference to any of them], but bring them up [tenderly, with lovingkindness] in the discipline and instruction of the Lord.'

So from this we can learn some more important behavioural traits of good fathers…

BE PATIENT

Surely, what makes us provoke our children to anger is an absence of our patience towards them. I have been praying for more patience for many years and it seems God's favourite way of answering that prayer is to put more tractors in front of my car when I am in a hurry to get somewhere! To be serious, patience is something I am slow to put into effect. I am gradually learning to be more patient with each hurdle the Lord puts in my path, but I am willing to admit I still have a long way to go!

The key point about exasperating our children is that it causes them to **resent us** instead of what God commands them to do, which is to **honour us** (as their parents). In effect when we exasperate our children, this results in us leading them into the temptation and sin of resentment.

BE TENDER

We also see from this Scripture that our love towards our children is to be tender, and that we are to demonstrate to them loving-kindness. I do not believe I need to elaborate on this – it speaks for itself.

TEACH YOUR CHILDREN THE WAYS OF GOD

Paul then tells us a key duty in terms of our spiritual responsibility as a father. He says we are to bring up our children *'in the discipline and instruction of the Lord.'*

Let me ask you a question. How often do you sit down with your children and read and apply the Scriptures to them? If your children are babies in their cots, do you ever sit by their bedside and read Bible stories to them each night when you put them to bed, even though they may not understand? I cannot prove it, but I believe such an act of love subconsciously affects the child for the good. I believe something beneficial happens in the spirit-realm.

In these hectic times with so many daily practical priorities vying for our time, spending quality time with our children can be a difficult struggle.

Yet, this isn't a suggestion of Paul's. It is really a *command* - a God-ordained Word of instruction to you and me as fathers.

You see, if it were just a nice idea - an option - then this Scripture would be worded something like this:

'Fathers, if you could make the time to do this, then I would like to suggest it would be a good idea if you might bring up your children in the discipline and instruction of the Lord.'

No, let me remind you that this Scripture simply and clearly states:

'Bring them up in the discipline and instruction of the Lord.'

In fact, God's people were told to do this right back in the Old Testament at the time that God gave the Law to Moses. In Deuteronomy chapter 6 verses 5 to 7, God spoke these words to the people of Israel.

'You shall love the LORD your God with all your heart and mind and with all your soul and with all your strength [your entire being]. These words, which I am commanding you today, shall be [written] on your heart and mind. You shall <u>teach them diligently to your children [impressing God's precepts on their minds and penetrating their hearts with His truths]</u> and shall speak of them when you sit in your house and when you walk on the road and when you lie down and when you get up.' (Author's emphasis).

That was God the Father's first command – love Me more than you love anyone or anything, *and tell your children to do the same.*

In Chapter One of Volume One, I reminded you that you are called to be the spiritual head of the wife, and discussed what that does and doesn't mean. You are also the spiritual head of the home. With regard to your children, your wife is your God-given helper, as we learned from Genesis chapter 3, so it is true that our wife is to *support us* in this role, especially when we are away from home.

There is no suggestion that the verse to instruct your children is *only* to take place while the children are young and living with their parents.

And so it begs the question, if your children are grown up, do you still make time to sit down with them and discuss spiritual insights and the instruction of the Lord? Granted it is more challenging, especially if they are married, as you must then prayerfully consider how this may impact on your son's wife or your daughter's husband. Inappropriate interference of parents-in-law is to be avoided at all costs.

Hopefully, you brought up your children to understand the command to marry another believer, because if their spouse is an unbeliever, it makes your position as spiritual instructor more difficult (See 2 Corinthians chapter 6 verses 14 to 17).

DO NOT PROVOKE YOUR CHILDREN TO ANGER

In the same way that Paul wrote to fathers in the church at Ephesus, he also wrote to the Christian fathers in Colossae:

"Fathers, do not provoke or irritate or exasperate your children [with demands that are trivial or unreasonable or humiliating or abusive; nor by favouritism or indifference; treat them tenderly with lovingkindness], so they will not lose heart and become discouraged or unmotivated [with their spirits broken]." (Colossians chapter 3 verse 21).

Since Paul felt it necessary to repeat this instruction, I can only assume that the problem of exasperating children was a common failing among fathers in the early Church.

The avoidance of provoking our children to anger is of paramount importance. If we look at what subtle differences there are between these two Scriptures in the books of Ephesians and Colossians, we see here that Paul adds the concern that our wrong behaviour may cause our children to *'lose heart and become discouraged or unmotivated [with their spirits broken].'*

So it follows from both passages that the best way we can avoid this is not to make demands of them that would be considered *'trivial or unreasonable or humiliating or abusive'.*

Furthermore, we must not show *'favouritism or indifference'*, but instead Paul repeats the command to treat our children *'tenderly (and) with lovingkindness.'*

So I will repeat these two here:

TREAT YOUR CHILDREN TENDERLY AND WITH LOVINGKINDNESS.

DO NOT SHOW FAVOURITISM.

Godly Discipline and Admonition

In **Chapter 12 of the book of Hebrews**, we learn that we are to discipline our children, just as God disciplines those He loves. Verses 4 to 11 read as follows:

'You have not yet struggled to the point of shedding blood in your striving against sin; and you have forgotten the divine word of encouragement which is addressed to you as sons,

"MY SON, DO NOT MAKE LIGHT OF THE DISCIPLINE OF THE LORD, AND DO NOT LOSE HEART and GIVE UP WHEN YOU ARE CORRECTED BY HIM;

FOR THE LORD DISCIPLINES and CORRECTS THOSE WHOM HE LOVES,

AND HE PUNISHES EVERY SON WHOM HE RECEIVES and WELCOMES [TO HIS HEART]."

You must submit to [correction for the purpose of] discipline; God is dealing with you as with sons; for what son is there whom his father does not discipline? Now if you are exempt from correction and without discipline, in which all [of God's children] share, then you are illegitimate children and not sons [at all]. Moreover, we have had earthly fathers who disciplined us, and we submitted and respected them [for training us]; shall we not much more willingly submit to the Father of spirits, and live [by learning from His discipline]? For our earthly fathers disciplined us for only a short time as seemed best to them; but He disciplines us for our good, so that we may share His holiness. For the time being no discipline brings joy, but seems sad and painful; yet to those who have been trained by it, afterwards it yields the peaceful fruit of righteousness [right standing with God and a lifestyle and attitude that seeks conformity to God's will and purpose].'

As a child, if I was disobedient I received an appropriate 'smack' from my father. A 'good hiding' was a punishment inflicted upon my backside by my father's hand. At the time, the slap was painful, it usually made me cry, and I tried to make sure I was never disobedient again. I can only ever remember receiving this correction once or twice. It quickly taught me to behave. At school, instead of a teacher's hand, a plimsoll was used. It was painful, but I never cried – I didn't want to embarrass myself in front of my school friends. Sadly, I received this school punishment often because that punishment was handed out for merely having poor hand-writing! Clearly, such punishment was NOT appropriate, since it didn't lead to an improvement in my handwriting, no matter how hard I tried. All it did was exasperate me, and others like me, who were punished in that way. The key is to correct in an appropriate way.

I look back and see the Bible's wisdom when it talks about using the 'rod of correction' towards a wayward child (Proverbs chapter 22 verse 15, and 1 Corinthians chapter 4 verse 21). When I became a father, I gave one of my sons an appropriate smack for swearing at his mother when he was aged around seven. He used a vulgar word he had clearly learned in the playground at school, since such language was never heard in our home. He cried as a result of the smack I gave him on his backside, but from that day until this, (he is now forty!) I have never heard him swear at his mother.

An appropriate rod of correction can work wonders in the upbringing of our children. Yes, I could have sat my son down and tried to have a quiet word about the right and wrong of swearing. All I can say is I have lost count of the number of times I have witnessed and heard a stressed parent telling their young child to stop being naughty in public, only for the child to continue in their naughty ways. *"If I have to tell you once more....."* says mum. *"This is the last time I will tell you!"* she will repeat. In response, I want to enquire *"Really? Why isn't your child behaving then?"* And the answer, of course, is because the child knows they will always be given another 'final warning', and another, and another, because experience has taught the child that their particular parent never follows through with any appropriate punishment or correction. How I pray that God will help such parents who are unwilling, or feel unable, to apply the Godly counsel of Holy Scripture...

THE LAW-MAKERS HAVE A ROLE TO PLAY TOO

Political correctness and 'good intentioned' recent UK legislation preventing parents from disciplining their children in an appropriate biblical way, has resulted in a rise in the number of children growing up to become loud, bad-mouthed, unruly, and altogether misbehaved in public. In my experience, this was generally not the case as recently as thirty years ago. Many modern-day children and youths seem to display a complete disrespect for discipline and for those in authority. With it there has been an increase in crime, with increasing numbers of people needing psychiatric care, and our prisons are bursting at the seams. Dare I suggest, like many of my peers, that, at another extreme, it has also resulted in the 'emasculation' of many of our young boys? No wonder increasing numbers of young people struggle today with gender and identity crisis - something unheard of a generation or two ago. For millennia, in all cultures, boys have been mentored by their fathers, and had the delight of knowing they would grow up to become a man, whilst girls have grown up into women; no confusion, no question.

In the above Bible passage from the book of Hebrews, chapter 12, whilst God is referring to the fact that as the perfect loving Father He disciplines, corrects and punishes us BECAUSE He loves us, it also clearly states that we fathers are to treat our children in the same way. The passage tells us why. Because, whilst *'no discipline brings joy, but seems sad and painful; to those who have been trained by it, afterwards it yields the peaceful fruit of righteousness [right standing with God and a lifestyle and attitude that seeks conformity to God's will and purpose].'*

I put it to you that if today's parents disciplined, corrected and appropriately punished their children in traditional biblical ways, our society would be a much better place to grow up and live in. Why? Because those who are trained in this way will enjoy the *'peaceful fruit of righteousness'* and be conformed *'to God's will and purpose'*. So, in short…

DISCIPLINE, CORRECT AND APPROPRIATELY PUNISH YOUR CHILDREN OUT OF LOVE FOR THEM, BUT NOT OUT OF ANGER.

Before I end this Chapter, I do not want to be misunderstood, and neither would I want to misrepresent the Word of God. One of the greatest sadnesses in life is being regularly misunderstood, it causes me great pain.

I want to clarify that by talking about 'disciplining, correcting and punishing' I am not talking about **abusing** anybody, especially so in the case of those we deeply love. God never abuses us; in fact, He often overlooks our sins because of His amazing grace and unconditional love. However, God is particularly keen to bring to our attention any sin we undertake that will cause us harm.

But, to use an obvious example, if your three year old son is about to put his hand into an open fire or run out into the road in front of a moving vehicle, any loving father would either shout at him to get his attention, or grab him as fast as he could to prevent the inevitable pain of injury. The raising of one's voice or rapid pulling back of the child from danger may very well result in the child getting upset and crying. That is sometimes the price one must pay for training the child and correcting his behaviour.

Deliberate sin and especially repetitive sin may need to be dealt with in a way that will also require punishment of the child. The punishment must be proportionate to the wrong behaviour. I, for one, believe in giving a child an appropriate smack as punishment for wrong-doing, accompanied with the reassurance to our child that we love them, and explaining that the punishment is meant for their good; to instruct them and deter them from repeating wrong behaviour. However, I would not condone adult aggression that would result in, for example bruising, beating etc. Beware too, of verbal or mental abuse of your child as a method of correcting. Abuse comes in many forms – not just physical - and is <u>not acceptable behaviour for a man of God under any circumstances!</u>

In 1 Corinthians chapter 5 verse 11 and also chapter 6 verse 10, Paul warns us not even <u>to associate</u> with 'revilers'. These are people who verbally abuse people, including brothers in Christ who do so (see Amplified translation of these Bible verses). If we are not to associate with such people, how much more so must we be careful in the choice of words that we speak to those we love?

SUMMARY

I would now like to summarise the eight key points that we have learned from the passages of Scripture I have highlighted concerning how to be a better godly father:

FATHERS ARE TO BE MERCIFUL.

FATHERS ARE TO LOVE UNCONDITIONALLY.

BE PATIENT.

BE TENDER.

TEACH YOUR CHILDREN THE WAYS OF GOD.

DO NOT PROVOKE YOUR CHILDREN TO ANGER.

TREAT YOUR CHILDREN TENDERLY AND
WITH LOVINGKINDNESS AND DO NOT SHOW
FAVOURITISM.

DISCIPLINE, CORRECT AND PUNISH YOUR
CHILDREN OUT OF LOVE FOR THEM, IN THE SAME
WAY GOD DOES TO THOSE HE LOVES.

As I have said earlier in this book, in order to carry out the instructions of Holy Scripture we will certainly need to be Christ-like, not fleshly; and that can only be achieved by being born again and by the infilling of the Holy Spirit, enabling us to crucify the flesh. We must eagerly seek the presence of the Holy Spirit in our lives, and allow Him to be for us, what we cannot be, in and of ourselves.

On a practical note, I would add that as a husband and father, we men have some tough decisions to make. For example, what kind of profession will you choose to embark upon in order to provide for your wife and children? How many hours a week will you be prepared to work for the greater good of yourself and your family? Ironically, 'modern day man' spends far too much time at work and away from the very people he loves. The result is wives who feel unloved, and children who grow up to be wayward because of their 'absent father'.

I read an article somewhere saying that a work/life balance survey carried out in January 2017 showed that one third of fathers regularly felt burnt out and 20% were working extra hours. About one third would take a pay cut to achieve a better work/life balance. Nearly half of working fathers would like a less stressful job so they can spend more time caring for their children.

Husband, father, I am appealing to you as one whose first marriage ended in divorce; consider very carefully the question of work/life balance. Don't be like so many men I know who admit to having the problem of being a 'workaholic' but put their head in the sand or say they will address it one day. 'One day' usually never comes. Instead, for the sake of your marriage, your wife and your children, consider this quote and do the right thing now. "No man ever said on his death bed, I wish I had spent more time at the office." [4]

Finally, as I am such a great advocate of Gary Chapman's book, **The 5 Love Languages**, I would draw your attention to two of his subsequent books that will help you become a better father, **'The 5 Love Languages of Children'** and **'The 5 Love Languages of Teenagers'** [5]. It is as important to learn your children's love languages and to respond to them, as it is to learn your wife's love languages and to respond to those. Knowing your children's love languages will also help you correct and discipline them more effectively.

I will leave you with these **'Ten Commandments for Child raising'**: [6]

1. **Teach them, using God's Word. (Deuteronomy 6:4-9)**
2. **Tell them what's right and wrong. (1 Kings 1:6)**
3. **See them as gifts from God. (Psalm 127:3)**
4. **Guide them in godly ways. (Proverbs 22:6)**
5. **Discipline them. (Proverbs 29:17)**
6. **Love them unconditionally. (Luke 15:11-32)**
7. **Do not provoke them to wrath. (Ephesians 6:4)**
8. **Earn their respect by example. (1Timothy 3:4)**
9. **Provide for their physical needs. (1Timothy 5:8)**
10. **Pass your faith along to them. (2 Timothy 1:5)**

When we obey God's Word for our lives as men, and apply God's Word fully in our role as fathers to our precious children, we *will* reap the rewards of our labour.

Chapter Three

HONOURING GOD AND PEOPLE
IN THE WORKPLACE

'Beware of any work for God that causes or allows you to avoid concentrating on Him. A great number of Christian workers worship their work. The only concern of Christian workers should be their concentration on God. This will mean that all the other boundaries of life, whether they are mental, moral or spiritual limits, are completely free with the freedom God gives His child; that is, a worshiping child, not a wayward one. A worker who lacks this serious controlling emphasis of concentration on God is apt to become overly burdened by his work. He is a slave to his own limits, having no freedom of his body, mind, or spirit. Consequently, he becomes burned out and defeated. There is no freedom and no delight in life at all. His nerves, mind, and heart are so overwhelmed that God's blessing cannot rest on him.'
Oswald Chambers [1]

The purpose of this book is to detail what God has to say to men about how we can become more like Him, overcome temptation and sin, and behave better towards those we love. In this chapter I would like to discuss what God has to say to us in the area of how to behave at work.

God's Word talks less about how we are to behave at work than it does about other aspects of our life. I suspect that is because in the days of the Bible, there were no factories churning out mobile phones, wrought iron gates, uPVC windows, garage doors, aircraft, ships, cars, widgets etc., etc. Furthermore, there were no 'global' businesses, as such. Most people worked on the land or ran uncomplicated businesses, or were employed by small business owners. Yes, some goods were exported, but nothing on the scale of today.

When we look at the fraud and corruption in some aspects of business in the twenty-first century, I believe if Jesus were to visit us today, He would have a lot to say about the way some businessmen and employees behave at work.

So what can we learn to help us behave in a godly way at work, and bring honour to God and our colleagues in the workplace?

Well, before we look at what the Bible specifically says about work, let's remember what Jesus considers the greatest Commandments to be...

" 'YOU SHALL LOVE THE LORD YOUR GOD WITH ALL YOUR HEART, AND WITH ALL YOUR SOUL, AND WITH ALL YOUR MIND.' This is the first and greatest commandment. The second is like it, 'YOU SHALL LOVE YOUR NEIGHBOUR AS YOURSELF [that is, unselfishly seek the best or higher good for others].' The whole Law and the [writings of the] Prophets depend on these two commandments." (Matthew chapter 22 verses 37 to 40).

Note that last verse - in effect, Jesus is saying everything you read in God's Word should take into account the importance of these two great commandments.

It seems clear to me therefore, if we want to know how to behave at work (whether that be working at home, in an office, factory, Government department, hospital, school – wherever is your place of employment), we need to ask ourselves two simple questions:

1. Is the way I work, or behave at work, honouring God?

2. Is the way I work, or behave at work, honouring other people?

What might honouring God and people at work look like?

Well, we will want to be honest in the workplace. We will want to do what is right, and what is just. We will want to act with integrity. We will not compromise the truth. These things, we will want to do always, if we want to honour God and our co-workers.

If we take a quick look at the Ten Commandments as they might apply to 'work', what can we learn? (The Ten Commandments can be found in Exodus chapter 20).

The First Commandment

"You shall have no other gods before Me". (Verse 3).

I want to move straight on to Commandment 2, because, in the context of this chapter, it ties in with the First Commandment.

The Second Commandment

"You shall not make for yourself any idol, or any likeness (form, manifestation) of what is in heaven above or on the earth beneath or in the water under the earth [as an object to worship]. You shall not worship them nor serve them….." (Verses 4 and 5a).

Firstly, we see that we are not to 'worship' work nor make it an idol (a substitute for God).

Reality Check Number One:

If work is more important to you than God, if it takes the place of God, then you are not honouring God at work! Many people have said to me things like, "I wouldn't know what to do if I didn't work," and "I don't know how I am going to cope with my retirement when I will have nothing to do." This is often an admission that work is the most important thing in a person's life.

If you think like that, then I would remind you that the world is full of **people in need**. If you have no work, or are retired and want something to do, why not decide to help some of those people in need?

You don't have to become an overseas missionary, because you will find that many people living in your local city, town, village (wherever you live) *are in need.*

Ask God what He wants you to do, and if it involves elderly people (for example), maybe you could start a regular church service at your local Retirement Home, or simply ask the manager of the home if you could visit lonely people who live there. You will be surprised how many elderly people are suffering intolerably, not necessarily because they are in bad health or destitute - although some will be - but simply because they have nobody to talk to from one day to the next. Michele and I have seen this for ourselves as a result of having led for the last three years a monthly church service at a local retirement complex where we live.

If that's not for you, start a home group or a Bible study group; cut the churchyard grass, work with young people. You get the idea?

If you are retired, or currently have no paid work, undertaking voluntary work instead of no work will give you a new opportunity to honour God and your fellow man and woman.

The Third Commandment

"You shall not take the name of the LORD your God in vain [that is, irreverently, in false affirmations or in ways that impugn the character of God]; for the LORD will not hold guiltless nor leave unpunished the one who takes His name in vain [disregarding its reverence and its power]." (Verse 7).

One of the next things we learn from the Ten Commandments is not to take the Lord's Name in vain. Not *blaspheming* at work will demonstrate to others that you are different, and is an early signal to co-workers that you are very likely a Christian. Going beyond that and also *not swearing* (using foul or abusive language) at work will definitely make you stand out!

The Fourth Commandment

"Remember the Sabbath (seventh) day to keep it holy (set apart, dedicated to God). Six days you shall labor and do all your work, but the seventh day is a Sabbath [a day of rest dedicated] to the LORD your God; on that day you shall not do any work..." (Verses 8, 9 and 10a).

A Commandment often overlooked within Christian circles is to keep the Sabbath Day holy. For Jews, of course, the Sabbath (Jewish 'Shabbat') starts on a Friday evening at sundown and ends on Saturday evening. For Christians, it is normal to take Sunday (the Lord's Day) as our Sabbath. Having said that, I know some Christians who will uphold Saturday as their Sabbath. Whilst not wanting to be legalistic concerning what day of the week, for Christians, is and is not the Sabbath, I do want to make an important point here.

Whichever day of the week is the 'Sabbath Day' according to your conscience, then it is clear from God's Word that we shall undertake no work on that day! God said that we must _rest_ (from work) on the seventh day (of _each week_). That is a *command*, not a suggestion. Personally, I believe this command was given to us by God because the great and awesome Creator of the universe - who knitted you and me together in our mother's womb - created us with the in-built need to rest once every 7 days. We were not designed to be able to function healthily, *without* regular rest.

Failure to rest on one day a week produces physical, emotional and psychological consequences, and I have seen and continue to see many men (believers and unbelievers) suffering the consequence of 'burn-out' due to their rebellion and their sin of ignoring the Fourth Commandment.

Sadly, although most of us know that a great many, and I believe the *majority*, of illnesses and premature deaths are caused by stress related factors, few of us men accept that truth, and for reasons best known to ourselves (and the devil!), we ignore the warning signs created by God within our bodies and minds.

I plead with you dear reader to obey this Commandment so that you will not be one of those many men who suffer, due to over-work and refusing to obey God's Holy Word in this matter.

Instead, **rest from work one day every week!**

The Fifth Commandment tells us to honour our mother and father. If you work for one or both of your parents, this is an important Commandment to keep in mind! The Amplified version renders it this way:

'Honour (respect, obey, care for) your father and your mother, so that your days may be prolonged in the land the LORD your God gives you.' (Exodus chapter 20 verse 12).

Will you honour your parent(s) if you work for them? Will you respect and even take care of them at work? If you will, God's promise is to prolong your life.

If you will not, then you are bringing dishonour to God at work.

Next up, come the final five Commandments, and I think you will agree these have a great potential to cause us temptation at work.

The Sixth Commandment:

'You shall not commit murder (unjustified, deliberate homicide).' (Verse 13).

At first sight, you may not agree with me concerning the potential for this Commandment to cause us temptation at work. Murdering a co-worker or the boss? "I wouldn't do that" I hear you say.

Well maybe not, but consider these words of Jesus to the crowds when He was preaching to them (the Sermon on the Mount). *"You have heard that it was said to the men of old, 'YOU SHALL NOT MURDER,' and 'Whoever murders shall be guilty before the court.' But I say to you that everyone who continues to be angry with his brother or harbours malice against him shall be guilty before the court."* (Matthew chapter 5 verses 21 and 22).

It doesn't say here that Jesus considers 'getting angry' to be as bad as murder, but I believe that, so far as God is concerned, all sin is sin and, unlike us, He doesn't grade them on a scale of one to ten. Please know that I am NOT a theologian, so I cannot say this conclusively to you. But, remember that sin is 'missing the mark' (see Volume One Chapter Four of this book) and God's Word tells us that any kind of sin deserves our death (Romans chapter 6 verse 23), whether murder or anger!

So if you want to honour God and people at work, do not get angry with people or with circumstances. Righteous anger that is focussed on finding a solution to the issues at work, is OK, but not fleshly anger.

<u>**The Seventh Commandment**</u> straightforwardly reads like this:

"You shall not commit adultery." (Verse 14).

However, in the Amplified Bible, there is a note which says this:

'Jesus amplified this commandment in Matt 5:27, 28. Not only is adultery forbidden, but also any act of sexual impurity or unchastity, and any form of pornography or other obscenity.'

I do not have statistics to back up what I am about to say, but I believe adultery is a *major area of weakness for men* at work. Despite not having looked at any statistics that may be available, I am confident in this statement: if we have not succumbed to this ourselves, most of us men know of individuals who have fallen into temptation with a woman at work.

When you come to think about it, many of us men may find ourselves in a work environment where we actually spend more time with a woman at work than we do with our wife! Depending on our work, that woman (or women) could be a secretary, PA, teaching assistant, supervisor, nurse, laboratory technician, police officer, factory co-worker, literally anybody, it all depends on our vocation.

Whilst many godly men may be able to deal with this situation without any kind of struggle or conflict, the potential is there for the wrong kind of thoughts to surface.

What do you do if you are overcome with lustful thoughts towards a woman at work? First is to recognise the fact that such behaviour is not honouring God. Second is the recognition that this is not honouring your wife (or come to that the woman concerned), and third is the admission that this is sin. We must all confess and repent of the sin and ask God for forgiveness. If you struggle in this area at work, I strongly recommend you urgently find an accountability partner to confide in, and if the problem persists then drastic action may be necessary.

What do I mean by drastic action?

Ask for a transfer to another department or find another job! Before you laugh at my suggestion, see what Jesus says to those of us who take sin lightly:

'If your eye causes you to stumble and sin, pluck it out and throw it away from you [that is, remove yourself from the source of temptation]; it is better for you to enter life with only one eye, than to have two eyes and be thrown into the fiery hell.' (Matthew chapter 18 verse 9).

Furthermore, because I want to be vulnerable and open with my readers, I want to share with you that I am speaking to you as one who decided to take this drastic action myself when I was in my late forties, due to an infatuation with a female co-worker. I chose to follow what I believe, with the benefit of hindsight, was God's leading, and leave a senior position with a multinational company and went to work for a smaller independent company in the same field, to prevent myself from doing something that would have had an awful, life-changing impact on my life and my walk with God.

Coming back to the Seventh Commandment, *"You shall not commit adultery."*

You will recall I drew your attention to the Amplified note: *'Jesus amplified this commandment in Matthew 5:27, 28. Not only is adultery forbidden, but also any act of sexual impurity or unchastity, and any form of pornography or other obscenity.'*

I feel a need to bring this note to your attention because of the rapid global spread of the free availability and use of pornography (particularly via the internet). Many of us have the use of a company computer/tablet/smart phone etc., and the temptation for some to access sensual, obscene or pornographic images whilst working, is very high, particularly if we work at home or are away on a business trip and are alone in our hotel room late into the evening.

Many are the men in leadership in the Church, let alone those at work, who have been caught out in the very act of inappropriate use of computers, and some have fallen unceremoniously from their previous high status and position (see Volume One Chapter Four for help with this whole area of sin).

The Eighth Commandment

"You shall not steal [secretly, openly, fraudulently, or through carelessness]. (Verse 15).

Whilst at first sight this is clear and easy to understand, I still fell foul of this Commandment in my very first job in sales.

Consider for a moment your own definition of the verb 'to steal'.

Have you considered the following, or similar acts, as stealing?

1. Using the company's franking machine to pay for postage of a few personal letters?

2. Using company time or company resources to type up some personal emails or to do a little internet shopping?

3. 'Borrowing' a few company envelopes, rubber bands, paper clips for personal use (which of course you never replace).

4. Fiddling expenses. Whilst, in the past, I have overheard company executives brag about how they fiddle the Tax Authorities of thousands of pounds (by lying), I also want to bring to your attention here such seemingly trivial acts of fiddling as: claiming fuel for a journey of e.g., 45 kms which was actually only 35 kms; claiming for the cost of a crate of wine as a Christmas present for a client, which you actually enjoyed at home yourself, etc....!

The point is that before God, such acts are lying or deception, and God's Word tells us that a day will come when we will all have to give an account to God for the things we have done. We read this in Romans chapter 14 verses 10 to 12:

'But you, why do you criticize your brother? Or you again, why do you look down on your [believing] brother or regard him with contempt? For we will all stand before the judgment seat of God [who alone is judge]. For it is written [in Scripture],

"AS I LIVE, SAYS THE LORD, EVERY KNEE SHALL BOW TO ME,
AND EVERY TONGUE SHALL GIVE PRAISE TO GOD."

So then, each of us will give an account of himself to God.'

The Ninth Commandment

"You shall not testify falsely [that is, lie, withhold, or manipulate the truth] against your neighbour (any person)." (Verse 16).

I have observed people who 'have an axe to grind', deliberately drop a co-worker in the mire with a small untruth or by withholding some truth so as to discredit them. Others specifically lie or share a confidence with the boss for the sole intention of giving their boss a reason to discipline a co-worker. I find this particularly disturbing to watch and listen to, not only in the work-place but also in news reports, particularly in the world of politics.

Another dishonouring act I have witnessed over decades in industry is the number of times in meetings I have heard managers putting forward an excellent idea which was actually the idea of one of their subordinates, but the manager has shamefully taken the credit for it, in order to put himself in a positive light before his boss and his peers.

We must realise that God will one day expose incidents like this, and whatever we do dishonestly for our own personal gain, God will bring it crashing down. If He chooses not to do it in this world, then we will have to account for it before Him on Judgement Day.

The Tenth Commandment

"You shall not covet [that is, selfishly desire and attempt to acquire] your neighbour's house; you shall not covet your neighbour's wife, or his male servant, or his female servant, or his ox, or his donkey, or anything that belongs to your neighbour." (Verse 17).

Where do we start with this one? Ok, at the beginning! *'Covet'* means 'selfishly desire' or 'attempt to acquire'.

Let me remind you of the purpose of this chapter. We are looking at ways which will honour God and people in our place of work.

If we desire, for selfish purposes, something belonging to our employer or co-worker, then there is an inevitable reason to attempt to steal it. Stealing is usually pre-empted by the sin of coveting.

If we desire to be promoted in order solely to earn more money, or because we have no respect for our current line manager, then are we not coveting a promotion with wrong motives? If, on the other hand, we are seeking a promotion in the interests of making better provision for our wife and family, then this is an honourable motive. Any selfish motive will not honour God at work.

What is it that we must not covet in the work environment? Somebody's house, somebody's wife (we have dealt with this), a female servant (we have dealt with this also), an ox, a donkey? Well let's simply focus on the last phrase – we must not covet *'anything that belongs to'* our employer.

Is there anything, or any person that you desire, or would like to take, or attempt to acquire from your place of work? If so, you are dishonouring God and your employer if you carry through on those sinful thoughts and desires.

Next, I want to take a look at….

Scriptures specifically concerning 'work'.

There are a number of things that the Holy Scriptures specifically 'command' us to do concerning work.

I was intrigued to find that the word 'work' (and its derivatives) is mentioned no less than 663 times in the Amplified Bible! And the very first time we read this word in the Bible, we are reminded that the first worker of all time was of course God!

'And by the seventh day God completed His work which He had done…' (Genesis chapter 2 verse 2).

Jesus too was a worker. All the good things He did were described in the New Testament as His 'works', and in John chapter 4 verse 34, Jesus declares:

"My food is to do the will of Him who sent Me and to completely finish His work".

God and His Son were workers - what about you?

You may recall that it was because of The Fall (the sin of Adam and Eve in the Garden of Eden) that man's punishment was to have to toil on the land. Prior to The Fall, working on the land would have been a delight, after all, living in the Garden of Eden with God was perfect in every way. However, because of Adam and Eve's rebellion against God which brought about The Fall, God cursed the ground so that their work became a real burden to them. This was their punishment – the consequence of their sin.

We can conclude that the type of work undertaken on the land back in the days following God's cursing of the land, was very exhausting. Noah's father describes it in these words when his son was born *"This one shall bring us rest and comfort from our work and from the [dreadful] toil of our hands because of the ground which the Lord cursed."* (Genesis chapter 5 verse 29).

Staying with the book of Genesis, we learn that it is right for employees to be paid for their work: *"Then Laban said to Jacob, "Just because you are my relative, should you work for me for nothing? Tell me, what should your wages be?"* (Genesis chapter 29 verse 15).

Masters and Servants

As well as references to 'work', we also find the Bible referring to the role of 'masters and servants'. In Bible days, it was common for wealthy people to employ servants.

Well, shall we agree that in the New Testament, where Paul is talking about 'masters and servants' he is also talking about employers and employees? Would you agree that is fair?

If so, then we can see a number of principles that we should follow.

First, let's take a look at some principles which apply to you, if you are an employer (a 'master').

The Employer.

There are a number of New Testament Scriptures that instruct us. Here are some that I believe are important.

In the **Gospel of Matthew,** we read:

"When evening came, the owner of the vineyard said to his manager, 'Call the workers and pay them their wages, beginning with the last [to be hired] and ending with the first [to be hired].'" (Matthew chapter 20 verse 8).

Now, if you know the parable Jesus was teaching, from which the above sentence is extracted, you will know that Jesus is teaching a particular and extraordinary fact about how God treats His children and His teaching is, to say the least, most surprising. Nevertheless, I have selected this passage to show that, irrespective of the specific point Jesus was making, if you are an employer, your employees must be paid the rate you set (in the first verse of this passage you will discover that the rate was set at the time of hiring).

In his letter to Timothy, a young man that he is training up to become a church leader, Paul says:

'For the Scripture says, "You shall not muzzle the ox while it is treading out the grain [to keep it from eating]," and, "The worker is worthy of his wages [he deserves fair compensation]." ' (1 Timothy chapter 5 verse 18).

Like Jesus, Paul is instructing masters that people are worthy of being paid the wage agreed and he adds that the wage should be a fair one. That is to say, not the least you can get away with, nor necessarily higher than the market rate (although that would be a wonderful and godly approach to your workers), but a wage that is fair.

I may be labouring the point a little before summarising, but in Matthew chapter 10 Jesus sends out His disciples with an encouraging address including these words:

"Do not take gold, or silver, or [even] copper money in your money belt, or a provision bag for your journey, or even two tunics, or sandals, or a staff; for the worker <u>deserves his support</u>." (Verses 9 and 10, author's emphasis).

That word *'support'* has a financial connotation; He means the people receiving and benefiting from the work of His disciples should take care of them by providing food, drink and shelter. Clearly, Jesus instructs here that a worker deserves his pay!

So, Point Number 1 is:

Pay your employees a fair rate, the agreed rate, in a timely fashion.

Let's continue with God's instructions to employers.

In Paul's letter to the Colossians chapter 4 and verses 1 to 6 we read the following:

'Masters, [on your part] deal with your slaves justly and fairly, knowing that you also have a Master in heaven.

'Be persistent and devoted to prayer, being alert and focused in your prayer life with an attitude of thanksgiving. At the same time pray for us, too, that God will open a door [of opportunity] to us for the word, to proclaim the mystery of Christ, for which I have been imprisoned; that I may make it clear [and speak boldly and unfold the mystery] in the way I should.

'Conduct yourself with wisdom in your interactions with outsiders (non-believers), make the most of each opportunity [treating it as something precious]. Let your speech at all times be gracious and pleasant, seasoned with salt, so that you will know how to answer each one [who questions you].'

In this Scripture, I see four more instructions to employers:

Point Number 2 – **Deal with your employees justly and fairly.**

Point Number 3 – **Pray, both for your employees and your business.**

Point Number 4 – **Talk to people about your faith; witness!**

Point Number 5 – **Speak pleasantly with people, showing them grace. By doing so, God will give you wisdom in dealing with people.**

Paul also offers employers wise counsel within the Ephesian Church:

"You masters, do the same [showing goodwill] toward them, and give up threatening and abusive words, knowing that [He who is] both their true Master and yours is in heaven, and that there is no partiality with Him [regardless of one's earthly status]." (Ephesians chapter 6 verse 9).

Here Paul has clearly observed that some (Christian) employers have treated their employees in an arrogant way. He puts them in their place by reminding them that 'God is the real boss'; in God's sight, human bosses are equal in standing to their employees! God treats us all the same and I have to say that, having worked in the business world all my life, it is a rare thing indeed to find a truly humble boss or owner of a business; one who is able to treat all his workers with grace. Paul is reminding followers of Christ, and us today that there is no place for abuse or threatening words and behaviour in the workplace. So this leads us to….

Point Number 6 – treat your employees with humility and respect.

Now let's take a look at some principles which apply to you if you are an employee (a 'servant').

The Employee

In Proverbs chapter 25 and verse 13, it says *'Like the cold of snow [brought from the mountains] in the time of harvest, so is a faithful messenger to those who send him; For he refreshes the life of his masters.'*

Point Number 1 – Be *faithful* to your employer.

In the previous section *'The Employer'* I quoted from Ephesians chapter 6. That same chapter has something to say to employees…

'Slaves, be obedient to those who are your earthly masters, with respect for authority, and with a sincere heart [seeking

to please them], as [service] to Christ — not in the way of eye-service [working only when someone is watching you and only] to please men, but as slaves of Christ, doing the will of God from your heart; rendering service with goodwill, as to the Lord, and not [only] to men, knowing that whatever good thing each one does, he will receive this back from the Lord, whether [he is] slave or free.' (Ephesians chapter 6 verses 5 to 8).

There are many interesting points in that Scripture that I wish to highlight. I'll list below the key points that I see in this passage…

Point Number 2 – <u>Be obedient to your employer.</u>

Point Number 3 – <u>Treat them with respect and seek to please them.</u>

Point Number 4 – <u>Please them when they are watching you and when they are *NOT* watching.</u>

Point Number 5 – <u>Whatever your work involves, do it unto God.</u>

Point Number 6 – <u>God rewards obedient, faithful, diligent employees.</u>

Point number 2 above is clearly an important one as Paul repeats this instruction to the Colossian Church. ***"Servants, in everything obey those who are your masters on earth, not only with external service, as those who merely please people, but with sincerity of heart because of your fear of the Lord."*** (Colossians chapter 3 verse 22).

Point number 3 above is also something Paul repeats, this time to his young student Timothy. At the beginning of 1 Timothy chapter 6, he says that we must honour and respect (unbelieving) masters, and in the case of believing masters, we are to show them even greater honour and respect!

Whilst on the subject of showing bosses respect, Peter goes even further by saying that we are to do so, ***"not only to those who are*** *good and kind, but also to those <u>who are unreasonable</u>."* 1 Peter chapter 2 verse 18 (author's emphasis).

I find Paul's two letters to Timothy very helpful to men generally, and also to all people in leadership. There is a well-known verse in his second letter that I want to highlight in the context of work.

'Be ready in season and out of season' (2 Timothy chapter 4 verse 2 NKJV).

In this verse, Paul is telling his 'pupil' Timothy that he is to preach – in season and out of season. Part of Timothy's calling was preaching. That was his work, if you like. What we learn here is that when God calls us to work, we are to do it whether we feel like it or not.

If you are called to full time Christian ministry, be ready to do that work to the glory of God when you wake up on a high, and when you wake up on a low and your flesh says – **"I feel rubbish today, I think I'll stay in bed".** The Word of God says 'do it anyway' – 'Go the extra mile' (Matthew chapter 5 verse 41).

Now let us consider what we might do, or be asked to do at work.

Must we go to work?

Well, I suppose we could spend a lot of time debating that question, could we not?

For example, what if you have inherited a fortune from a rich family member? It could be tempting to invest that money wisely and live off the interest. On the other hand, maybe you could give it all away!

What if you have disabilities? Perhaps you should live off the incapacity payments provided by the Government, although I would not imagine such payments to be adequate. Maybe you could consider some work that is conducive with your reduced ability?

When I set out to write a series of training modules (which

resulted in the publishing of this book), I decided that, as with my preaching style, as far as possible, I did not want to give opinions. My opinion is no more valid than another's. What I felt God had asked me to do was to 'disciple men' and by that I believe He meant that I was to teach from <u>His Word.</u>

My objective, therefore is to make clear to readers what the Bible says about the topics I have covered in this book. And one clear teaching from the New Testament in answer to the question "Must I go to work?" is this:

"For even when we were with you, we gave you this rule: "The one who is unwilling to work shall not eat." (2 Thessalonians chapter 3 verse 10, NIV).

Although Paul does not mention it, he surely did not mean that it applies to those who are infirm or have a disability. However, if you are able-bodied, this 'rule' is for you. Go to work! If you have difficulty finding work, personally I would encourage you to consider self-employment. It doesn't work for everyone but I found it very rewarding during a season of my own life.

Next, must we always do what our employer tells us to do?

In the context of masters and servants, I showed earlier from Scripture that we are to obey the orders of our employers.

But what if we are asked to do something that is clearly wrong in the eyes of God?

If part of your job description involves doing something against God's will, then my advice would be to explain to your employer why you do not feel you could undertake that part of your role. If the employer values you as an employee, they may decide to ask another employee to take on the part of the work that is contrary to your conscience or your faith. In the event that they insist you do something that your conscience is uneasy about then, personally I would refuse to undertake the work and face the consequences.

However, I fully understand that many believers may not be in a place - either in their relationship with God or with their spouse (especially if the spouse is an unbeliever) - where they would be willing to lose their job. In such a situation, pray to God and ask Him for His guidance. Ask Him to find a new more suitable position for you quickly while you continue with the work in the meantime. Seek every opportunity to find more appropriate employment.

I want to encourage you by telling you honestly and sincerely that God has been faithful to me in the area of financial provision, ever since I took the decision to tithe my income, even through times of hardship, and I thank Him regularly for His faithfulness towards me. I share this with you to encourage you to respond to God's promise to be faithful to you if you will do this (See Malachi chapter 3 verses 8b to 10 and my reference to this Scripture in Volume One of this book, Chapter Two).

There have been a number of recent cases where Christian employees in the UK have lost their jobs as a result of changes in legislation. One such example has been brought about by the UK Government's introduction of 'same-sex marriage,' in blatant rebellion to God's Holy Word. Marriage registrars, who are Christians, who refuse to conduct 'same-sex marriage' services have had to resign or be sacked, even though their employers could, in my opinion, be considerate and respect the employee's faith and simply ask him or her to officiate over marriages that God approves of, i.e. marriages between a man and a woman. Some have resigned and had to seek work elsewhere. There will be great woe for those who persecute followers of Christ. Those in positions of authority and leadership will not escape this divine appointment of God's judgement.

If a single task that you have been asked to do is clearly against God's will then once again, explain to your employer why you cannot do it. The employer may ask a co-worker to take on the assignment.

Some time ago, I was asked by an employer to do something that I considered unethical. It involved a business deal. I explained to my boss (who was not a Christian) why I was unable to do what he asked, and he respected my reasons. He knew I was a Christian as I often talked to him about aspects of my faith. I believe God had given me favour with this man. He and I talked about a way I could do what he was asking me to do without it conflicting with my business ethics. Subsequently, the business deal was brokered in a way that I felt at peace within my spirit.

Are there any biblical examples we can follow?

There is one that comes to mind, from the Old Testament. The context is master and servant but as I have already said, this can also be applied to the employer/employee relationship.

In the time of the birth of Moses, the greatly feared Pharaoh (King of Egypt) told the midwives that when delivering Hebrew boys, they were to kill every one of them. The midwives refused. As you read the account of this in Exodus chapter 1 and verses 17 to 21, take particular note of how God rewarded the midwives despite them having to lie to Pharaoh about the reason they didn't kill the Hebrew boys:

'But the midwives feared God [with profound reverence] and did not do as the king of Egypt commanded, but they let the boy babies live. So the king of Egypt called for the midwives and said to them, "Why have you done this thing, and allowed the boy babies to live?" The midwives answered Pharaoh, "Because the Hebrew women are not like the Egyptian women; they are vigorous and give birth quickly and their babies are born before the midwife can get to them." So God was good to the midwives, and the people [of Israel] multiplied and became very strong. And because the midwives feared God [with profound reverence], He established families and households for them.'

What if we are asked to work on the Sabbath Day?

If we lived in Old Testament times, the question would never arise. It was unheard of to work on the Sabbath. The punishment for working on the Sabbath as declared by God was physical death (Numbers chapter 15 verses 32 to 36).

Today, we live under the New Covenant of grace and, as a result, something has changed. We no longer live according to any of the civil or ritual laws of the Old Testament, although we still live under the moral law of the Old Testament. The Billy Graham web site puts it like this:

'The moral laws—those against lying, stealing, immorality, etc.—show us how far we fall short of God's will and how badly we need salvation as a free gift, earned by Jesus' death on the cross (Galatians 3:24).

Once we accept God's free gift of eternal life through repentance from sin and faith in Jesus, the moral law becomes a guide for how we live out our new life in Christ by the power of the Holy Spirit (Galatians 5:16-26). The civil laws of Israel have passed away, since the church is not a nation.

The ritual laws of sacrifice, priesthood, and temple have been fulfilled in Jesus, and are no longer applicable to the church (see the book of Hebrews). However, the basic moral law of the Old Testament is clearly reflected in the New Testament guidelines for the Christian life (e.g. Colossians, chapter 3) and is summarized by Jesus in Matthew 22:37-40.' [2]

Although we live under God's Gospel of grace, the Ten Commandments still underpin the Christian's faith. Jesus did NOT come to end the law. Jesus said He came to FULFIL the law, not make it obsolete! When asked what were the greatest Commandments, He didn't say – **"None; they don't apply any more"**, He answered the question and told them which were the greatest (See Matthew chapter 22 verses 36 to 40).

As I mentioned earlier in this Chapter, in the Book of Genesis, we see that on the seventh day God rested from all His work (Genesis chapter 2 verse 2). I believe that the reason He commands us to rest is that He alone knows what is best for us, since He created us.

Every person knows what effect working constantly, and never resting, has on their body. So it is no wonder that resting one day a week is included in God's Ten Commandments. Sin (living according to the deeds of our flesh – that is our sinful nature) results in death (Romans chapter 6 verse 23, and Romans chapter 8 verse 13). The key question is what day of the week is the Sabbath Day? As I mentioned earlier, in Jesus' time (and for the Jews today), that day was Saturday. For Christians that day is Sunday. Does it matter? According to some it *does matter*. As I said earlier, for me it is a matter of conscience, but I may not be right. However, I found a worthwhile paper, a compelling biblical justification that God will find us accountable if we do not rest on His Sabbath Day (Saturday)[3], which I would encourage you to read. You will find the link in the Notes Section relating to this chapter of the book.

Why have I given this further insight into the Fourth Commandment? I have done so in order to reinforce the biblical command that we should **NOT** work on the Sabbath Day.

Is it right to work in a controversial industry?

What am I referring to as 'controversial' industries?

Well the list could be endless, but here are just a few examples: tobacco, nuclear power, gambling, alcoholic beverages, drugs (legal or illegal), nightclubs.

I don't believe there is a straightforward answer to the question I have posed, particularly as you would be hard-pressed to find a biblical answer, other than those Scriptures that tell us to refrain from certain lifestyles and types of behaviour.

Personally, I believe this is a matter of conscience for each of us before God. I believe if you become a Christian while working in a questionable industry or job, or if you are considering applying for such a position, you need first to prayerfully consult the Lord.

Secondly, we need to discover what His Word tells us.

If you hear from God by His Spirit, or if you discover there is nothing in His Word to condemn the work of the company, then also take into account the nature of the role you are considering within the Organisation.

In other words, what is it you are being asked to do?

Examples:

1. We all know tobacco is harmful to health. Thirty-five years ago I was employed by a global adhesives manufacturing company, and a technical colleague of mine was an overt Christian. He was a young God-fearing man. He worked as a development chemist in our company and worked with products for use in the Tobacco industry. When we talked about our different jobs (I was a sales manager in the industrial woodworking sector) he told me he knew of the potential clash of interest between the market sector in which he was engaged and his faith. However, he felt that his job gave him the opportunity to develop safer, more responsible adhesives for use in that sector.

    On the other hand, as part of my product portfolio, I had to sell solvent-based adhesives. I was professionally trained by the employer and was well aware of the potential risks to health for users of such products. In this role, I took the opportunity to make a point of stressing to customers and users the importance of using the correct solvent extraction systems and personal protective equipment. I also worked hard to persuade the managers of the companies to convert to alternative safer adhesive types.

    Did my colleague and I make the right choices? Only God knows, but, in both cases, our consciences were clear before Him.

2. Supposing you have the opportunity to work in a nuclear power plant but believe nuclear power is dangerous or against the will of God. Supposing the position on offer is that of Health & Safety Manager. You might consider that although the industry plays havoc with your conscience, the position gives you a God-given opportunity to ensure proper controls are in place to protect workers and the public.

(Footnote, I personally believe nuclear power has the potential to bring much good to the world's population. As with so many of God's resources, man has the choice to use them for good or for evil, e.g., uranium can be used to produce electricity or nuclear weapons; stainless steel is used to make swords as well as spoons).

Some people do not believe a Christian should become a politician. Many people believe that politicians, in order to be 'successful', have to be, at one extreme corrupt or at the other extreme at least, shall we say, able to be *economical with the truth*. However I, and many others, believe that the best hope we have for creating a godly society is if more Christians pursue a career in politics and become vocal members of either the Government or the main Opposition Party. What better way to bring change to our secular society? My favourite example of a most amazing Christian politician is that of the tenacious, British Member of Parliament, William Wilberforce who, despite being ridiculed for twenty years by colleagues in the House of Commons, saw his hard work to abolish slavery become law in 1833, just 3 days before he died.

What if we are struggling to succeed at work?

I believe it is God's will for you to succeed at work. After all, Jesus came that you may *'have and enjoy life, and have it in abundance [to the full, till it overflows].'* (John chapter 10 verse 10).

To my way of thinking, that Scripture implies that Jesus would want to bless you in your place of work in order that through working diligently and being successful, you might abound in the workplace and reap the rewards of your success physically, psychologically and financially. In the Bible, you are called to tithe 10% of your income to the local church (literally to bring ten per cent into the storehouse) and therefore the more you earn at work, the more money can be given back to God for His work to abound in the local church and local community.

If you are in a bad place psychologically at work; if you are surrounded by ungodly co-workers; if you have a bad boss, or you are simply not fulfilled in the workplace then talk to God about it. Pray. Ask Him whether He has put you there for a reason or whether you should apply for a different job elsewhere. Once you have prayed, listen to the still small voice of Jesus (remember He is God!). You may find that when you ask Him about your dilemma He is testing your attitude or your faith. Or you may find soon after you have prayed that a new employment opportunity opens up for you.

There is a wonderful story in the Gospel of Luke, chapter 5. Jesus, at the outset of His ministry, is looking to see whom He should chose to become His disciples. Which young men would have faith in Him? Who would obey Him? Whom could He rely on, when the going gets tough?

Will you obey Him at work - when He suggests you do something that makes no 'common sense'?

Well, take a look at the story.

One day, a group of hard-working young men were at work. They had an unproductive, disappointing shift. It was a night shift and they were fishermen. They caught nothing.

You probably know the story well. In the morning, Jesus appeared on the scene. The men would have known that He was not a fisherman, as He was preaching, and so they probably thought He was a prophet. When He had finished talking to the crowds, Jesus told these experienced fishermen to *'go out into deep water and lower the nets for a catch.'*

One of the young men was called Simon (he would later become Simon Peter, one of Jesus' disciples). This was Simon's reply, *"Master, we worked hard all night [to the point of exhaustion] and caught nothing [in our nets], but at Your word I will [do as you say and] lower the nets [again]."* (See Luke chapter 5 verses 1 to 11).

How would you have replied?

Let's say you are struggling to be successful at work. You are having a bad time. "Maybe it's time to find another job", you are probably thinking. But Jesus says, "Go and do again, what you just did because this time you will be successful".

You have a choice to make. Obey or disobey. Surely, Simon was thinking, "In the natural I know from experience this is a completely illogical thing to do. There just aren't any fish in the mood for biting right now!"

BUT, Simon obeyed.

What was the result of his obedience? His work and his entire future was transformed...

'When they had done this, they caught a great number of fish, and their nets were [at the point of] breaking; so they signalled to their partners in the other boat to come and help them. And they came and filled both of the boats [with fish], so that they began to sink. But when Simon Peter saw this, he fell down at Jesus' knees, saying, "Go away from me, for I am a sinful man, O Lord!" For he and all his companions were completely astounded at the catch of fish which they had taken; and so were James and John, sons of Zebedee, who were partners with Simon [Peter]. Jesus said to Simon, "Have no fear; from now on you will be catching men!" After they had brought their boats to land, they left everything and followed Him [becoming His disciples, believing and trusting in Him and following His example].'

Please don't misunderstand me, I *am* not saying if you are struggling to be successful at work, stick at it. What I am saying is, if you are struggling, talk to God. Pray about it; seek His Word - and obey what He leads you to do.

So, I close this chapter by suggesting to you that if you need or want a supernatural solution to your problems at work, seek the Lord. He knows just the answer for you. As the hymn writer exhorts us:

> *'Trust and obey, for there's no other way*
> *To be happy in Jesus but to trust and obey.'* [4]

<u>Postscript</u>.

In the context of work and providing for our family, I have to say I find some of the laws in the UK very difficult to classify as fair or just. For example, in Criminal Law, when somebody murders a person in cold blood, whilst they may be sent to prison for a very long time, the victim's next of kin receive no monetary compensation from the murderer, nor from the State, for the murder of their loved one.

This seems particularly unfair in the case of a woman whose husband (who let's say is the family breadwinner) has been killed. Suddenly due to no fault of the husband or the family, the woman is left possibly penniless and left to fend for herself. There is no financial restitution for such atrocities under Criminal Law (in the UK). How can such an example be right?

Compare such a situation with an Old Testament law in the book of Exodus:

> *"If men quarrel and one strikes another with a stone or with his fist, and he does not die but is confined to bed, if he gets up and walks around leaning on his cane, then the one who struck him shall be left [physically] unpunished; <u>he must only pay for his loss of time [at work], and the costs [of treatment and recuperation]</u>*

<u>*until he is thoroughly healed.*</u>" (Exodus chapter 21, verses 18 and 19, author's emphasis).

I believe this is an important principle concerning how we should treat people whose sinful or evil actions result in an innocent person being left unable to work. How much more so if the innocent person is killed! Can you imagine how much better some people might behave if we reintroduced some laws that employ a bit more of our ancestors' ways?

Whilst I appreciate that prison acts as a strong deterrent for some, my point is that the victim does not receive any *personal redress* from the perpetrator, something the above Scripture would remedy if made law today.

Chapter Four

LOVING OUR PARENTS IN DIFFICULT TIMES

"Honour (respect, obey, care for) your father and your mother, so that your days may be prolonged in the land the LORD your God gives you." (Exodus chapter 20 and verse 12).

Let me ask you a question. Do you love you father?

Do you love your mother?

Is it easy for you to love either or both of your parents?

These may seem like odd questions to many readers but I fully understand that you may have good reasons for having issues in this area of your life.

Maybe you were born the son of a rape victim.

Or perhaps your mother tried to abort you before you were born.

It could be that your father or mother never loved you. They perhaps left the family home when you were very young, and so you felt abandoned.

There are many reasons why people struggle to love, let alone honour, their parents.

Before we look at what the Bible has to say about loving our parents in good times and bad, I want to reassure you that whatever mental or physical scars might have been inflicted upon you - either by your parents as they brought you up, or by virtue of having absent parent(s) – your very existence is no accident. You were meant to be born. You were meant to be, here upon the earth.

If you struggle with who you are, and if you struggle with your parents, let me tell you an important truth. The Bible says God knew you before you were born AND He knit you together in your mother's womb – regardless of the circumstances that surrounded the moment of your conception (See Jeremiah chapter 1 verse 5).

The thing is, your body is simply a vessel in which the real *'you'* lives. You are spirit, you have a soul, and you live in a body.

If you have a bad opinion of yourself, consider this: a prostitute called Rahab was in the lineage of Jesus (see Matthew chapter 1 verse 5). Clearly, Rahab found favour with God. It seems that God rewarded her in the most unexpected way for protecting the Israelite spies who undertook a reconnaissance of Jericho prior to its invasion and capture (see Joshua chapter 2).

Hundreds of years later, we learn of God's special love for a different prostitute. She enters the scene in Luke chapter 7 (see verses 36 to 50), where it is recorded that, weeping with a repentant heart, she kissed Jesus' feet, and poured a precious ointment on them. A Pharisee cursed her, but Jesus showed her an agape love and told her that her sins were forgiven.

In John chapter 8 we read a wonderfully gracious account involving an adulteress who was thrown at Jesus' feet by a bunch of hypocritical and self-righteous men. Jesus showed her agape love too, and with the wisdom of His Words to her accusers (all men), He saved her from being stoned to death - *"He who is without [any] sin among you, let him be the first to throw a stone at her."* (Verse 7).

King David, a married man, had sex with Bathsheba, the wife of one of his loyal soldiers (i.e., committed fornication and adultery). She later bore him a son - Solomon - whom God loved so much He gave him more wisdom than any human being who has ever lived in the history of the world. Solomon, not David, was subsequently chosen by God to build His Holy Temple. God loved David, but he was held to account and had to bear the consequences of his sin, which resulted in the death of David and Bathsheba's first son and included the forfeiting of being the one God chose to build His Temple.

The point I'm wanting to get across is this: God **loves you**, whatever the background of your birth, or your subsequent life, whatever you have done, or may do. Even if our upbringing may have been difficult, God commands each of us to love our parents. And, if we will do that, He promises a blessing for us. In Exodus chapter 20 and verse 12, God gave us this Commandment:

"Honour (respect, obey, care for) your father and your mother, so that your days may be prolonged in the land the LORD your God gives you."

God promises that if you will <u>obey Him</u> by honouring, respecting, obeying and caring for your parents, your days will be prolonged in the land where you live (the land the Lord your God has given you).

Tragically, my observation (and I am not alone in this) is that – in recent times in the Western World - of all the Commandments that seem to be overlooked most by Christians, two of them stand out: the Fourth Commandment (concerning honouring the Sabbath) and the **Fifth Commandment concerning honouring our parents.** For millennia, in almost all cultures, respect for parents has always been one of the most important social norms.

Many Christians today are noticing an unparalleled attack upon God's Holy Word in these End Times. Indeed, Paul tells us there will be a great falling away before Jesus returns in triumph (See 2 Thessalonians chapter 2).

Furthermore in Matthew chapter 24 verses 10 to 12 Jesus tells us that before His imminent return, *"many will turn away from the faith and will betray and hate each other"* and *"because of the increase of wickedness, the love of most will grow cold."* (NIV).

Whether or not Jesus' return is imminent, it seems to me that there has been a conscious or unconscious reduction in respect for our parents in recent decades.

I have made this point because I believe God is particularly concerned about this gradual erosion in the attention His children are demonstrating towards His Holy Word. If we fail in our attention and obedience to His Word, then consequences will ensue.

Having made my point, I will now turn to applying the Commandment of **honouring our parents.**

If you are fortunate enough to have had wonderful parents, then loving them, respecting them, obeying and caring for them is likely to be much easier than if your relationship with your parents has been difficult. I realise that goes without saying, **but** God's Word doesn't include an 'exemption clause' telling us that *'where there are issues with your parents you don't have to bother with honouring, respecting, or caring for them'!*

Instead, what we find in Scripture are passages advising us what to do when there are relational conflicts so that we can resolve them; and I discuss those in the next Chapter.

So, I will proceed on the basis that you have the desire and *accept the need* to obey God's Fifth Commandment to honour your father and mother. If there are issues that need to be dealt with to make your obedience more possible, I will assume you will at least attempt to resolve those issues by applying some of the principles outlined in the next Chapter (Resolving Conflict).

How do we honour our parents?

What does it mean then, to honour our parents, and how might that look in the twenty-first century?

Before we look at this, I just want to clarify that the Commandment to honour our parents applies irrespective of our parents' age, or ours. It is **not** solely a Commandment for young children. Why do I say that? Because the Scripture I have cited clarifies that one aspect of the translation of the word 'honour' includes *'to care for'*.

Whilst many young children do care for parents who have health issues or disabilities, it is clear to me that the intention behind this phrase is not that the duty of caring is restricted to young children only. It is clear that our duty of caring for our parents extends into their old age, which can mean we, as their children, may be in our 50's 60's or even 70's if our parents live into their 90's!

If I have not convinced you, please allow me one more opportunity to do so. In the book of James, the disciple tells us that *'Religion that God our Father accepts as pure and faultless is this: to look after orphans and widows in their distress...'* (James chapter 1 verse 27).

If God expects followers of Christ to look after widows (in general) in their distress, how much more does He expect us to look after our widowed parent in their old age?

Now I've clarified the point that honouring our parents does not end when we 'fly the nest', let's look at *how* we can continue to honour our mother and father, once we have left them and set up our own home.

The Amplified translation of the Bible gives us some clues by qualifying **'honour'** with the words: **'respect, obey, care for'.**

The word *respect* means *'an act of giving particular attention, i.e., consideration'* and also *'having a high and special regard for, as in esteem'.* [1]

It follows therefore that God wants us to give particular attention to what our parents may say to us, particularly if our parents are followers of Christ and if their counsel is always according to the

Word of God, as written in the Holy Bible, as opposed to so-called 'spiritual' teaching from sources that are contrary to God's Word. He also commands us to show them special consideration.

If our parents love us, then the godly advice they give us will come from a heart of love. They will want what is best for us. They are a generation older than we are, and with age comes wisdom. Well usually! Therefore their wise words, if acted upon - even if at the time we feel sceptical about those words - may well reap great benefits for us. This requires humility on our part, of course! As adult children, we often think that we know best and may think we know better than our parents, even if they are Christians. Such thinking is rooted in pride.

I have found myself on occasion trying to give godly advice to one of my grown-up unbelieving sons, and often is the time I thought to myself afterwards sarcastically, 'OK, son, you know best!' God requires us to speak out in faith and truth to whomever may seek our advice, but I believe we are to be like Jesus and when people walk away without accepting our godly advice or instructions, we have to leave them to face the consequences. We are to give our disappointment to God; this will enable us to cope with the fact that our loved one has rejected godly counsel. (See Mark chapter 10, verses 17 to 23).

What if it is clear that our parents are not giving us sound advice?

Then you have the choice to show them love, respect, courtesy and gratitude for offering their advice but not take it, or discuss with your parents why you disagree with them. It is absolutely possible to respect and esteem our parents without necessarily agreeing with them (in love). However, resenting our parents for offering advice or godly counsel and treating them badly afterwards is sinful and we will be accountable to God on the Day of Judgement for such action, unless we confess and repent of it.

We are called to express our love and respect towards them even though we may not agree with what they say. But if our parents' advice or counsel is biblical and we have an issue with it, then we (as their children) need to examine ourselves as to why we are resisting or rejecting our parents' godly counsel, whatever age we are.

In what ways should we *show consideration* to our parents?

Another change that has occurred in recent years is that it has become much easier to relocate, live and work hundreds of miles from our parents and wider family, and even to emigrate to other parts of the world. A decision to do so, clearly has a huge effect on our ability to show consideration to our parents in their times of need. Whilst a phone call or 'video call' is a great blessing and comfort to them, it is no substitute for being with them in person; only then can we drive a parent to hospital when the need arises, or sit at their side and listen or advise when they need reassurance.

But if we do live near to them, here are a number of ways we can show consideration to our parents. I include here some ways we can care for our parents as well.

In times of need.

If you have been raised by loving parents, then it may help to remember that for perhaps more than twenty years of their lives, your parents have housed you, fed you, and provided in many different ways for your well-being while you grew up and in many cases, even long after you have left home to go to University or set up your own home. In short, they have invested a great deal of their time, love and finances into you! Perhaps we should all consider that when our parents reach older age and may become frail or ill, it is time to repay them for all they have done for us and invested in us over the years.

I have met many elderly folk who have been left alone to fend for themselves, or been put into some kind of Retirement Home while their children get on with their lives. This statement isn't intended to create false guilt amongst readers; there are many reasons why older folk are in Retirement or Care Homes and often it is their own personal decision, or in their best interests. There are great benefits to be enjoyed too by older people who live in well-maintained and well-managed homes. However, many of the people I have met feel very lonely, particularly if family members and especially their children, do not make a point of visiting them regularly.

<u>Especially at times of illness or bereavement.</u>

My father died in hospital at the age of ninety. Three years earlier, we moved him to be near where we live, so that we could keep an eye on him. He wanted to live in the safety of a Retirement Complex, but I have to confess that I did not visit him as often as I should have, and certainly not as often as he would have liked. There were mitigating circumstances but that is not the point. During periods of illness was a time when he particularly wanted more attention from me, his son. He appreciated nurses and doctors and care-workers visiting, but it was most of all his loved ones he wanted to visit and chat to him.

Over the years, Michele and I have visited many elderly folk during times of bereavement. They all tell us how important it is to them that their next of kin make time to help them through the loss of their spouse. Sadly, soon after the funeral, it is so often the case that children quickly have to get back into their daily routines, and their parent who is now widowed can find himself or herself left to cope without their spouse being there anymore.

As hard as it is for so many of us, 'respect' includes accommodating the needs of our parent(s) when it would be easier to put our own needs first.

<u>To show our gratitude</u>

The words, 'thank you' are two very precious words. Throughout their lives, most parents show remarkable acts of love and service to their children. Let us remember to show our gratitude to our parents for all that they have done in the past, as well as what they continue to do for us as their adult children. If your mother loves flowers, why not take some with you next time you visit? If your father likes a chat down the pub, then why not offer to take him there, next time you are passing? My father loved going out for meals, and so we took him out regularly so that he could enjoy a change of scenery from staring at the four walls of his home.

Acts of service

If your parents are in middle age or older, do you check to see if they need any help with the chores around the home? It's normal for older folk to want to be independent and claim they are perfectly capable of coping, but it's good to keep an eye out for tell-tale signs that they need help, e.g., perhaps the trees in the garden need a younger man to climb up and lop off some overhanging branches? Or maybe you notice that the floors or work surfaces of their home have an accumulation of dirt or spillages which their failing eyesight has overlooked.

If you are in full time employment and spare time is at a premium for you, it might be that you need to persuade an elderly parent that some paid 'home help' is a good investment.

Obedience

The Amplified Bible includes the word 'obey' in its explanation of what is meant by *honouring* our parents.

Paul also makes clear that we are to obey our parents in his letter to the Colossians (chapter 3 verse 20) which reads:

"Children, obey your parents [as God's representatives] in all things, for this [attitude of respect and obedience] is well-pleasing to the Lord [and will bring you God's promised blessings]."

When we are young, we know that it is right to obey our parents, and when we misbehave, then godly parents might use 'the rod of correction' to encourage or punish us and it usually has the desired effect! However, as we grow up and become adults, a conflict can arise where we may think we know better than our parents. How then do we deal with the Commandment 'honour (obey) your parents'?

I believe if we look at Ephesians chapter 5 and the first few verses of Ephesians chapter 6, we see that *obeying our parents* applies to when we live in our parents' household. Let me explain….

Paul is discussing the roles of husbands and wives and how we are called to love, respect and care for each other deeply. The context is the family unit in the home. Paul describes the husband as the *'head of the wife'* in the same way as Christ is the head of the Church. Paul goes on to say in chapter 6 verses 1 to 4 (NIV): *"Children, obey your parents in the Lord, for this is right. "Honour your father and mother"— which is the first commandment with a promise — "so that it may go well with you and that you may enjoy long life on the earth. Fathers, do not exasperate your children; instead, bring them up in the training and instruction of the Lord."*

So here we see that within the home, children are to obey their parents, but note the 'pre-requisite' – that fathers should not exasperate their children. If the father (head of the household) brings up his children in the training and instruction of the Lord, the assumption is that godly children will find it both right and respectful to obey their parents.

Furthermore, in Ephesians chapter 5 verse 31, Paul repeats the Genesis chapter 2 Scripture concerning children leaving home to get married: *"For this reason a man shall leave his father and his mother and shall be joined [and be faithfully devoted] to his wife, and the two shall become one flesh."*

If, when they get married, the children leave their parents' home, it seems clear to me that at that point, the children are set free from the requirement to obey their parents, since the command to obey parents (according to Paul) was within the context of the family home. What's more, the Scripture here tells us that the man shall be *faithfully* devoted to his wife. For me, this precludes being faithfully devoted to his parents.

In summary, I believe it is clear that the act of *obeying our parents* is restricted to whilst we live in their home, whilst the act of *respecting* and *caring* for our parents is a lifelong command. Having said that, we are still free to obey certain requests made by our parents when we have <u>left their home</u>, as an act of love and respect for them!

There are some other Scriptures we can look at to help us with this subject of honouring our parents.

In Genesis chapter 26 we find that, as adult children, we have a responsibility not just to honour our parents but also to ensure we are not a source of worry or grief to them. Here we find that Esau married two women who were *'a source of grief to [Esau's parents] Isaac and Rebekah.'* (Verse 35).

Clearly, if Esau's wives were a source of grief to Esau's parents, then they were not honouring Esau's parents (their own parent's in-law). Why didn't Esau correct the wrong behaviour of his wives?

Well, whilst the passage doesn't say so, it is entirely possible that Esau didn't honour his mother and father after his younger brother Jacob connived with their mother Rebekah to deceive their elderly father Isaac who had failing eyesight, into giving Jacob the birthright that Isaac intended, quite rightly, to pass to Esau prior to his death. (See Genesis chapter 27).

Furthermore, if Esau no longer honoured his parents, then it follows logically that he would have instructed his two wives not to honour them.

Whether my supposition is correct or not, I believe the above passage infers that, if we are married, we must honour our parents-in-law as well as our parents. I believe another passage of Scripture that suggests this to be true is John chapter 19 verses 26 and 27. This passage blows me away! Jesus, is in agony and is dying on the Cross, and yet His very last act of love and concern was for the future wellbeing of <u>His mother</u>, since He would no longer be at her side to care for her....

"'So Jesus, seeing His mother, and the disciple whom He loved (esteemed) standing near, said to His mother, "[Dear] woman, look, [here is] your son!" Then He said to the disciple (John), "Look! [here is] your mother [protect and provide for her]!" From that hour the disciple took her into his own home.'

If John - Jesus' esteemed friend - was to take Jesus' *mother* under his roof as his 'mother', how much more should we honour and care for our parents and also the parents of our spouse?

Dishonouring our parents deserves death, according to God's Word.

In Romans chapter 1, Paul talks about the wrath of God being revealed from heaven *'against all ungodliness and unrighteousness of men who in their wickedness suppress and stifle the truth.'* He goes on to list a large number of sins that these people commit. **Included** in this list is the fact that they are *'disobedient and disrespectful to parents'* (verse 30). He concludes the chapter by saying *'Although they know God's righteous decree and His judgment, that those who do such things deserve death, yet they not only do them, but they even [enthusiastically] approve and tolerate others who practice them.'*

This is the first time in the New Testament we learn that failing to honour our parents *deserves* death! We may not *actually* die (physically), but parts of our life or ministry may 'die' in the sense that God's protection and blessing may be removed from us due to our failure to honour and respect our parents.

Taking care of a widowed parent

In 1 Timothy chapter 5, verses 3 and 4, Paul is chiefly talking about honouring widows, but note how children are to respond to the needs of their widowed parents:

"Honour and help those widows who are truly widowed [alone, and without support]. But if a widow has children or grandchildren [who are adults], see to it that these first learn to show great respect to their own family [as their religious duty and natural obligation], and to compensate their parents or grandparents [for their upbringing]; for this is acceptable and pleasing in the sight of God."

The message here is that if we are not only a child of an elderly parent but also a grand-child, we have a responsibility to take care of our parent/grandparent in the event of them losing their spouse. Paul writes (as I said earlier) that it is, in effect, a way of thanking them for the sacrifice they made to us in bringing us up lovingly when we were young. Such behaviour on our part will please the Lord and, I am sure, result in Him blessing us (as reflected in the Fifth Commandment).

As our parents and grand-parents reach old age many of them begin to suffer from varying degrees of frailty and declining health. As a result, the demands on us, their children, increase and in some cases increase greatly. Dealing with the increasing demand in these stressful days of the twenty-first century can be a great struggle for us.

Some will give up work and become, in some cases, full time carers. The financial implication of such a sacrifice can be huge. Others may arrange (with their parents' consent) to move their parents into assisted living complexes or full time care homes.

The Bible doesn't mention the suitability of care homes and it doesn't advise us concerning giving up our work and source of income when our parents need our full-time support. In those ancient days, family circumstances were very different; families were generally larger and they lived together or close by. Health care was insignificant and people were not generally kept alive (when their health declined) with the use of long-term medication.

Today I believe God would say to you and to me, *"Honour (respect, obey, care for) your father and your mother, so that your days may be prolonged in the land the LORD your God gives you."*

You will likely interpret that command in a different way to me and to others, as the circumstances of your ageing parents' dotage unfolds. Talk to God (pray) about your personal family difficulty and He will guide you to do what is right in His sight. God is looking at your heart, your integrity; and He will judge us all on that basis when it comes to how well we honoured our mother and father in our younger years of living at home with them, and also during their old age.

Chapter Five

RESOLVING CONFLICT

"The only person you can change is yourself." [1]

When I was an adolescent fifteen year old year old boy, I thought I knew everything.

Today, fifty years later, I realise I still have a lot to learn! And when I compare my knowledge with that of God, then I really do realise how tiny and insignificant my knowledge is. After all, in 1 Corinthians chapter 1 verse 25 we read, *'The foolishness of God [is not foolishness at all and] is wiser than men [far beyond human comprehension], and the weakness of God is stronger than men [far beyond the limits of human effort].'*

That Scripture brings me down to earth.

I left school and went to work at the age of sixteen as an engineering apprentice, and noticed that the men I worked with actually knew a lot more about mechanical things than I did, and a lot more about life too!

They would sometimes talk about their wives and the issues they had in their marriages. Those issues, they would say, were of course always the fault of their wife (!)

At eighteen, I started courting, and was married at the age of 22.

28 years later, that marriage ended. I was shocked and heart-broken. I had no idea anything major was wrong with our relationship.

As a result, I now find myself constantly warning men who

think they are happily married, *"Watch Out, I thought I was happily married too; don't take your wife or your marriage for granted. Keep working at it."*

Why do things go wrong?

In case you haven't noticed, we live in a fallen world. Despite what you think, *you* are not perfect. Your wife isn't, either.

In his book **'What Did You Expect?'**, Paul David Tripp puts it far better than I. He says this...

'Most of the troubles we face in marriage are not intentional or personal. In most marriage situations, you do not face difficulty because your spouse intentionally did something to make your life difficult. Yes, in moments of anger that may happen. But most often, what is really happening is that your life is being affected by the sin, weakness, and failure of the person you are living with. So, if your wife is having a bad day, that bad day will splash up on you in some way. If your husband is angry with his job, there is a good possibility that he will bring that anger home with him.'

Tripp then says something very profound:

'God loves your spouse, and he is committed to transforming him or her by his grace, and he has chosen <u>you</u> to be one of his regular tools of change. So, he will cause <u>you</u> to see, hear, and experience your spouse's need for change so that <u>you</u> can be an agent of his rescue.' (Author's emphasis). [2]

My wife Michele has known this truth for some time and puts it into effect far better than me. She is regularly sharing with me in private, the behaviour or speech I exhibit from time to time which is ungodly. I don't always like to hear the truth about myself, especially from my wife, and on many occasions it has caused me to get annoyed with her or sulk like a child for a while. God's grace has enabled her to live with my childish behaviour. When I read the above paragraph some time ago in Tripp's book, it was as if God switched a light on in my spirit. It was only really then that I realised God was using Michele to help try to correct me, because He loves us all so much, and He wants our lives to be joyful and to bring glory to Him. We do not bring glory to God when we behave in an ungodly manner!

So, when there are conflicts in our relationships, how do we deal with them?

Is there an effective 'conflict resolution' technique that always works?

Because we are talking about human beings, nothing is 100% effective, BUT, I want to say that what follows is, in my experience, not only effective at helping resolve difficulties between spouses, but indeed between any two individuals, whether colleagues, friends, parent and child, or somebody else.

I will begin by looking at what the Bible has to say to help us.

Key Passages of Scripture

In the context of conflict resolution, the first thing I note from Scripture is that Jesus tells us to *avoid conflict* in the first place!

How are we to do this? Jesus tells us to forgive and go on forgiving others. One of Jesus' foremost disciples asks his Master, how many times we should forgive? This is what we read in Matthew chapter 18 verses 21 and 22:

'Then Peter came to Him and asked, "Lord, how many times will my brother sin against me and I forgive him and let it go? Up to seven times?" Jesus answered him, "I say to you, not up to seven times, but seventy times seven." '

The clear inference of Jesus' words is that we are to go on forgiving indefinitely, not literally to stop forgiving after we have forgiven 490 times!

In Matthew chapter 5 and verse 22 Jesus warns us about getting angry and continuing in our anger towards others by unforgiveness and by harbouring malice in our hearts. He says,

"I say to you that everyone who continues to be angry with his brother or harbours malice against him shall be guilty before the court; and whoever speaks [contemptuously and insultingly] to his brother, 'Raca (You empty-headed idiot)!' shall be guilty before the supreme court (Sanhedrin); and whoever says, 'You fool!' shall be in danger of the fiery hell."

Another Scripture to take into account is the following one, where Jesus gives us advice concerning when a brother or sister in Christ sins against us (causes conflict). Matthew chapter 18, verses 15 to 17 says:

"If your brother sins, go and show him his fault in private; if he listens and pays attention to you, you have won back your brother. But if he does not listen, take along with you one or two others, so that EVERY WORD MAY BE CONFIRMED BY THE TESTIMONY OF TWO OR THREE WITNESSES. If he pays no attention to them [refusing to listen and obey], tell it to the church; and if he refuses to listen even to the church, let him be to you as a Gentile (unbeliever) and a tax collector."

So Jesus instructs us to try to resolve a conflict one-to-one with the perpetrator. If this fails, then we are to involve one or two godly men or women. If this still fails, we are to take the issue to the Church. If the issue remains unresolved, despite the church leaders being involved, we are to treat that person like an unbeliever. That will involve giving to God the issue you have with the other person, and laying it at His feet. We are not to harbour resentment in our hearts. God *will* one day vindicate us.

It is how to resolve the conflict in a one-to-one situation, particularly in the case of a loved one, that I want to focus on, in the remainder of this Chapter.

Let me begin this aspect by telling you that there are two Scripture passages that are *extremely* important in helping us learn how to do this.

These Scriptures are so important that I have found that the devil will do all he can to hide these passages from us; and, what's more, if we should stumble upon them, he will then do his best to hide their meaning. So, let's bring them out into the light shall we?

The first passage comes from the mouth of Jesus - our Lord and Saviour.

The second passage comes from the Apostle, Paul - the writer of two thirds of the New Testament. These two Scriptures are closely linked…

First:

"Blessed [spiritually calm with life-joy in God's favour] are the makers and maintainers of peace, for they will [express His character and] be called the sons of God." (Matthew chapter 5 verse 9).

Second:

' "Be angry, and do not sin": do not let the sun go down on your wrath, nor give place to the devil'. (Ephesians chapter 4 verses 26 and 27 - NKJV).

As it so often does, the Amplified version of the Bible brings to life the hidden meaning of this second Scripture:

'BE ANGRY [at sin—at immorality, at injustice, at ungodly behaviour], YET DO NOT SIN; <u>do not let your anger [cause you shame, nor allow it to] last until the sun goes down.</u> And do not give the devil an opportunity <u>[to lead you into sin by holding a grudge, or nurturing anger, or harbouring resentment, or cultivating bitterness]'.</u> (Ephesians chapter 4 verses 26 and 27, author's emphasis).

I expect you are thinking, *"What does the author mean, that the two Scriptures are linked?"* Well, allow me to explain.

Going back to the time of my first marriage, I was a *peacekeeper*. Almost every time there was a problem, I swept it under the carpet.

I pretended it wasn't really a problem. *"Time is a great healer"* my dear Mum always used to say, and I found that if I didn't mention to my spouse that something was annoying me, it was an effective way of keeping the peace. It seemed to work for 28 years (for some it lasts a much shorter time) but then suddenly it was as if a time-bomb went off. The shock of learning the truth that peace-keeping can only keep the emotions under control for a limited time was very painful, not only for my first wife and me, but other people's lives were affected too - *forever.*

But, soon into my second marriage with Michele, I learned that 'keeping the peace' is not the same thing as 'making peace'.

So, here is my point...

The advice Paul gave to the Ephesian Christians to not let the sun go down on their anger, means *sort out your differences <u>as soon as possible.</u>*

Jesus, in the above Matthew chapter 5 Scripture, tells us that makers and maintainers of peace express God's character and will be called the sons of God.

When we merely keep the peace, we are remaining silent and *not addressing the issue*; we are instead letting the issue go *unchecked and unresolved.*

BUT, *making peace* means RESOLVING THE CONFLICT!

When should we make peace (resolve the conflict)? As soon as physically possible (before sundown – i.e., before the end of the day). Why so soon? To prevent the devil getting a foothold.

That is why I believe those two Scriptures are linked closely.

The devil wants you to take offense at your wife's words or actions. He will make you think that some innocent comment that your wife makes is a personal attack on you. When you take offence at something your wife may say to you, before you know where you are, you can discover that your mind is racing away with itself and you find yourself imagining something like e.g., 'how much better moving in with the pretty young woman down the road might be'. I have allowed such lies to come into my mind on *several* occasions in the past.

The longer you leave it before you make peace (resolve the conflict), the longer the devil has to cause you to get angrier with the other party. This is why, not only Paul exhorts us to make up quickly, but also Jesus does. In Matthew chapter 5 verses 25 and 26 He warns us to make up quickly. He reminds us that if we fail to make up quickly with the person we have wronged or offended we will suffer consequences, especially if we have to go to court over the matter.

So, I see these two Scriptures interconnected, as follows:

Make peace – i.e., resolve the conflict – and do it as soon as the conflict has arisen. BUT, if tempers are flared then take time out, wait until the emotion has died down, if necessary wait until the end of the day, 'before the sun goes down.' Then, and only then, when you have calmed down, put into practice the hard work of peace-making.

How do *we* make peace?

I'd like to go back a few steps before we look at some of the techniques in resolving conflict i.e., 'making peace'.

Somebody once said, *"Nobody goes to work in order to do a bad job."* If you think about it, that is true for the vast majority of people. It's the same at home, and in relationships.

If you are married, the likelihood is you and your spouse married each other because you *fell in love*. At that time, you were probably looking at each other most of the time, through 'rose tinted spectacles.'

Neither of you could do anything wrong, courting each other was wonderful, life was bliss. The truth is, however, that after we marry and move in together we find that living with a fellow human being who has feelings, perhaps different to our own, and preferences that may seem positively alien to us, will throw up issues from time to time that need to be resolved. It does NOT mean that you are incompatible and it does NOT mean that you made a mistake in getting married! This is perfectly normal and everybody can relate to this, to a greater or lesser degree.

Later on, maybe children arrive on the scene; the wife (usually) is up all night taking care of the new arrival(s), you - the husband - decide it's prudent financially to work extra hours to pay for the baby, stress levels increase for both partners and tempers get a little frayed.

It suddenly becomes apparent that there is more to married life than the blissful utopia of being 'in love.'

It's 'wake up' time! You do, after all, live in a fallen world, and both your wife and you are imperfect. One of you probably has a shorter fuse than the other, and you both need help.

Well, the good news is that help is at hand. The normal places we go to for help (parents, a trusted confidante, or chatting with mates down the pub) may not actually be that helpful, depending on how you were brought up and whether your trusted friends are fellow believers.

If you are a Christian, then you know the wisdom of seeking help from God, both through prayer and by checking out His Holy Word.

We see from the above Scriptures that we are to be peacemakers, and that we are not to let the sun go down on our anger, so we understand God's advice is to sort the issue out today.

But…, there may be all sorts of reasons why that goal is seemingly impossible e.g., it may be that you've got to go back to work, the boss is waiting, or your wife isn't exactly in the mood for sorting this out because the children are crying, or the in-laws are coming round this evening for dinner and… and… and… HELP!

Ok, so where do we begin?

If you have attended **'The Marriage Course'** I referred to in Volume Two Chapter 1, then you will remember there was a section in the course devoted to this very issue, and so my advice is to go and find the Course Booklet and turn to the Chapter entitled 'Resolving Conflict' [3]. Take a look at the notes you made about each other in the exercises. You might remember something useful that you have neglected to do, which may be contributing to your relational conflict.

If you haven't attended that, or a similar course, then read on (and, while you are at it, book yourself and your wife onto such a course as soon as possible!).

There are a number of steps to learn, if you are to become experienced and successful in mastering the art of conflict resolution.

I believe the first thing to remember is that, deep down, you and your spouse *love each other*. Just because it doesn't necessarily *feel like* your spouse loves you at the moment of them upsetting you (or vice versa), it is usually the case that they do love you, probably very much indeed! It's simply that at that moment they don't *like your behaviour* very much.

The issue that has caused the misunderstanding, pain, or anger, is not primarily down to the fact that you or your spouse have caused the issue. The cause of any issue is usually due to the behaviour that has been exhibited by the person, or by the words that have been spoken.

Behaviour, actions and words; *these* are the things that cause conflict. Yes, somebody has carried out that wrong behaviour or spoken those careless, painful words, but try to understand and believe that *something*, not *somebody*, has caused those hurtful words or that wrong behaviour. Whilst we cannot change others, we can change the things we say and we can change our behaviour.

Others can too!

So, whilst *somebody* has performed the behaviour or spoken the words - i.e., created an issue that has caused conflict - the first point is this:

Separate the person from the issue.

The issue that needs resolving has been caused by sin. In the case of careless words the cause could have been a genuine misunderstanding. But the process that follows is designed to uncover the misunderstanding or the sin.

What has caused that sin is what needs to be established, because until we establish the cause, it is very difficult to resolve the issue.

We will now come on to how we uncover that cause. It will help to remember that sin can be caused by self, other people, or the devil.

Before we move on, I want to remind you that if you are a Christian, you are in a battle. The battle is against the devil and his forces in the spiritual realm. One of the devil's number one battlefields is the home. He hates marriage. He hates love. He hates it greatly when you are getting along just fine with your loved ones! That is why what I wrote in Volume One, Chapter Three is so important. We need to take great care to ensure we have placed our spiritual armour on – every day. This is our first line of protection and defence against the enemy.

One tiny chink in our armour and in pops the enemy to kill, steal and destroy. The book of James is full of Scriptures that help to explain the sinful reasons why conflicts arise in our lives.

Two classic verses on the subject of sin and its consequences are found in James chapter 1 verses 14 and 15:

"Each one is tempted when he is dragged away, enticed and baited [to commit sin] by his own [worldly] desire (lust, passion). Then when the illicit desire has conceived, it gives birth to sin; and

when sin has run its course, it gives birth to death".

It works like this: you crave for something you *don't* need; soon you reach a point where you *must* have it; then you *will* have it at all costs; by this stage the desire can be so great that if someone gets hurt, you *don't* care. Usually someone does get hurt, and often it is the one you love most. In effect, James is saying that sin is like a slippery slope; once you get onto the slope it's hard to get off. Someone gets hurt, and so conflict arises. The better thing to do is don't allow yourself to get on the 'slippery slope' in the first place!

James also points out the danger of *words*. In James Chapter 3, we learn that the tongue is a small part of the body, and yet it boasts of great things. It can contaminate our entire body and wreak havoc, both for us and for others. It needs to be tamed! James tells us the tongue is *'a restless evil [undisciplined, unstable], full of deadly poison'*. See James Chapter 3 verses 5 to 10.

No wonder Jesus warns us, *"All you need to say is simply 'Yes' or 'No'; anything beyond this comes from the evil one."* (Matthew chapter 5 verse 37, NIV). What He is saying is *"Speak the truth, don't exaggerate the truth or slightly mislead with your words; be known for being a man of your word!"*

Just one chapter later, James repeats that the reason for our quarrels and conflicts is our craving and lusting for what we do not have. We become jealous and so covet other people's possessions, which can lead to theft and even murder he says (See James chapter 4 verses 1 to 5).

Uncovering the cause of the conflict.

We will now come on to how, in the context of resolving conflict, we establish what has caused the sin, which resulted in the conflict we want to resolve.

I said that first of all we need to separate the person from the issue.

The issue is that someone has sinned, however deliberate or unintentional that sin might have been.

You need to understand that what your spouse believes to be sin may *not* be something you believe to be sin, and vice versa. Arguing, defending or justifying our actions will not help matters and will usually only exacerbate the situation. If you have caused hurt to someone by your words or actions, then that is a sin, and it *should be* understood by both of you as sin. The purpose of the next stage of the process we need to go through, is to help the other party understand that they have hurt the aggrieved party by their sin.

The task now is to agree that the issue needs to be discussed and understood by both parties in order to understand how and why the issue arose. Only then can it be resolved. Quality time will be required to be set aside in order to undertake this task fully. If this stage is hurried it runs the risk of resulting in a compromise instead of the need for complete understanding and an ability to apologise, forgive, reconcile and move forward, *'remembering their sins no more'* (Hebrews chapter 8 verse 12b).

Establishing what sin has caused the issue.

For some people this stage can be completed in 10 to 15 minutes, for others it can take an hour or more. It is imperative that both parties allow the other to talk *uninterrupted*, for as long as they need in order to feel **heard, validated** and **understood**.

This can be difficult for some. If you are impatient, like me, you will want to bypass the process in order get to the end quickly. Believe me, you may get away with that a few times, but you will NOT resolve the conflict to the other person's satisfaction and the issue will not be fully resolved even if it appears to have been, and will eventually re-surface at some future point.

There are many courses in improving listening skills. That fact alone should make most of us realise that listening is not natural for many of us!

For example, I am very good at talking a lot and interrupting often, but very poor at listening! I was trained in a professional capacity and was informed that in order to demonstrate good listening skills I should do certain things while the other person is talking to me. For example, I was taught that I should nod my head from time to time and mutter words like "uhah", "yes", "mmmm", "I know", etc., at appropriate points while the other is talking. The idea was that such affirming actions and words would make the other person feel that I was listening intently. For the most part, I found that worked, or so I thought! However, if I do this kind of thing whilst my wife is talking to me, it interrupts the flow of what she is trying to say, and she will stop talking to me if I do it!

In order to help me better listen to Michele, she wrote down for me her definition of the word 'listen'...

L = **Listen** with your ears, your heart, your mind and your soul.

I = **Invoke** an atmosphere of gentleness, understanding, validation and determined resolution.

S = **Stop** yourself when you feel the urge to interrupt.

T = **Treat** the other person with courtesy and respect.

E = **Embrace** the opportunity to learn and grow in silence and humility.

N = **Never** assert what you 'want' over what the other person **needs.**

I therefore recommend you find out what makes your wife (or whoever the other party is, with whom you are seeking to resolve conflict), feel that you are genuinely listening to them, before undertaking deep discussions to resolve conflict or address sensitive issues. It helps Michele if I sit opposite her, if possible with one hand over my mouth to prevent me from interrupting her, and maintain good eye contact whilst she is talking to me. I trust it goes without saying that the TV, radio, mobile devices, tablets etc., are completely out of bounds during this important time together!

So, it is important to start the process by planning a time to sit down and talk with no distractions. It might be as soon as the conflict has taken place or it might be later the same day, whichever you both feel is best.

Listen intently and do not interrupt.

The purpose of the discussion that is about to ensue is fourfold.

Firstly, it is to give the aggrieved party an opportunity to make clear to the other why they felt hurt by what was said or what was done to them.

The **second** objective is to ascertain what the other person actually meant when they said the things that caused the offense or why they did the things that caused the offense. Sometimes there is a misunderstanding and this can be discovered during the discussion.

Thirdly, it gives the party in the wrong, an opportunity to apologise, and ask for forgiveness.

Fourthly, it creates an opportunity to try to discuss and agree on how the person who caused the conflict can behave differently (for the better) in order to try to ensure there is no reoccurrence of the issue in the future.

So, how do we start the conversation? It can feel a little awkward to begin with. I suggest words to this affect...

"Darling, we agreed we would take time to talk this evening about an issue that caused me to get very upset earlier today. Can I explain to you what made me upset, so that you can understand why what you said (or what you did) hurt me?"

The other party is to agree with that reasonable request.

You then add that you would like the other party to listen until you have finished talking completely and *at no time* to interrupt. You tell the other person that when you have finished talking they may then respond fully to what you have said. If the one who is doing the listening needs to clarify something that you are saying, it is best if they either remember what it is they need to clarify, or write it down, so they do not interrupt you, but they wait until you have completely finished talking, before seeking clarity.

This is because it is rude to interrupt, and the apparently innocent act of interrupting - even to seek clarity - could further exacerbate the way that the person speaking is feeling. When interrupted, frustration will often arise and the person speaking may speak louder in order to drown out the person interrupting. The very act of interrupting during a conflict resolution exercise can often inflame the situation and make it very difficult subsequently, to resolve. I have experienced and witnessed the adverse consequences of making this mistake many times.

I cannot reiterate enough times, that the golden rule of listening when resolving conflict is **do not interrupt.**

When the other person has finished speaking, then and only then is it the turn of the other party to respond to what they have heard.

Both parties must focus on the issue and not attack the other person. As soon as you say something like *"You always do that"* or *"How many times have I got to tell you not to do that before you will change your behaviour,"* the other party will see such statements as an attack on them personally and inevitably retaliate, even if they know that what you are saying is true. Focus on ways to attack **the issue** rather than the person, with comments more like… *"I need you to understand why your behaviour upsets me,"* or *"The reason I feel hurt is because the negative words you said about me 'You'll never amount to anything' remind me of how my father spoke negative words* *over me – it upset me so much when I was young."*

After listening to each other, two things should become clear. It should become clear what the person causing the issue has done or said to make the issue arise, also what they meant by their words or behaviour and why they said/did it.

The next step is to agree on the way forward. Once clarity has been achieved, an apology is essential, followed by an exchange of ideas on what might be done to try to avoid a reoccurrence of the issue in the future.

What constitutes an apology?

I have found over the years that for men, in particular, saying the word "sorry" is all they feel a need to do in order to apologise to another person that they have wronged. In some cases that may be adequate. However, it wasn't until I read a book called **'The Five Languages of Apology'** [4] that I came to understand that making a meaningful and genuine apology requires a much more sincere action on my part.

The co-authors have counselled people for decades, and in so doing have discovered there are essentially five different ways in which people feel a complete apology has been made. These are, *expressing regret, accepting responsibility, making restitution, genuinely repenting and requesting forgiveness.*

A genuine apology should include all of the five aspects mentioned above. So, you might say something like this:

"I am really sorry for how my careless words upset you just now. I should have thought before I spoke and not allowed myself to say those words. They are not true – I spoke them in anger. I promise to think harder before I speak next time and want to apologise to you and ask you to forgive me for my thoughtless act. Perhaps you would allow me to cook dinner for you tonight to make up in some way. I want you to know that I love you deeply."

Such an apology will usually be received with love and acceptance, provided it is said and meant *sincerely*.

What can be agreed to prevent a reoccurrence of the issue?

Supposing the issue is that, you the husband, have made a habit of going down the pub every Friday night after work, and each week your wife has no idea what time you will be home. She has made it clear that this upsets her.

Suppose you learn from the conflict resolution exercise that she doesn't have an issue with you going to the pub. What annoys her is that you never call to let her know what time you will be home. Consequently, some nights the dinner she has cooked for you has to be thrown away, the kids don't get to see their dad before they go to bed, and all manner of other more 'minor' issues arise for your lonely wife.

You explain to her that the reason you don't call is because once you get into discussion with the lads you simply lose all sense of time. In any case you say that phoning one's wife with an ETA is not considered very 'macho' for a man trying to keep up appearances with the lads, lest they make fun of you for being 'under the thumb'.

Well, firstly I would put it to you that loving your wife in a caring and understanding way is **far** more important than looking 'macho' in front of the lads. What kind of lads are you spending time with if they ridicule you for calling your wife while you are with them?

I would suggest a reasonable way of ensuring the conflict doesn't arise again (assuming you really must meet with your friends after work every Friday evening) is to agree to always be home by a set time. Explain to your friends why that is so, or if you and your wife agree that arriving home at an agreed time isn't necessary, then instead, promise to always phone your wife with an ETA, if necessary by phoning her from outside the pub to avoid any embarrassment from your friends.

Next, we will look at an example of what the act of resolving conflict might look like in reality. But before I do that, I want to summarise the advice given in this chapter so that we can consider all of the aspects I have covered in this chapter within the conflict resolution example that follows.

Whatever is agreed, the onus is then on the offender to come through for the spouse and ensure they do everything they are able to do in order not allow the issue to re-occur. If you are the culprit, pray that God will help you with self-control!

Summary of this Chapter

1. Issues of conflict are caused by sin, weakness, or failure in a person or in both persons. [5]

2. God wants to help your spouse improve for the better and He will use you to bring that about! [6]

3. Be a peace*maker* and in so doing you will express God's character.

4. Do not give the enemy a foothold – deal with the conflict before the end of the day.

5. *Resolve* the conflict – don't ignore it, it will NOT go away on its own.

6. Separate the person from the issue.

7. DEAL with the issue (bad behaviour or careless words), not the person.

8. Establish what sin or misunderstanding caused the issue.

9. Listen, validate and understand the other person. Do not interrupt.

10. Apologise.

11. Agree a way forward.

Practical example of a conflict resolution exercise

In this example, let us assume that your wife likes going

shopping every Saturday afternoon whilst you like to watch your favourite soccer team. On one such occasion, your team is playing a really important game. Whilst your wife is out shopping you are seated in the stadium and you get a phone call from her to say her car has broken down. You get angry that she thinks you should come and fix it and, as a result of the conversation, she hangs up on you. You watch the game and arrive home a little late because - let's face it – since you and your wife have fallen out with each other, the last place you want to go to at that point in time is home.

You walk through the front door hoping to find a forgiving wife with dinner on the table but you are greeted, unsurprisingly, with "Oh, nice of you to come home eventually! Your dinner's gone cold. You do remember how to use the microwave don't you?"

You start moping about, whilst your wife lets you know that she has had to pay a garage £500 to fix the problem, while you were having a great time at the soccer match. You can't take any more and the conversation deteriorates into a slanging match.

Eventually, you agree to sit down a little later and try to make up.

The following is what a positive conflict resolution session might look like:

Firstly, you will ensure you are both sitting in an appropriate way to maximise listening skills and shut out all possibility of unwanted distractions. Switch off, or put on 'silent mode' all phones including the house land-line. Switch off TV, radio and other electrical devices that could distract you. If people can see through the room window, then shut the curtains so that no-one can see that you are at home, and do not answer the door-bell to visitors.

The time you are about to spend together is _far more important_ than watching the TV, answering phone calls, or greeting unwanted guests. It is amazing what resources the devil will muster up to prevent you from having effective quality time together to resolve the very conflict in which he has engulfed you!

The first thing to remember is that the conflict has been caused by sin. We are going to separate the person from the issue. So we are going to find out how the situation arose by listening fully to each other.

The husband could start by saying, "Darling I want to resolve the conflict that has arisen between us and I would like you to explain to me what it was that caused the conflict to arise. I promise to listen without interrupting you; until you tell me you have finished talking."

Husband, you will then listen to your wife <u>without</u> interrupting. It is essential you listen with no agenda of your own, for example, by filtering out things you don't want to hear!

In your marriage vows, you will recall that you promised to love and cherish your wife. My wife Michele, has explained to me that to her and to most women she knows, the word 'cherish' means LISTEN!

Now it is important to understand that women are 'wired' differently to men, particularly with regard to feelings.

When your wife has finished talking, whatever you think about what she has said, you need to be sure to validate her feelings, together with the reason she feels the ways she does. Women's feelings are not 'silly emotions'. Their feelings are real and they need validating. You may not understand your wife's concerns and feelings, but that does not mean they are irrelevant. Any attempt to pour scorn on the way she feels will be received for what it is: arrogant, unloving and unhelpful!

You must show your wife respect and empathy even if you don't necessarily agree with what she has said. The fact is you have hurt your wife and as such, you have an obligation to hear her concerns before you attempt to resolve the issue.

Also it will help greatly to recognise that it takes a great deal of courage for many women to tell their husband exactly what they are thinking, in the knowledge that their husband may well be upset or annoyed by their remarks. So, be sure to begin to respond by thanking her sincerely for sharing with you everything that is concerning her.

Secondly, if you did not understand any aspects of what she said, ask your wife to clarify those particular points.

When you think you are sure you have understood what she has said, then tell her in your own words what you think she has said, in order to check you have completely understood her. It is normal that what she will have said will have highlighted the sin that has led to the conflict.

So depending what you have heard her say, you might respond like this:

"So, firstly, I want to thank you for taking the time to share with me your true deep feelings about how my behaviour upset you. If I understand you correctly, the thing I did that upset you most was that I wasn't willing to leave the soccer stadium when you needed me to help you with the car break down. In addition, you were further upset by the fact that I came home late and didn't take the trouble to call you. Is that correct?"

If you have overlooked something, or you have not correctly understood your wife, the check question I have suggested gives her a chance to clarify.

If my account of what was said in this 'imaginary example' was correct, you have now uncovered the sins that led to the conflict:

1. Your selfish act of not being prepared to leave the soccer stadium to assist your wife in her moment of need.

2. Your selfish act of not calling your wife with your ETA, when you deliberately didn't return home when expected.

If your wife agrees with your assessment, then you are ready to move on. If she does not agree with your assessment, then further clarification will be required, both parties remembering not to interrupt while the other party is talking.

Remember to address the issue, not the person. Many men at this stage would respond to their wife with a defensive statement along these lines...

"Let me tell you why I didn't come to your help, dear. The ticket to watch the game cost me £50, it was the most important game of the season for the team and to be honest there was no way I was going to leave the game to attend to a car breakdown, when I told you during the phone call that all you needed to do was call the local garage. After all, as it turned out I wouldn't have been able to fix it anyway!"

One of the reasons many men would give this kind of response is because, in the mind of many men, what I have just stated above is entirely logical. The problem is it is also <u>egotistical and devoid of any compassion, understanding and empathy</u>.

Such a defensive statement simply 'fuels the fire' and the most likely outcome is that the conflict worsens rather than it becoming resolved.

Why is this?

It is because instead of *validating* how your behaviour made your wife feel, you have in effect told her why (in your opinion) it was *unreasonable* **for her** to expect **you** to come to her rescue! You have acted *selfishly* because what you are saying to the most important person in your life is that in her moment of need, a soccer match was more important to you than her.

In this example, it may well seem logical to you that the problem would have been solved by a garage break-down company, but your wife's needs at that moment were to be <u>embraced and supported by her husband</u>, not the person at the garage who sorted out the problem.

Furthermore, to come home late, without calling to let your wife know, is <u>immature and selfish</u> because it takes no account of her needs and may cause her to become anxious or worried that something has happened to the person she loves, albeit she probably doesn't *like* you very much at that moment!

I have learned these things for myself – the hard way, and at some cost – so I cannot encourage you enough to put these tried and tested ideas into effect.

The best type of response, instead of the defensive one I have just outlined, is to be gracious and apologetic; saying something like this…

"Now that I fully understand why my behaviour caused you pain, darling, I want to say how sorry I am about it. I was wrong. I should have left the soccer game as soon as you called. I was wrong to place the soccer game above the importance of you and your wellbeing. I am also sorry that because I was annoyed about the whole event, and I couldn't enjoy the game as much as I had hoped, I kept away from you and came home late because I knew you would be annoyed with me when I came home. Not coming home on time and not calling you was childish of me. Please forgive me for my selfishness."

I believe with confidence that in most cases, any reasonable wife would now forgive you, and would feel very loved and cherished by your mature response.

Finally, to complete the process, you need to discuss how you might respond in the future should a similar event arise. So you might say…

"I would like to reassure you that in future, should a similar issue arise, if you tell me you need me, I will do my very best to come through for you darling. I want to make sure you know that I love you deeply, and your welfare and wellbeing is my number one priority, even though I failed to demonstrate it on this occasion."

Whatever your conflict may be about, if finding a way forward is not so clear, and becomes a sticking point to resolving this issue, you might instead ask your wife to share her ideas on how you could avoid a reoccurrence of the conflict. In such a case, a conversation addressing the following question is advisable...

"Can we discuss and agree how you would like me to respond in future should something similar arise?"

Listen to her ideas and evaluate whether her suggestions are reasonable and something that you could do to demonstrate your love for her. However long the conflict resolution takes, do not give up until you are **both** happy with the outcome.

A few final tips.

Resolving conflict does not come naturally to many of us. As we learn to 'dwell with' our spouse, we will discover what they are naturally good at doing and what they struggle to do. It is a good idea to share out the workload at home according to our natural strengths. Try to play to each other's strengths like a team would do. This will help avoid issues and conflict. So for example, if your spouse doesn't like washing-up or can't do gardening, you do them instead, assuming you are able. Also, if possible, try to work with your spouse to improve weaknesses, always remembering that if they are not willing to co-operate for whatever reason, the only person you can change is yourself!

Financial Issues.

One of the most common issues arising in the home concerns finances. If only one person is in paid employment, then one way of minimising the potential for conflicts arising over financial matters is for the breadwinner to accept that the money earned belongs jointly to both the husband and the wife. If you, as the husband are the breadwinner and your wife does not undertake paid employment, remember that she contributes to the marriage in her own way. Housework and child rearing should not be looked upon as something the 'stay at home' spouse does for free!

Let me help you understand this principle. Supposing you were to place a monetary value on each of the jobs your wife does at home from the moment she wakes to the time she goes to bed, you may well find that it equates to more than you, the breadwinner, earn from paid employment!

If your wife, for some reason, finds herself in a position due to ill-health, where she is unable to undertake this precious and godly role of being the homemaker, along with the God-ordained role of raising your children, then the monetary value you have calculated for the work your wife does, would have to be paid to somebody else instead. I would strongly recommend, therefore, that you let your wife know just how much you value her obedience to God in choosing to stay at home, unpaid, to run the home and raise the family for a significant period of her life.

Would you, dear brother-in-Christ, be willing to do what she does perhaps for twenty or more years with no pay? I hope you would agree with me that our wives deserve a medal for what they do! In the event that it is you and not your wife that is a stay at home 'househusband', then let me tell your wife that *you* also deserve a medal!

In a situation where both of you go out to work, then husband and wife should *share* the burden of housework *and* the role of bringing up the children.

Finally, whenever issues arise, always remember to pray together about them. God is in the business of resolving conflicts supernaturally as well as naturally.

It breaks God's heart that so many people, including followers of Christ, have held life-long grudges because of their selfish unwillingness to forgive and to do the hard work of *making* peace. My prayer is that many readers will find that this chapter, together with other recommended reading I have suggested, will help you to learn this God-ordained art of making peace and resolving conflict.

<u>I'd like to end the chapter with this point:</u>

If you are married, when you are trying to resolve conflict, it might help to remember that on your wedding day, you and your spouse made vows to each other. Depending on whether you were married in a civil ceremony or a church setting, the exact vow you undertook, before witnesses, may have been a variation on the following pledge to live together *'from this day forward; for better, for worse, for richer, for poorer, in sickness and in health, to love and to cherish, till death us do part; according to God's holy law.'*

Some readers may benefit from reading that last sentence again <u>slowly</u>, to let the power of those solemn vows sink in.

Let me encourage you to ask yourself, *"Am I consistently demonstrating to my wife that I love, honour and cherish her in all these aspects of our married life?"*

If the answer is "Yes" and your wife agrees that you are, then that is great!

If, however, you are not doing so, then may I encourage you to apply, **<u>NOW</u>**, those principles I have outlined in so many of the chapters of the two volumes of this book, before it's too late.

How I wish I had understood and learnt much sooner, what God has subsequently taught me about His purpose in every aspect of a man's life, and has laid on my heart in the writing of this book….

Epilogue

ARE YOU UP FOR IT?
– PLAYING *YOUR* PART IN GOD'S PLAN

'We are condemned to salvation through the Cross of Christ. But discipleship has an option with it – "If anyone..." (Luke 14 v 26). The Bible Training College exists so that each of you may know whether or not God has a man here who truly cares about proclaiming His gospel and to see if God grips you for this purpose. Beware of competing calls once the call of God grips you.' [1]

Man of God, congratulations! You have made it to the end of this book, which I have written under the conviction of the Holy Spirit.

I believe God asked me to write this book because many of His men are being defeated by the devil and his demons, daily. God's 'End Times Church' has been weakened because many men who have been chosen by God will not come through for Him. They are not standing strong and overcoming. They are not leading the Church in the direction God expects and demands of His leaders. Instead, many are listening to Satan's lies and falling by the wayside or even teaching a false gospel. The chapters of this book are set out to help God's men overcome, step up to the plate, and correct their behaviour where it is falling short.

God wants to use *you.*

God has given you a great personal gift (a personal talent). Have you discovered it yet? Has God awoken you to it? Perhaps you are not convinced that you have a gift at all. Well, take heart,

Moses was given a vision that he would set God's people free from slavery in Egypt. He had the vision as a young man, but spent forty years tending sheep before he finally received the call. God had to refine Moses before He could use Him to set His people free. He has to refine us all. For some of us it takes God four years, for others, forty. I had to wait twelve years for God to do His deep work of refining me, once He had given me the vision of wanting to help to disciple men.

Perhaps you have been listening, as I have done, to Satan's lies…. *"You will never amount to anything." "You might be a Christian, but you are a sinner, so God has discounted you."*

LIES, LIES, DAMN LIES!!! God has NOT discounted you. If you are caught up in sin today, and/or in the past, God simply asks you to confess it to Him and then turn from those ways (repent). He will then use you powerfully and mightily to bring down Satan's strongholds and take back ground for His Kingdom's sake. He has chosen you and He needs you to say **"Here am I, send me".**

He is desperate to send YOU! You may already know in what aspect of your life or work He wants to use you.

He isn't just looking for 'natural leaders', intellectuals or highly qualified theologians, but if you are any of these, He will use you too! God looks first at the heart of the man!

He is looking right now into your heart. He wants to awaken you to His truths, dear reader. He has a plan for you and is asking *"Will you turn to me? Will you turn back to me so I can fulfil My plan for your life?"*

And if your cry is "Yes Lord, Here I am, send me," then you will be amazed time and again at what God will do through you.

Let me encourage you right now to pick up a Bible and read Jeremiah chapter 1 and imagine God is speaking to you personally, the same words He spoke to His chosen 'instrument' Jeremiah. God will use you, if, like Jeremiah you will obey Him.

Nobody who knows me would have thought I would be capable of writing this book, and neither did I. But, by faith and obedience I was able to do so, by God's grace (despite all manner of attacks on me by the enemy).

Look at the Bible characters God used. Would you have chosen them? Abraham – lost faith and slept with his servant girl so as to have a child – but NOT the one God promised him. Abraham's promised miraculously-born son (Isaac) was born to his barren wife Sarah, but not until *after* Abraham's sinful lack of faith, which caused him to sleep with Hagar, his wife's Egyptian slave-girl. King David was the only recorded 'Man after God's Own Heart' in the Bible – but he committed adultery and arranged for the woman's husband to be murdered. Jesus' disciple, Peter, disowned Him three times. But still God used these and countless other Bible characters mightily to achieve His works.

God will use you if you will humble yourself. Bow down before Him in the privacy of your prayer closet and say *"Here I am God, send me."*

Will you do this today?

Warning!

Hold on a moment, you need to know that if you will tell God you want Him to use you and that you are available, there will be a cost.

If you decide to stand up and be counted - with other brothers in Christ - and walk into your God-ordained destiny, achieving whatever unique plan God wants you to undertake for Him, there will be struggles along the way. The battle will hot up the moment you step out for God. Paul was flogged, shipwrecked and imprisoned (see the Book of Acts). Nehemiah was ridiculed and faced much opposition when he said **"Yes"** to God and returned to Jerusalem to rebuild the city walls (see Nehemiah chapter 4). Jesus was spat upon, mocked, and then crucified! Consider these facts carefully before you decide whether or not you are up for it. Consider also these verses from Matthew Chapter 10 which concerns instructions for Jesus' disciples - you and me. Within that chapter, Jesus issues these *warnings* to those who will follow Him:

"Do not think that I have come to bring peace on the earth; I have not come to bring peace, but a sword [of division between belief and unbelief] (verse 34).

And he who does not take his cross [expressing a willingness to endure whatever may come] and follow Me [believing in Me, conforming to My example in living and, if need be, suffering or perhaps dying because of faith in Me] is not worthy of Me. Whoever finds his life [in this world] will [eventually] lose it [through death], and whoever loses his life [in this world] for My sake will find it [that is, life with Me for all eternity]. (Verses 38 and 39).

If you do choose to step out into your God-ordained destiny - instead of accepting the comfortable status quo – then you will discover a new kind of freedom. There will be excitement, adrenalin rushes and blessings. There is no feeling like experiencing the blessing God gives freely when you are in His will, walking in His ways, and going about His business! God loves to reward you when you obey His Word and sacrifice your *own will* for *His Will.* He promises to be with you. If you will step out and go, God will turn up. Everything you need in order to win the battle and achieve His will for your life is promised to you if you will be faithful, strong and courageous!

"And what more shall I say? For time will fail me if I tell of Gideon, Barak, Samson, Jephthah, of David and Samuel and the prophets, who by faith [that is, with an enduring trust in God and His promises] subdued kingdoms, administered justice, obtained promised blessings, closed the mouths of lions, extinguished the power of [raging] fire, escaped the edge of the sword, out of weakness were made strong, became mighty and unbeatable in battle, putting enemy forces to flight." (Hebrews Chapter 11, verses 32 to 34).

THE Code [2]

As I have warned you many times throughout this book, if you are determined to seek out God's unique plan for your life, making Jesus your Lord, and determined to follow Him from this day onwards, you will find yourself in a spiritual battle. But, if you are prepared to battle against everything that sin, the world and the devil will place as a barrier before you, the rewards in this world and the next will be wonderful. To help you along this new road, I hope you will gain immense encouragement from reading and reflecting upon something that Christian Vision for Men (CVM) refers to as **'THE Code – it's time for a new kind of man.'**

THE Code was conceived by Carl Beech, President of CVM, and finalised after a very long time of prayer and with the support of a team he brought together to seek after God. THE Code is to be found in a book of the same title co-authored by Carl Beech, Andy Drake & Ian Manifold. [3]

CVM is the UK's foremost Christian Men's Organisation.

'THE Code…

1. *Jesus is my Captain, Brother, Rescuer and Friend.*

2. *I owe everything to Him. I will do anything for Him.*

3. *I will unashamedly make Him known through my actions and words.*

4. *I will not cheat in anything, personal or professional.*

5. *I will look away from the gutter, but be prepared to pull people out of it.*

6. *I will keep my body fit and free from any addictions.*

7. *I will put the welfare of those closest to me before my own welfare.*

8. *I will treat all men and women as brothers and sisters.*

9. *I will lead as He would lead. I will honour my leaders*

provided this also honours Him. I will follow Him in company with my sisters and brothers.

10. *I will use my strength to protect the weak and stand against the abuse of power.*

11. *I will protect the world that God has made.*

12. *If I fail I will not give up. He never gives up on me.'*

My final words…

If you are not a Christian, my prayer for you is that Jesus will appear to you in a personal encounter, revealing to you that He is the Messiah, the Saviour of all who will believe in Him. I pray that you will repent of your sins and put your faith in Jesus Christ to save you, and that you will then live your life in obedience to His Holy Word, so that you can experience all the rewards of living a life in Him.

If you are a woman and have read this book, I pray that what I have written, but more importantly what God's Word says, will inspire you to encourage and help the man in your life to be all that God is calling him to be.

To every Christian man who overcame fear and read this book, my prayer for you is that you will be brave, and BELIEVE that God has a unique plan for your life that only *you* can fulfil for Him! Walk in His ways with faith and courage, and obediently apply all you have learnt, or have been reminded of (in the message of this book), and in so doing, become the MAN AFTER GOD'S OWN HEART which He created you to be…

VOLUME TWO - Notes

Chapter One

1. Tearfund is a UK based Christian Charity 'called to follow Jesus wherever the need is greatest'. Tearfund primarily focuses on supporting those in poverty and providing disaster relief for disadvantaged communities. See www.tearfund.org

2. © *The UCB Word for Today*, from the daily reading of 30th June 2010. The UCB Word for Today is a free daily devotional resource written by Bob and Debbie Gass, available from UCB (United Christian Broadcasters), www.ucb.co.uk.

3. Taken from *What Did You Expect?: Redeeming the Realities of Marriage* by Paul David Tripp, © 2010. Used by permission of Crossway, a publishing ministry of Good News Publishers, Wheaton, IL 60187, www.crossway.org

4. Ibid. Page number 88

5. Ibid. Page numbers 88 to 89

6. Ibid. Page number 92

7. Ibid. Page number 36.

8. Ibid. Page number 36.

9. *The 5 Love Languages: How to Express Heartfelt Commitment to Your Mate* ISBN 1-881273-15-6, and *The 5 Love Languages, Men's Edition: The Secret to Love That Lasts* ISBN 978-0-8024-7316-5, both titles by Gary Chapman. Used by permission.

10. The Marriage Course is produced by Alpha International at Holy Trinity Brompton, Brompton Road, London, England SW1 1JA. *The Marriage Course Guest Manual* is published by Alpha International ISBN 1-902750-27-6. See www.themarriagecourse.org Used by permission.

11. The Marriage Preparation Course is produced by Alpha

International and the topics covered are as follows: 1. Communication 2. Commitment, 3. Resolving Conflict, 4. Keeping Love Alive 5. Shared Goals and Values. See www.themarriagepreparationcourse.org Used by permission.

12. www.thefreedictionary.com

Chapter Two

1. Centre for Social Justice, 10 Greycoat Place, Westminster, London SW1P 1SB.

2. The Father Code, a website written by Jack Thurston https://thefathercode.com/the-9-devastating-effects-of-the-absent-father/

3. John Newton, 1725 to 1807.

4. This quote is believed to be attributed to the late Senator Paul Tsongas in his book *Heading Home.* Others have attributed it to Barbara Bush, Harold Kushner, or a friend of Senator Paul Tsongas.

5. *The 5 Love Languages of Children* by Gary Chapman and Ross Campbell ISBN 978-0802412850. *The 5 Love Languages of Teenagers* by Gary Chapman ISBN 978-0802412843. Used by permission.

6. I originally read this in Jim George's book: *A Man After God's Own Heart* page 101. ISBN 978-0-7369-5969-8. Jim George attributes this quotation to J. Daniel Bacon as cited by Roy B. Zuck, in his book *The Speaker's Quote Book* p. 51. © Copyright 1997, 2009 by Roy B. Zuck. Published by Kregel Publications, Grand Rapids, MI. Used by permission of the publisher. All rights reserved.

Chapter 3

1. *My Utmost For His Highest – An Updated Edition In Today's Language* by Oswald Chambers, edited by James Reimann.

ISBN 0-929239-57-1, first paragraph of his entry for April 23rd. Used by permission.

2. https://billygraham.org/answer/which-of-the-hundreds-of-old-testament-laws-are-applicable-to-us-as-christians/

3. https://www.logosapostolic.org/bible_study/RP208-1PenaltyBreakingSabbath.htm

4. *'When we walk with the Lord'* hymn written by John Henry Sammis (1846 – 1919).

Chapter 4

1. https://www.merriam-webster.com

Chapter 5

1. Joyce Meyer, Joyce Meyer Ministries. www.joycemeyer.org

   This quotation is something I have heard Joyce Meyer use several times in her TV broadcasts.

2. Taken from *What Did You Expect?: Redeeming the Realities of Marriage* by Paul David Tripp, © 2010, pages 23 to 24. Used by permission of Crossway, a publishing ministry of Good News Publishers, Wheaton, IL 60187, www.crossway.org.

3. The Marriage Course is a resource produced by Holy Trinity Brompton, Brompton Road, London, England SW1 1JA. *'The Marriage Course Manual'* is published by HTB Publications. ISBN 1-902750-27-6. www.themarriagecourses.org Used by permission.

4. *The Five Languages of Apology – How to Experience Healing in All Your Relationships* by Gary Chapman and Jennifer Thomas. ISBN: 1-881273-79-2, ISBN -13: 978-1-881273-79-0. This book has since been re-released as a revised/updated edition with a new title: *When Sorry Isn't Enough: Making Things Right with Those You Love.* Used by permission.

5. *Taken from What Did You Expect?: Redeeming the Realities of Marriage* by Paul David Tripp, © 2010, page 23. Used by permission of Crossway, a publishing ministry of Good News Publishers, Wheaton, IL 60187, www.crossway.org.

6. Ibid. Page 24

Epilogue

1. *My Utmost For His Highest* by Oswald Chambers ISBN 0-916441-83-0. Used by permission.

2. *THE Code – it's time for a new kind of man* is a rule for living produced by Christian Vision for Men. Used by permission of Carl Beech, President CVM. The book is co-authored by Carl Beech, Andy Drake & Ian Manifold - ISBN 978 0 85721 0227. See on-line studies at www.codelife.org and www.cvm.org.uk

3. Ibid.

RECOMMENDED READING:

Wild at Heart: Discovering The Secret of A Man's Soul by John Eldredge. ISBN 0-7852-6694-1.

The Way of the Wild Heart – A Map for The Masculine Journey by John Eldredge ISBN 10: 0-7852-8868-6.

You Have What it Takes by John Eldredge ISBN 978-0785288763.

My Utmost For His Highest by Oswald Chambers ISBN 0-916441-83-0.

25 Truths about Demons and Spiritual Warfare by David Diga Hernandez ISBN 978-1-62998-765-1.

The 5 Love Languages: How to Express Heartfelt Commitment to Your Mate by Gary Chapman ISBN 1-881273-15-6.

The 5 Love Languages, Men's Edition: The Secret to Love That Lasts by Gary Chapman ISBN 978-0-8024-7316-5.

The Five Languages of Apology – How to Experience Healing in All Your Relationships by Gary Chapman and Jennifer Thomas ISBN: 1-881273-79-2, ISBN -13: 978-1-881273-79-0. This book has since been re-released as a revised/updated edition with a new title: *When Sorry Isn't Enough: Making Things Right with Those You Love.*

Why Men Hate going to Church by David Murrow. ISBN 978-0-7852-6038-7.

Finishing Strong by Steve Farrar. ISBN 1-57673-726-8.

Iron Men by Nathan Blackaby. ISBN 978-1-78259-672-1.

MERE CHRISTIANITY by C S Lewis. ISBN 978-0-00-746121-9.

The Screwtape Letters by C S Lewis. ISBN 0-00-628060-9.

Being God's Man… In the Face of Temptation by Arterburn, Luck & Wendorff. ISBN 978-1578566815.

Spadework by Carl Beech. ISBN 978 1 84427 259 4.

A Man After God's Own Heart by Jim George
ISBN 978-0-7369-5969-8.

What Did You Expect? - Redeeming the realities of Marriage by Paul
David Tripp. ISBN 978-1-84474-474-9.

Respectable Sins by Jerry Bridges. ISBN 978-1-60006-140-0.

*COME ON CHURCH! WAKE UP! Sin Within the Church and What
Jesus Has to Say About It* by Michele Neal.
ISBN 978-1-62136-316-3.

Total Forgiveness by R T Kendall. ISBN 978-0-340-75639-3.

Discipleship by David Watson. ISBN 978 1 444 79201 0.

GO AND Sin no More – A call to holiness by Michael L. Brown.
ISBN 978-0-615-73019-6.

God in Work by Christian Schumacher. ISBN 0-7459-4043-9.

Every Man's Battle by Stephen Arterburn. ISBN 978-0307457974.

CONTACT THE AUTHOR

You can contact me and you can read
some of my sermons by visiting
www.thechristianbookformen.com

For details of my wife's books visit her website
www.michelenealuk.com

or follow her on Twitter @MicheleNealUK